New Frontiers in Regional Science: Asian Perspectives

Volume 23

New Frontiers in Regional Science: Asian Perspectives

This series is a constellation of works by scholars in the field of regional science and in related disciplines specifically focusing on dynamism in Asia.

Asia is the most dynamic part of the world. Japan, Korea, Taiwan, and Singapore experienced rapid and miracle economic growth in the 1970s. Malaysia, Indonesia, and Thailand followed in the 1980s. China, India, and Vietnam are now rising countries in Asia and are even leading the world economy. Due to their rapid economic development and growth, Asian countries continue to face a variety of urgent issues including regional and institutional unbalanced growth, environmental problems, poverty amidst prosperity, an ageing society, the collapse of the bubble economy, and deflation, among others.

Asian countries are diversified as they have their own cultural, historical, and geographical as well as political conditions. Due to this fact, scholars specializing in regional science as an inter- and multi-discipline have taken leading roles in providing mitigating policy proposals based on robust interdisciplinary analysis of multifaceted regional issues and subjects in Asia. This series not only will present unique research results from Asia that are unfamiliar in other parts of the world because of language barriers, but also will publish advanced research results from those regions that have focused on regional and urban issues in Asia from different perspectives.

The series aims to expand the frontiers of regional science through diffusion of intrinsically developed and advanced modern regional science methodologies in Asia and other areas of the world. Readers will be inspired to realize that regional and urban issues in the world are so vast that their established methodologies still have space for development and refinement, and to understand the importance of the interdisciplinary and multidisciplinary approach that is inherent in regional science for analyzing and resolving urgent regional and urban issues in Asia.

Topics under consideration in this series include the theory of social cost and benefit analysis and criteria of public investments, socio-economic vulnerability against disasters, food security and policy, agro-food systems in China, industrial clustering in Asia, comprehensive management of water environment and resources in a river basin, the international trade bloc and food security, migration and labor market in Asia, land policy and local property tax, Information and Communication Technology planning, consumer "shop-around" movements, and regeneration of downtowns, among others.

Researchers who are interested in publishing their books in this Series should obtain a proposal form from Yoshiro Higano (Editor in Chief, higano@jsrsai.envr.tsukuba.ac.jp) and return the completed form to him.

More information about this series at http://www.springer.com/series/13039

Yuzuru Miyata • Hiroyuki Shibusawa
Indrawan Permana • Any Wahyuni

Environmental and Natural Disaster Resilience of Indonesia

 Springer

Yuzuru Miyata
Department of Architecture
and Civil Engineering
Toyohashi University of Technology
Toyohashi, Aichi, Japan

Hiroyuki Shibusawa
Department of Architecture and Civil
Engineering
Toyohashi University of Technology
Toyohashi, Aichi, Japan

Indrawan Permana
Department of Architecture,
Faculty of Engineering
Palangka Raya University
Kalimantan Tengah, Indonesia

Any Wahyuni
Directorate General of Highways - Ministry
of Public Works of Indonesia
Makassar, Indonesia

ISSN 2199-5974   ISSN 2199-5982   (electronic)
New Frontiers in Regional Science: Asian Perspectives
ISBN 978-981-10-8209-2   ISBN 978-981-10-8210-8   (eBook)
https://doi.org/10.1007/978-981-10-8210-8

Library of Congress Control Number: 2018932983

Printed on acid-free paper

This Springer imprint is published by the registered company Springer Nature Singapore Pte Ltd. part of Springer Nature.
The registered company address is: 152 Beach Road, #21-01/04 Gateway East, Singapore 189721, Singapore

Introduction to Environmental and Natural Disaster Resilience of Indonesia

Disaster Prevention and Environmental Economics Research in Indonesia

Indonesia is a prominent country with a land area of approximately 1.9 million square kilometers and a population of 217 million. Although the country experienced a major economic structural reform in the late 1990s, its economy has regained stable growth in recent years as a result of the skillful economic and fiscal management by the present administration. Indonesia is a nation with immense potential and is endowed with abundant human and natural resources. The conditions faced by Indonesia—geographical location, archipelagic region, tectonic formation, largest population, and tropical climate—place the country in the highest disaster risk category for tropical geo-hazards, including earthquakes, volcanic eruptions, landslides, floods, and forest fires. Over the years, Indonesia has repeatedly experienced the same types of disasters. Earthquakes, volcanic eruptions, tsunamis, floods/debris flows, landslides, slope failures, and wildfires are especially frequent, and measures to control and reduce these disasters are needed urgently.

Natural disasters often undo many years of physical and human capital accumulation and can lead to a slowdown in the speed of convergence toward a steady-state economy within the country context. The world has recently faced a sharp surge in the frequency of extremely severe natural disasters, and the effects have been devastating. Indonesia is highly prone to natural disasters given its location between the Ring of Fire and the Alpide belt. In the past several years, Indonesia has been subjected to numerous natural disasters, among them the devastating earthquake and tsunami that occurred in Aceh and Nias at the end of 2004 and which claimed more than 225,000 lives. The Asia Pacific Disaster Report prepared by the UN International Strategy for Disaster Reduction (UN/ISDR) and the UN Economic Commission for Asia and the Pacific (ESCAP) on October 26, 2010, reported that during the 1980–2009 period in Asia Pacific countries, Indonesia was ranked fourth in terms of experiencing natural disasters, with approximately 312 cases, was ranked second in terms of the highest number of deaths, at approximately 191,164 people, and had economic losses of at least US\$ 22.5 billion. These statistics alone make disaster prevention study a high research priority for growth economists seeking to identify the optimal policies for addressing the impacts of rapid-onset events, especially in the context of developing countries such as Indonesia.

The causes of the high frequency of severe disasters have become popular research topics, and the findings have improved the understanding of the relationship between human activities and the environment. In defining the negative effects, frequent natural disasters are linked to low economic growth rates and reduced household consumption over time, without any sign of economic recovery. Regarding the positive effects, natural disasters promote economic growth, improve agricultural and construction outputs and capital formation, and address fiscal and trade deficits through the rebuilding and recovery process.

The resulting regional economic status after a natural disaster can be influenced strongly by how the recovery activities are managed. Aside from being a disaster-prone area, Indonesia is also experiencing many advances in economic development. As home to 260 million people, it is one of the world's major emerging economies and emitters of greenhouse gas (GHG) emissions. According to its National Council on Climate Change, the country emitted approximately 2.1 GtCO2 in 2005, or about 5% of global GHG emissions, and contributed 0.6% only to world gross domestic product.

At the global level, 57% of GHG emissions originate from fossil fuel combustion. Unlike China and India, most of Indonesia's emissions do not originate from industrial activities. In fact, 38% of the country's total emissions are from peatland (with the majority caused by fires) and 35% are caused by changes in land use. In a country with the third largest tropical forests in the world, this situation will continue to reflect considerable environmental degradation and health costs, a decrease in agricultural productivity, and material damage. Under a business-as-usual scenario, emissions from peat fires, land use, and forestry are expected to grow to 1.64 GtCO2 by 2030 (from 0.91 GtCO2 in 2005), bringing Indonesia's estimated total GHG emissions to 3.3 GtCO2 according to the country's Second National Communication under the United Nations Framework Convention on Climate Change (UNFCCC).

Indonesia's economy is anticipated to grow by 5.2% in 2017 and 5.3% in 2018 as the effects of fiscal consolidation dissipate and as private activity increases, supported by modestly rising commodity prices, improving external demand, and increased confidence attributable to reforms. Considering the increasing economic opportunities and environmental impacts in Indonesia, research focusing on environmental policies will provide substantial assistance in designing proper regional policies and in maintaining sustainable economic growth in general.

Significance of Targeting Palangkaraya and Makassar

Palangkaraya is a small-medium-sized city in Central Borneo, Indonesia. It is the largest city in the Kalimantan and is located strategically in the heart of Borneo. Similar to the other urbanized cities in Indonesia, Palangkaraya is facing an irregular land use pattern in which its flood-prone areas are being occupied illegally for residences. The country's first President Soekarno suggested Palangkaraya—in the interior area of less developed and heavily forested Kalimantan—as a potential replacement for Jakarta.

Palangkaraya is the capital of the Central Kalimantan Province in Indonesia, and a population of 19,000 lives near Kahayan River, an area that experiences daily flooding. Numerous illegal residents reside in this flooded area, and they are significantly exposed to both natural and living environment risk. The main cause of this flooding is the deforestation of the agricultural area surrounding Palangkaraya. Palangkaraya provides an interesting object for environmental disaster prevention economics with respect to natural hazards from floods and environmental destruction. In this study, we develop a new analysis model for environmental disaster prevention economics by describing land use in a flooded region and the movement of illegal residents, focusing on Palangkaraya as the research object. Although this study focuses on one region in Indonesia, many similar areas exist in the Indonesian and Southeast Asian regions. The content of this book provides sufficient general versatility to adhere to similar problems in other areas.

As the "Gateway to Eastern Indonesia," Makassar's economy is booming as the country's east develops and demands more commodities. Economic growth in Makassar exceeds the national average and reached 9.23% in 2014. The same is occurring with the ever-growing population. With 1.8 million residents, Makassar is a large market that shows significant promise. Aside from the economic growth, Makassar faces environmental issues also, such as reclamation area issues and greenhouse gas emissions.

Makassar has experienced rapid urbanization in the last two decades and is now the fifth largest city in Indonesia. Makassar also experiences rapid changes in land use. Between 1990 and 2000, as much as 24% of the total agriculture land and 16% of the paddy cultivation area was converted to other uses, namely, housing and commercial. Approximately 49% of the city's gross domestic product (GDP) is derived from the manufacturing, hotel and restaurant, and tourism sectors. These industries are located mostly along the coast and are at risk of flooding and a rise in the sea level. Another consequence of urbanization is the increasing number of motor vehicles. In 2012, the number of cars was 1.7 million, reflecting a 12% annual growth rate. Inadequate infrastructure in terms of the road network and a poor public transportation system are the main causes of frequent traffic jams in the city. Thus, Makassar provides an interesting perspective for studying the interaction between infrastructure and changes in environmental policy.

Toyohashi, Aichi, Japan   Yuzuru Miyata
Toyohashi, Aichi, Japan   Hiroyuki Shibusawa
Kalimantan Tengah, Indonesia   Indra Permana
Makassar, Indonesia   Any Wahyuni

Contents

Part I
Analysis of Illegal Settlements in Palangkaraya City, Indonesia – Urban Economics Studies

Chapter 1
Issues of Illegal Settlements in Palangkaraya City

1.1 Introduction

The last millennium marked a symbolic transition in the evolution of human settlements through which the world's people become more urban than rural. The rapid population growth in cities gives rise to concerns about the changing nature of the relationship between rural and urban. In 2003, people who live in city areas of developing countries accounted for 48%, or approximately three billion people, of the world's population; moreover, by 2035, half of the world's poor people are projected to live in urban areas (UN-HABITAT 2006, 2010).

Furthermore, vivid evidence exists that points to the phenomenon that the dynamics of urban interactions in various linkages—ranging from economic linkages, social linkages, political and administrative linkages, and service linkages—contribute strongly to morphological changes in city and urban areas. These linkages, in particular, economic linkages in sectors such as industries, services, and households, boost urbanization and are widely recognized for their contributions to the appearance of irregularities in land use patterns in urban areas. Such irregularities are configured by the misuse of vacant lands, including flood-prone areas, hill slopes, vacant land alongside railways, vacant land under high-voltage transmission towers, and others, for residential functions. In addition, settlements usually take a slum formation in which an illegal settlement is typologically included.

This study presents urban economics models, namely, the partial equilibrium model and the general equilibrium model, to analyze Palangkaraya city in the Central Kalimantan Province, Indonesia. This study aims to provide systematic explanations of the existence of illegal settlements in the city. Similar to many small-medium-sized cities in Indonesia, Palangkaraya city faces an irregular land use pattern from illegal settlements covering flood-prone areas in urban regions. In addition, as the city became more populated, the quality of the surrounding natural environment and the forests in surrounding rural areas apparently started declining.

© Springer Nature Singapore Pte Ltd. 2018
Y. Miyata et al., *Environmental and Natural Disaster Resilience of Indonesia*,
New Frontiers in Regional Science: Asian Perspectives 23,
https://doi.org/10.1007/978-981-10-8210-8_1

In fact, some areas in Palangkaraya city, particularly residential areas alongside the riverbank, face frequent floods. This study seeks a better understanding of such misuse of flood-prone areas in Palangkaraya city in the midst of urbanization growth and the devastating effects of deforestation.

The models enable analytical studies on irregular urban land use patterns in Palangkaraya city, particularly the appearance of illegal settlements in flood-prone areas. The primary effort has been devoted to identifying interactions between urban economic agents and flood occurrences and to determining how dynamic interactions configure land use patterns in Palangkaraya city. As a result, such appropriate urban policies aimed at addressing the problem can be derived analytically and assessed to promote sustainable development.

1.2   Main Issues

Urbanization has been regarded widely as a trigger for the increase in urban problems in many cities around the world. These urban problems range from the cities' physical structure to social and urban environmental problems. For instance, in Indonesia, many cities are undergoing radical changes in their physical form, not through territorial expansion only but also through internal physical transformations given the rapid urbanization that has been occurring starting three decades ago. The morphological change has resulted in the existence of irregular formations, such as the appearance of illegal settlements in flood-prone areas within cities.

Urbanization can yield important social benefits and improve the access to public services and the job market. However, at the same time, urbanization could result in increasing demand for services, including housing. The unmet demand for affordable housing, along with urban poverty, has led to the emergence of slums in many developing countries. Today, more than one billion urban residents around the world live in inadequate housing. They live mostly in slums with poor living conditions and insufficient services. One-quarter of all urban housing units in developing countries are temporary structures, and more than one-third do not conform to building regulations.

Furthermore, globalization, free-market policies, and Asian-Pacific integration have stimulated Indonesia's economic growth in the last three decades, which has been experienced as an "economic miracle." During this period, Indonesia could accelerate development throughout its territory through the support of rapid economic growth. In particular, urban areas in seven cities—Jakarta, Surabaya, Bandung, Semarang, Medan, and Makassar—within the Indonesian sovereignty were improved significantly by rapid development. In Java Island—the most populated island—massive circular migration is observed easily as thousands of workers commute daily on the long route to job sites. Urban areas are promising places for rural dwellers to escape the worsening rural impoverishment.

Among Asian countries, Indonesia is the fourth most populous country in the world, with 217 million people in 2004. The 2000 census showed that 36.34% of the population lived in urban areas. In 2015, at least 50% of the population lived in cities. The population in urban areas is increasing at 4.4% per year, much higher than the national population growth. This growth has placed more than 110 million people in approximately 60 cities. Although the average population growth was only 1.49% during the last census period (1990 to 2000), it was focused on urban areas and, in particular, high in the industrial growth areas of Riau, Belitung, Banten, and Maluku Utara. The 2001 average growth rate for urban households was estimated at 3.5–3.75% given an average household size of 4 persons (Hoek-Smit 2001) or an increase of approximately 800,000 urban households.

In 2000, 86,833,000 dwellers populated urban areas in Indonesia. Between 1990 and 1995, the fastest growing cities were Bandung at 3.1% and Makassar at 3.0%, indicating that growth did not occur solely in large cities. The facts showed also that growth occurred in small-medium-sized cities. Hence, urbanization and its problems occur also in small-medium-sized cities with populations less than one million.

Rapid urbanization and an inadequate ability to cope with the housing needs of people in urban areas have contributed to the expansion of illegal settlements in riverbank areas. As a region influenced by a tropical climate that features high humidity and rainfall, obviously the Central Kalimantan Province in Indonesia preserves many watersheds. Each watershed has a main river and tributaries. In addition, most cities, towns, and villages are obviously near rivers for access to waterway transportation and water resources. Therefore, most settlements, particularly in the downtowns of cities, are preferably constructed on riverbank areas.

The Central Kalimantan Province in Indonesia is on Kalimantan Island, the third largest island in the world. Land topography in the province is mostly flat in the south, where most of the cities, towns, and villages are located, and is slightly mountainous in the north, where rainforests remain but suffer from massive deforestation. In addition, hundreds of rivers flow from the northern region, which is characterized as highlands, to the southern region, which is characterized as lowlands. Therefore, given such natural characteristics, wetland areas exist and cover some of the lowlands in the south. Hence, most of the cities in the south, such as Palangkaraya, Sampit, and Pangkalan Bun, and towns, such as Kasongan, Pulang Pisau, Buntok, Muara Teweh, and Kuala Kapuas, obviously coexist with wetland areas.

Palangkaraya city, similar to other small-medium-sized growing cities in the Kalimantan region in which the largest areas of tropical rainforests still remain, is growing and experiencing urbanization. The city's rural–urban linkages that involve flows of goods, capital, labor, and information and technology exchanges are formed and actively interact in many ways to feed the development of its urban area and of its surrounding rural areas. Palangkaraya city, with an administrative size of 2678.51 km^2, has two faces. One of the city's faces is represented by industries, public and private offices, urban infrastructures and amenities, and dense settlements. Another face is represented by the countryside, including villages, agricultural land, and forests.

In addition, during the rainy season, a monsoon augmented by humid breezes from the Indian Ocean brings heavy rainfall to the region. The water naturally flows from the highland to the Java Sea in the south through river networks, henceforth configuring numerous watershed areas including the wetland areas. Because the city is adjacent to the watershed area and the river basin system, and because the forest at the upper river suffers from massive deforestations, Palangkaraya city is prone to destructive water inundation. In particular, floods threaten the settlements on the riverbank, including the settlements in flood-prone areas.

1.3 Study Motivations

The Central Kalimantan Province is preserving tropical rainforests of high bio-diversity and a huge wetland area. The area provides habitats for endangered species, such as Orangutan Kalimantan (*Pongo pygmaeus*), Bekantan (*Nasalis larvatus*), *Tarsius* (*Tarsius bancanus* Borneonus), Anggrek Ekor Tikus (*Paraphalaenopsis* spp.), Ikan Belida (*Notopterus chitala*), and others. Furthermore, according to calculations by the Wetland International Indonesian Program in 2004 (Wahyunto, Ritung, Suparto, and Subagjo 2004), the Central Kalimantan Province stores approximately 2.25 million hectares of wetland areas or approximately 14.65% of the province's size. The wetland area consists of an estimated 6.3 million tons of carbon content and is spread randomly in the regencies and cities of South Barito, East Barito, Pulang Pisau, Palangkaraya, Katingan, East Kotawaringin, West Kotawaringin, and Sukamara.

The wetland areas are scattered within the administrative areas of Palangkaraya city. In particular, the wetland's subsets, such as flood-prone areas, are misused frequently as residential areas. Such action is a kind of human intervention that disturbs the ecological functions of flood-prone areas. For instance, during housing construction projects, flood-prone areas become disheveled from digging, channeling, land-clearing, and land-filling activities. These treatments apparently distracted the carbon content in the ground, hence, emitting carbon into the atmosphere. Therefore, wetland areas should be protected from massive human interventions to reduce carbon emissions significantly, in line with the global mitigation activity for climate change.

The Central Kalimantan Province region lies on lowland topography and is widely dominated by flatlands. Six large rivers longer than 400 km exist—Sungai Barito, Sungai Katingan, Sungai Kahayan, Sungai Kapuas, Sungai Mentaya, and Sungai Seruyan—draining the lowland and, thus, forming complex river basin systems. Considering the natural conditions, henceforth the existence of flood-prone areas is inevitable within Central Kalimantan Province. These flood-prone areas comprise approximately 11% of the total size of the Central Kalimantan Province or 153,564 km^2. In addition, the flood-prone areas in the region are naturally connected to river basin systems near which most of the cities, villages, and settlements are located.

Furthermore, flood-prone areas alongside a river body essentially hold a hydrological function. By nature, these areas rule water charge and water discharge to and from the river body, hence, acting as flood control. During rainy sessions when the riverbank is exceeded by runoff, flood-prone areas slow and store the runoff, hence protecting the down river from devastating floods. The reverse is true in dry sessions when flood-prone areas function as water storage for the rivers. By disturbing and covering the flood-prone areas with building construction, their functions rapidly deteriorate, and floods become out of control. In addition, because flood-prone areas are periodically inundated and saturated by runoff water from water bodies, this condition allows for interchanges between aquatic and terrestrial components and provides storage for the runoff, which allows for infiltration and recharging of alluvial groundwater. Hence, ground for the habitats of particular species is created, thus, holding a biological function. Considering these reasons, flood-prone areas are critical areas in which preservation and conservation should be implemented rather than occupation by humans.

The Central Kalimantan authority recently launched a discourse on green government policies aimed at guiding and controlling the region's development. The discourse has attracted the attention of the public and stakeholders, including Indonesia's national government and many international organizations (WWF Indonesia 2012).

Furthermore, the Central Kalimantan Province is now the host to the implementation of Reducing Emissions from Deforestation and Forest Degradation (REED), an international initiative on climate change and forests under the UNFCCC and the Kyoto Protocol. REED, which is supported financially by Norway and other donor countries (Springate-Baginski and Wollenberg 2010), is conceptually aimed at significant participation in efforts to reduce carbon emissions. Developed countries that emit significant amounts of carbon should take responsibility to support developing countries in their efforts to preserve their forests and any potential carbon storages. In addition, carbon storage includes not only forests but also wetland areas. Therefore, in accordance with the REED pilot project, wetland areas including flood-prone areas in the Central Kalimantan Province should be treated delicately. In that sense, preservation and conservation must be among the initial actions rather than occupations.

Several occupied flood-prone areas alongside the Kahayan riverbank in Palangkaraya city were evaluated, which necessitates considering the background and questions such as why it was unexpectedly occupied and who engaged in the misuse. Historically, the river is a source of life that provides water and food, as well as waterway transportation. Therefore, inhabitants tend to live as close as possible to the source of life—the river. In the past, when forests at the upper river were yet untouched by human activities, the riverbank was once a safe place to live. Eventually, as wooden industries emerged, heavy downpours at the upper river could charge the water exceeding the river body. As a result, the occupied flood-prone areas become inundated. Therefore, these facts indicate that the hydrological function of flood-prone areas is actually fading, obviously increasing the risk of a flood for other riverbank settlements in the downtown area of the city. However, this deteriorating condition is simply avoided by low-income groups consciously settling in flood-prone areas and taking on the flood risk. Hereinafter, because infrastructure, facilities, and services are inadequate, the quality of living and the environment have worsened in flood-prone areas, creating an urban problem.

Furthermore, with the aim of restoring the occupied flood-prone areas, Palangkaraya city's authority has introduced resettlement policies. These policies have been initiated because the city authority realized that such dwellings have disturbed the critical functions of the flood-prone areas and have had no legal development framework. The resettlement policies offered dwellers a new residential site on the outskirts of the city. Although some effort was made to implement the policies, most of the inhabitants resisted them strongly because the new residential site is far from the city center and is not served by reachable transportation networks to and from the center.

Moreover, some urban economic scientists have introduced analytical methods and have conducted rigorous analysis of urban studies. Their achievements have placed milestones for scientific and analytic study in the urban economics field. Applying their approaches, current urban economics studies may become scientific and analytic. Therefore, this study is motivated to provide an analytical study and a rigorous analysis of the irregularities in the configuration of urban land use in areas of illegal settlements. Thus, from this attempt, scientific explanations are derived, and policies addressing the problem can be numerically simulated and assessed.

1.4   Originality

Urban economics studies, particularly studies on illegal settlements in urban areas of cities, are quite rare; however, some studies revealed significant results that augment our understanding of the urban phenomena. These studies have contributed to the broad recognition of the existence of slums in many urban areas. Yet, analytical methods that apply science have rarely been demonstrated in these studies. Henceforth, scientific explanations including numerical simulations on the phenomena were rarely found.

This study comes with rigorous analyses and scientific explanations regarding the existence of illegal settlements in flood-prone areas. The models constructed in this study were developed using standard urban economics theories. The maximization problem for both the production sector and households provides the bid rent function and the bid max lot size function in Palangkaraya city. Then, by inputting empirical data, several numerical simulations, including policy simulations, were conducted, and the results were discussed. Henceforth, this study considers these matters and, thus, can be regarded as putting forward an analytical method and a scientific analysis for such irregularities in land use patterns in which illegal settlement appears. This attempt has yet to appear in traditional urban economics.

Furthermore, this study employed the bid rent approach. This approach was first used by von Thünen (1826) to analyze agricultural land rent in rural areas. Subsequently, this approach was rigorously extended to the urban context by Alonso (1964) and followed by Muth (1969), Mills (1972a, b), Beckmann (1973), and

Solow (1973). The most recent study was done by Fujita (1989) and Fujita and Krugman (1995). In particular, Fujita (1989) solved a utility optimization problem to define the bid rent function, Ψ (u, r), which provides the maximum amount that consumers of residential space are willing to pay under utility, u, and at distance r from a central business district. However, in that study, Fujita neglected the heterogeneity of households and the land.

This study follows the approach of Fujita (1989). However, differently from Fujita (1989), which did not consider the heterogeneity of land quality, this study considers two types of land in the city: normal land and flood-prone areas. This approach reflects more real conditions of particular cities in which a river basin system and surrounding forests exist. Because no studies exist in the field of regional science that were applied to regions such as the Central Kalimantan Province, in which city development, river basin system, and forest degradation collide, this study can be regarded as a pioneer and as stimulating further scientific studies on regional development and environment problems in the Central Kalimantan Province.

1.5 Study Description

This study aims to analyze Palangkaraya city, a small-medium-sized city in the Central Kalimantan Province, Indonesia. Similar to other urbanized cities in Indonesia, Palangkaraya city faces such an irregular land use pattern in which its flood-prone areas are illegally occupied as residences. This study seeks scientific and systematic explanations for the existence of illegal settlements in flood-prone areas; hence, appropriate urban policies could be assessed analytically. As granted by nature, the city is characterized by different land qualities. Land in the city is qualified on the basis of damage to household assets from floods. Three areas in the city are so-called flood-prone areas that are inundated frequently by runoff from a river body. Apparently, floods cause damage at various levels to the household assets invested in the areas.

Furthermore, the existence of housing units in flood-prone areas can be identified as an illegality because they were built out of the legal framework—in this case, a lack of land title certificate and no building construction permits. Moreover, the flood-prone areas alongside river bodies hold the critical functions of hydrology, biology, and ecology, and their existence is protected by laws. Nonetheless, Indonesia's national acts on the environment, river, and regulation of public works by the Minister of the Republic of Indonesia and the city ordinance PERDA No.16/1982 of Palangkaraya city have acknowledged that areas alongside a river body, including flood-prone areas, must not be used for dwellings and must be left as open spaces to preserve their natural functions. Thus, these acts, regulations, and ordinances regard the occupation of flood-prone areas or areas alongside a river body as illegal. Given that point, the term "illegal settlement" is defined and refers to settlements built outside of the legal framework.

Furthermore, despite this restriction, the occupation of flood-prone areas for residential use in urban areas is a common phenomenon in urbanized cities, particularly in developing countries. These illegal areas are populated primarily by low-income households living in a high-density area, often without adequate facilities, infrastructure, and services. Therefore, because of the lack of accessibility to clean water, waste dumps, and healthy sanitation—as observed in many illegal settlements—living conditions have deteriorated to low standards. Although many studies exist on the urban phenomenon and explanations might have been derived, the necessity still exists to complement the results obtained from previous studies with explanations for basic questions, such as how did the settlements in flood-prone areas come into being, what models can be applied to analyze the phenomenon, and so forth. Therefore, in that sense, scientific explanations that result from applying analytical methods are expected to be formulated, thus, enriching the literature.

This study aims to provide such scientific explanations using an analytical method on the existence of flood-prone areas in the urban area of Palangkaraya city in the Central Kalimantan Province, Indonesia. This study constructed urban economics models to analyze the illegal settlements in the city. The models take into account flood occurrences and damage to household assets. This attempt is introduced by considering facts in the Central Kalimantan Province region, which is in a tropical climate with inevitable high precipitation. In particular, during the rainy season from September to December, rainfall is usually a maximum of 4000 mm per year. Severed by uncontrolled deforestation at the upper river, devastating floods could destroy some city areas, villages, and settlements near the river body.

This dissertation is arranged as follows.

Chapter 1 introduces the main issues addressed by this study and consists of the study motivations, originality, and description.

Chapter 2 provides the necessary background for this study, including urban issues through the world and, in particular, urban development issues in Indonesia. This chapter also elaborates on the urbanization process and, thus, urban development, which is primarily increased through dynamic interactions in sectors such as industries, services, and households. Such interactions, as found in many cases, have led to the appearance of slums in the form of illegal settlements in city areas. Furthermore, the specific characteristics of Palangkaraya city that emphasize the existence of illegal settlements in flood-prone areas of the city and the ensuing environmental problems are briefly described.

Chapter 3 presents the theoretical development of the partial equilibrium model. However, for the sake of simplification, the production side is neglected in the model; hence, household income is exogenously given.

Chapter 4 presents the development of the general equilibrium model. Significantly different from the partial equilibrium model, the general equilibrium model takes into account the agglomeration of the economy and the production sector. In that sense, the general equilibrium model is slightly closer to reality. Chapter 5 presents the conclusions and policy recommendations.

References

Alonso, W. (1964). *Location and land use*. Cambridge, MA: Harvard University Press.

Beckmann, M. J. (1973). Equilibrium models of residential land use. *Regional and Urban Economics, 3*, 361–368.

Fujita, M. (1989). *Urban economic theory. Land use and city size*. Cambridge, MA: Cambridge University Press.

Fujita, M., & Krugman, P. (1995). When is the economy monocentric? von Thünen and Chamberlin unified. *Regional Science and Urban Economics, 25*, 505–528.

Hoek-Smit. (2001). *Effective demand for low and moderate income housing, homi project, Kimpraswil, Government of Indonesia*.

Mills, E. S. (1972a). *Studies in the structure of the urban economy*. Baltimore: Johns Hopkins University Press.

Mills, E. S. (1972b). *Urban economics*. Glenview: Scott Foresman.

Muth, R. F. (1969). *Cities and housing*. Chicago: University of Chicago Press.

Solow, R. M. (1973). On equilibrium models of urban locations. In J. M. Parkin (Ed.), *Essays in modern economics* (pp. 2–16). London: Longman.

Springate-Baginski, O., & Wollenberg, E. (Eds.). (2010). *REDD, forest governance and rural livelihoods: The emerging agenda*. Bogor: The Center for International Forestry Research (CIFOR).

United Nations Human Settlements Programme (UN-HABITAT). (2006). *State of the world's cities 2006/7*. Routledge: The Millennium Development Goals and Urban Sustainability.

United Nations Human Settlements Programme (UN-HABITAT). (2010). *State of the world's cities 2010/11 cities for all: Bridging the urban divide*. Routledge.

von Thünen, J. H. (1826). Der Isolierte Staat in Beziehung auf Landwirtschaft und Nationalekonomie, Hamburg.

Wahyunto, E., Ritung, S., Suparto, W., & Subagjo, H. (2004). *Maps of area of peatland distribution and carbon content in Kalimantan, 2000–2002*. Wetlands International – Indonesia Programme & Wildlife Habitat Canada (WHC), Bogor.

WWF-Indonesia. (2012). *WWF-Indonesia Annual Report 2010–2011: Towards five decades of conservation in Indonesia*.

Chapter 2
Background of the Study

2.1 Urbanization and Slum Phenomena: A World Issue

Urban space is a product of three principal developments. The first is the growth of settlements in terms of size and number, including their spreading. The second is an increase in the population living in urban areas. The third is the transformation of society attributable to the realm that people who live in towns and cities follow an urban lifestyle, which can be distinctive from a rural lifestyle.

Moreover, urban spatial growth is the result of the combination of a natural increase in the urban population and net migration to urban areas (Firoz 2004). Urban growth is observed to be very closely linked with industrialization, commercialization, or overall economic growth and development. Finally, because most of the populations have grown more rapidly, urbanization must definitely address keeping peace with economic development, which is a continuous and rapid process.

World urbanization has been a prominent phenomenon since the prior century. In 2003, people who lived in the city areas of developing countries accounted for 48% of the world's population or approximately three billion people. In its report, the Department of Economics and Social Affairs of the United Nations (United Nations DESA 2004) indicated that by 2030, 60.8% of the world's population will live in cities, as shown in Fig. 2.1.

Population growth is expected to be particularly rapid in the urban areas of less developed regions, averaging 2.3% per year during 2000–2030 (see Table 2.1). Migration from rural to urban areas and the transformation of rural settlements to urban places are important determinants of the high urban population growth anticipated in less developed regions.

In addition, the region of Asia is projected to hold 55% of the urban population in 2030 (see Fig. 2.2), reflecting an increase of almost 50% from the 2000 urban population. This rate of increase is estimated as the highest among other regions,

© Springer Nature Singapore Pte Ltd. 2018   13
Y. Miyata et al., *Environmental and Natural Disaster Resilience of Indonesia*,
New Frontiers in Regional Science: Asian Perspectives 23,
https://doi.org/10.1007/978-981-10-8210-8_2

Fig. 2.1 Urban percentage of the world, selected periods 1950–2030

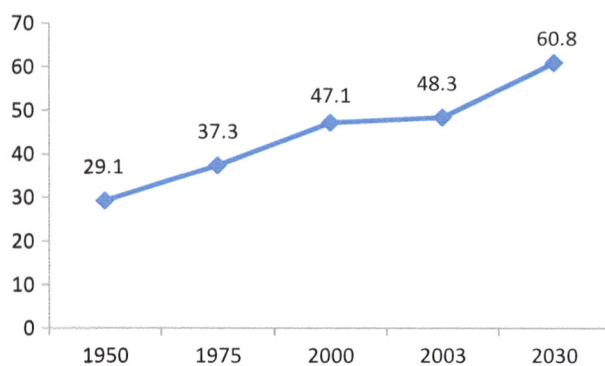

Table 2.1 Total, urban, and rural populations by development groups, selected periods, 1950–2030

Development groups	Population (billions)					Average annual rate of change (percent)	
	1950	1975	2000	2003	2030	1950–2000	2000–2030
Total population							
World	2.52	4.07	6.07	6.30	8.13	1.76	0.97
More developed regions	0.81	1.05	1.19	1.20	1.24	0.77	0.13
Less developed regions	1.71	3.02	4.88	5.10	6.89	2.10	1.15
Urban population							
World	0.73	1.52	2.86	3.04	4.94	2.72	1.83
More developed regions	0.43	0.70	0.88	0.90	1.01	1.45	0.47
Less developed regions	0.31	0.81	1.97	2.15	3.93	3.73	2.29
Rural population							
World	1.79	2.55	3.21	3.26	3.19	1.17	−0.03
More developed regions	0.39	0.34	0.31	0.31	0.23	−0.43	−1.05
Less developed regions	1.40	2.21	2.90	2.95	2.96	1.46	0.06

Source: Department of Economics and Social Affairs, United Nation (2004)

indicating that the most rapid urbanization within the next 20 years is expected to occur in the cities of Asia.

Rapid urbanization with highly paced social and economic development in Asia is creating growth in city and town populations, leading to a shortage of infrastructure provisioning and increasing traffic congestion, provoking environmental degradation, and evoking a housing shortage. These issues became major problems faced by cities and towns in pursuing sustainable development.

Increased urbanization has led to a concentration in the number of industrial units and other service sector activities that are located mainly in the core of cities. Hence, as a consequence, numerous complex problems have emerged that have created an unbalanced situation in urban centers, especially social and economic conditions. The migration has strained infrastructural facilities in cities to the breaking point. The intermixing of various land uses has created confusion and chaotic conditions.

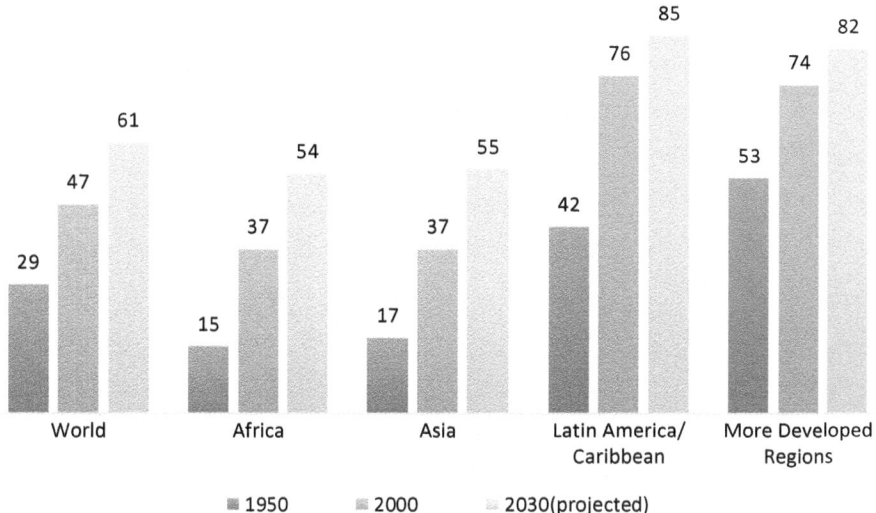

Fig. 2.2 Trends in urbanization by regions, selected periods 1950–2030 (*Source*: Department of Economics and Social Affairs, United Nations 2004)

An acute shortage of housing exists in urban areas, with the result that metropolitan areas and cities throughout the nation face a grim situation given the rapidly increasing number of shanty dwellers, squatters, pavement dwellers, and slums.

Most developed countries, developing countries, and less developed countries are facing this problem of growing slums within their city areas. Slums are universal in character; however, not a single country has completely nullified their appearance in its urban areas. Infrastructural facilities, such as housing, safe drinking water, transportation, health care, educational institutions for children, and parks, have become woefully inadequate and will soon reach a critical stage that threatens civilized existence itself. Today, more than one-fifth of the urban population lives in slums and squatter settlements (UN-Habitat 2010).

Definitions and concepts of slums vary from country to country depending on the socioeconomic conditions of the concerned nations. Slums are often characterized as areas of a city with inadequate housing, deficient basic requirements, overcrowding, and congestion. Slums are also defined as areas with buildings unfit for human habitation. Also embodied in the definitions of a slum are phrases such as dilapidation, overcrowding, faulty street arrangements, and lack of ventilation, lighting, or sanitation facilities or a common combination of those factors. In addition, slums are definitely a detriment to safety, health, and morals.

A slum phenomenon has been internationally recognized as inevitably accompanying urban growth in most developing countries. According to a UNESCO report, a slum is represented by a building, a group of buildings, or an area characterized by overcrowding, deterioration, insanitary conditions, or absence of facilities and amenities, and—because of some or all of these conditions—the health, safety, or morals of its inhabitants or the community are endangered (Anderson 1959). An

Fig. 2.3 Population of slum areas at midyear, by region and country 2001 (*Source*: UN-Habitat 2001)

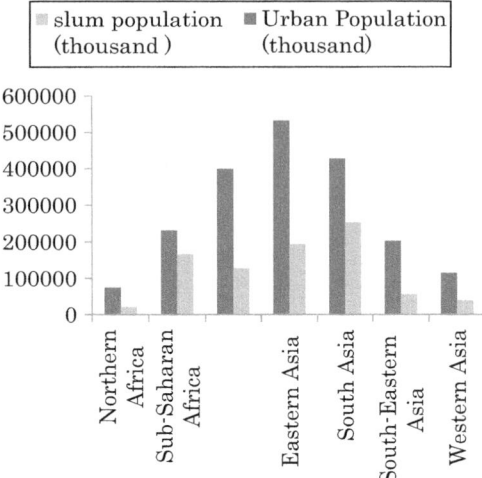

urban slum includes high-density dwellings, such as high-rise apartments, and squatter settlements and shantytowns, where people occupy vacant land and illegally build shacks for themselves. Many illegal settlements are built on land poorly suited for housing, for instance, on flood-prone areas or steep hillside that are especially subject to damage from natural disasters.

Slum residents usually lack security of tenure or the right of legal access to and use of the lands and buildings they occupy. Each year, several million urban dwellers are forcibly evicted. An estimated 20–40 million urban families are homeless, some because they have been evicted and others because they cannot afford housing, even illegal.

The situation is worse in sub-Saharan Africa, where 60% of urban housing units are temporary structures and approximately half do not conform to building regulations. Sub-Saharan Africa has the highest slum percentage, at 71.9%, relative to its urban population, indicating that slum areas dominate these urban areas. Developing countries in South Asia have the highest average slum percentage, given the contribution of India, which has the largest slum population (see Fig. 2.3).

It is particularly difficult for the urban poor to obtain tenure because property registration processes are inefficient, complicated, and expensive. The process is even more difficult for informal settlements. Many governments hesitate to legalize such dwellings out of fear of encouraging even more illegal settlements.

However, legal housing is typically too expensive or scarce for the urban poor. Outdated government regulations that control land acquisition and housing construction, coupled with the rapid urban population growth, have made land scarce and, in turn, has inflated housing prices. Estimates from various countries show that low-income households would need 15–30 years to save 30–50% of their incomes to afford a legal house that meets minimum standards. In reality, most of the urban poor earn too little to save any money at all. They also lack access to credit from commercial lending institutions.

Table 2.2 Percentage of urban population living in slums in the 2000s

Country	Percentage
Indonesia	54
Bangladesh	47
India	36
Philippines	28
Sri Lanka	21
Thailand	16
Malaysia	15
Republic of Korea	1

Source: UN-ESCAP (2000)

Considering the slums in Indonesia relative to those in other countries shows that, in the 1980s, as the urbanization rate in Indonesia's mega cities rapidly increased, the percentage of the urban population living in squatter and slum settlements became the highest relative to other countries, such as Bangladesh, India, the Philippines, Sri Lanka, Thailand, Malaysia, and the Republic of Korea. This percentage is more than half, on average, at exactly 54% of the urban population living in slum and squatter settlements. Table 2.2 shows the percentage of the urban population living in slum.

2.2 Urban Housing Problems: Slum Trigger

The impact of urbanization on the urban space, the urban environment, and the quality of life is tremendous. Often, the provision of infrastructural facilities lags far behind the pace of urbanization. As a result, cities could easily face a severe shortage of water, sewage, developable land, housing, transportation, and other urban services.

Deteriorating infrastructure, weak municipal institutions, and poor delivery systems have constrained the urban economy and its ability to generate employment, income, and services for the poor. The impact of urbanization may be considered in the context of urban infrastructural services comprising water supply, sanitation and solid waste management, and land and the urban environment.

The urban housing sector has been recognized in terms of public policies and investments; however, the sector's priority has generally been considered very low. The housing crisis continues to be daunting and manifests itself in many ways: growth of slums and haphazard development, overcrowding and deficient services, increasing homelessness, and speculation in and profiteering from land and houses.

The provision of formal housing is beyond the affordability of the poor. Often, infrastructural provision is overwhelmed by an increasing population that created the housing shortage. As an example, according to Suhandjaja (1991), the housing shortfall in urban areas in Indonesia is approximately 864,000 dwellings (Table 2.3).

Also noticeable is that most of the housing stock is temporary. Moreover, as of the early 1980s, almost one-third of all urban area constructions were temporary

Table 2.3 Urban housing shortage, Indonesia

	Number
Total urban housing stock	10,826,000
Total number of households	11,690,000
Estimated shortage of dwelling	864,000

Source: CBS (1989) and Suhandjaja (1991)

Table 2.4 Quality of urban housing stock, Indonesia

Quality of dwelling	1961		1983	
	Number of units	Percent	Number of units	Percent
Permanent dwellings	431,000	20.0	2,419,000	37.0
Semipermanent dwellings	539,000	25.0	2,096,000	32.5
Temporary dwellings	1,185,000	55.0	1,935,000	30.0
All dwellings	2,155,000	100.0	6,450,000	100.0

Source: Suhandjaja (1991)

(Table 2.4). A similar proportion of the housing stock, approximately 30.6%, was also smaller than 40 m^2 in size (CBS 1989), and a large proportion of low-income households lack access to electricity and a piped water supply (Urban Institute 1989). Thus, these urban problems are compounded by the illegal status of many squatter settlements in urban areas; the use of marginal sites in areas liable to flooding, including flood-prone areas; and the absence of infrastructural provisions.

Urban space is a product of three principal developments. The first is the growth of settlements in term of size and number, including their spreading. The second is the increase in the population that lives in urban areas. The third is the transformation of society attributable to the belief that people living in towns and cities follow an urban lifestyle that can be distinctive from a rural lifestyle.

Moreover, the urban spatial growth is the result of a combination of the natural increase in the urban population and the net migration to urban areas (Firoz 2004). Urban growth is observed to be very closely linked with industrialization, commercialization, or overall economic growth and development. Finally, as most populations grow more rapidly, urbanization will definitely fail to keep pace with economic development, which is a continuous and rapid process.

2.3   Typology of a Slum

Distinctions between types of slums appearing in cities are often made on the basis of combinations of physical location, the legality of land ownership and built structure, urban zoning, land occupation, and informal construction. For instance, a clear separation exists between slums proper, on the one hand, and shanties or spontaneous housing, on the other hand. Table 2.5 shows the typology of the slum. The term "slum" often refers to inner-city residential areas that were built a long time ago and that have prevailed through urban planning, zoning, and construction

Table 2.5 Typology of slums

A. Metro core	1. Formal
	(a) Tenement
	(i) Hand-me-downs
	(ii) Built for poor
	2. Informal
	(a) Squatters
	(i) Authorized/legal
	(ii)Unauthorized/illegal
	(b) Pavement dwellers
B. Periphery	1. Formal
	(a) Private rental
	(b) Public housing
	2. Informal
	(a) Pirate subdivision
	(i) Owner-occupied
	(ii) Rental
	(b) Squatters
	(i) Authorized/legal
	(ii) Unauthorized/illegal
	3. Refugee camps

Source: Davis (2006)

standards but also that, over time, have progressively become physically dilapidated and are overcrowded by the lowest-income groups. The term "illegal settlement" often refers to illegal or semi-illegal urbanization processes or unsanctioned subdivisions of land on which illegal occupation occurred by squatters who erected housing units, usually without formal and legal permissions. This type of slum is typically referred to as a shanty or a squatter settlement.

2.4   Dynamics of Indonesia's Urbanization

Today, many Indonesian cities face rapid population growth. Between 1995 and 2005, Indonesia experienced a 39% increase in its urban population that outpaced other East Asian countries by a wide margin. A substantial number of rural households became urban households without even changing location. In Indonesia, the definition of urban is based on characteristics such as density, number of amenities, and the share of income from agriculture, all of which are subject to changes.

From 1971 to 1990, the percentage of the population living in urban areas increased from 17.1% to nearly 28.8% nationally, which results in a rate of increase of approximately 40.62% (see Fig. 2.4).

Evidence from surveys showed that the movement toward urban areas, particularly to West Java, Southeastern Sulawesi, Kalimantan, and other islands, stemmed

Fig. 2.4 Rate of
Indonesia's urbanization
1950–1970 and 1970–1990
(*Source*: United Nations,
World Urbanization
Prospect 1993)

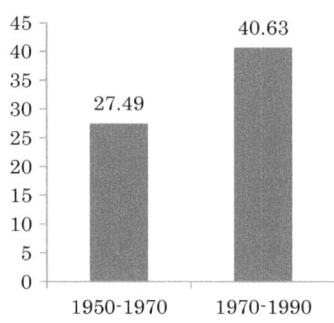

not from the innate lure of cities but from the lack of employment in rural areas.
Migrants seemed to view the pollution, crime, anonymity, and grinding poverty of
the city as short-term discomforts that eventually give way to a better life.

Economic activity is becoming more concentrated in large cities and their surrounding areas. The four largest metropolitan areas generate approximately
one-third of the national GDP and account for approximately 14% the country's
total population. Table 2.6 shows that, in 2006, Jakarta and its surrounding cities
contributed approximately 20% to Indonesia's GDP, followed by greater Surabaya
6%, greater Bandung 3%, and Makassar 1%.

Cities surrounding major metropolitan areas also contribute to and benefit from
their proximity to these areas. Metropolitan Jakarta's contribution to GDP is
enhanced from the large number of sizable urban areas surrounding DKI Jakarta.
In East Java, the industrial center moved away from the capital city of Surabaya to
the surrounding cities of Sidoarjo and Gresik. In effect, this move created an
integrated regional (metropolitan) economy with an average annual growth of
approximately 7%. In contrast, the population growth in Surabaya city is negative,
whereas this growth in surrounding cities is positive because people tend to move to
the outskirts of a metropolitan area.

The flow of people from rural to urban areas was massive during the rapid
development in urban areas of primate cities under the freedom era. The Indonesian
government under Soekarno's regime, followed by Soeharto's regime, adopted
national economic development policies. Many cities and towns developed rapidly
during these regimes, created employment in infrastructure constructions and other
sectors, and provided a better quality of life by setting up urban facilities and
amenities. This "radiating light" of cities attracted the rural population to leave
agricultural activities. The rural–urban flow then became unbearable and, as time
passed, went beyond the capacity of cities to absorb.

Table 2.6 Populations and gross regional domestic product, 2006, in most urbanized cities in Indonesia

Name	Provinces	Population	Population growth	Number of poor	Real GRDP	Growth	Share to national
JABODETABEK		15,202,546	2.0%	1,701,300	309,879	6.0%	20.0%
Greater Bandung	West Java	6,450,386	1.0%	714,200	40,370	7.0%	3.0%
Greater Surabaya	East Java	7,676,518	0.2%	1,037,800	102,174	6.0%	6.0%
Greater Makassar	South Sulawesi	1,521,158	2.0%	148,200	12,260	8.0%	1.0%
Total		30,850,608		3,601,500	464,683		30%

Source: Statistics Indonesia (2007)

Table 2.7 Urban population in Indonesia, 1980–2006

Year		Java	Outer Islands	Indonesia
1980	Total population (000)	91,269.5	55,665.4	146,934.9
	Urban population (000)	22,929.4	9916.4	32,845.8
	Proportion of urban population	0.251	0.177	0.224
	Share of urban population (%)	69.8	30.2	100.0
1990	Total population (000)	107,581.3	71,049.9	178,631.2
	Annual rate of population growth 1980–1990 (%)	1.65	2.47	1.97
	Urban population (000)	38,341.5	17,092.3	55,433.8
	Proportion of urban population	0.357	0.238	0.310
	Share of urban population (%)	69.2	30.8	100.0
	Annual rate of urban population growth 1980–1990 (%)	5.28	5.95	5.37
2000	Total population (000)	120,429.3	83,026.7	203,456.0
	Annual rate of population growth 1980–1990 (%)	1.11	1.56	1.35
	Urban population (000)	8874.4	26,369.8	85,244.2
	Proportion of urban population	0.847	0.328	0.419
	Share of urban population (%)	69.1	30.9	100
	Annual rate of urban population growth 1980–1990 (%)	4.38	4.43	4.40
2006	Total population (000)	–	–	225,500
	Annual rate of population	–	–	1.40
	Urban population		–	94,710.0
	Proportion of urban population	–	–	0.42

Source: Firman (2004)

2.4.1 Patterns of Indonesia's Urbanization

Among 20 countries with populations larger than 50 million, Indonesia is ranked in the middle-low level, slightly more than Thailand, Vietnam, India, Ethiopia, Pakistan, Congo, and Bangladesh (Population Reference Bureau 2006). In 1950, Jakarta was the only city in Indonesia with a population of more than one million. Only 30 years later, by 1980, three additional cities—Surabaya, Bandung, and Medan—reached one million people. Then, in 1990, seven additional cities, including Semarang, Yogyakarta, Palembang, and Ujung Pandang (now Makassar), joined this statistic. During the last three and a half decades, Indonesia has undoubtedly faced a massive transformation from a predominantly rural to an urban society.

The share of the urban population between Java and the outer islands has remained constant since 1980, at almost 70% for Java and 30% for the outer islands, as shown Table 2.7. From 1980 to 2000, the total urban population in Java increased from almost 23 million to nearly 59 million, whereas the population in the outer islands increased from 10 million to 26 million. These growth figures confirm that the major agglomeration of the urban population occurred in Java.

Indonesia is shifting from a primarily rural economy to an economy based on industry and services. Despite a large number of individuals still living in rural areas, agriculture currently represents approximately 16% only of Indonesia's GDP. Manufacturing represents approximately 26%, and all industry and services primarily located in urban and peri-urban locations amount to approximately 83.6% of GDP. Manufacturing has been the fastest growing segment of the economy and, since 1981, has grown more than three times as fast as the agricultural sector.

This shift is driving rapid demographic change. In 1975, just 20% of Indonesians were city dwellers; however, more than 60% are expected to be urban dwellers, by 2025. Greater Jakarta has an urban agglomeration of more than 17 million people. The three next largest cities—Surabaya, Bandung, and Medan—have agglomerations between 3 and 4 million. After these cities are five other cities in the range of one million inhabitants and then a very large number of medium to small cities. Different approaches are needed to support these different types of urban areas. In particular, the large number of smaller cities is a challenge for development institutions. Since 2001, Indonesia has been in a decentralization era. Many urban investment functions officially shifted from central ministries to local governments, resulting in a major change in governance and significant effects on regional development.

Administratively, Indonesia is divided into 33 provinces. In each province, the percentages of the population living in urban and rural areas vary. In some provinces, such as Kepulauan Riau, Jawa Barat, DI Yogyakarta, Banten, and Kalimantan Timur, the urban population is larger than the rural population, including DKI Jakarta, which in fact has no rural population. However, in general, the total rural population is 57.86% higher than the urban population, as shown in Table 2.8. Therefore, in the vast majority of provinces in Indonesia, rural areas—in which most agriculture activities occur—are still places of living for many people.

2.4.2 Rural–Urban Linkages

Indonesia is an agriculture-based country. More than 60% of the Indonesian population is farmers living in rural areas. However, despite low-income gains, farmers are never weary and continue to persistently plant rice and other agricultural commodities. Living in such marginal conditions means that most farmers cannot afford higher education and adequate healthcare for their families. For years, most of the government's development programs have been concentrated in Java Island, the most populous island of Indonesia. This policy has fostered population and development imbalances within the archipelago of Indonesia, resulting in increasing numbers of poor landless farmers in rural areas. In contrast, significant land with huge potential is available in the outer islands; however, the land cannot be productive because of low population density.

Table 2.8 Percentage of Indonesia's population by areas and provinces, 2000

Province	Area	
	Urban (%)	Rural (%)
Indonesia	**42.14**	**57.86**
1. Nanggroe Aceh Darussalam	28.75	71.25
2. Sumatera Utara	42.64	57.36
3. Sumatera Barat	28.93	71.07
4. Riau	34.59	65.41
5. Jambi	28.32	71.68
6. Sumatera Selatan	33.78	66.22
7. Bengkulu	28.33	71.67
8. Lampung	21.24	78.76
9. Kep. Bangka Belitung	43.04	56.96
10. Kepulauan Riau	76.01	23.99
11. DKI Jakarta	100	na
12. Jawa Barat	50.31	49.69
13. Jawa Tengah	40.19	59.81
14. DI Yogyakarta	57.64	42.36
15. Jawa Timur	40.88	59.12
16. Banten	52.17	47.83
17. Bali	49.74	50.26
18. Nusa Tenggara Barat	35.08	64.92
19. Nusa Tenggara Timur	15.46	84.54
20. Kalimantan Barat	26.4	73.6
21. Kalimantan Tengah	28.14	71.86
22. Kalimantan Selatan	36.21	63.79
23. Kalimantan Timur	57.75	42.25
24. Sulawesi Utara	36.66	63.34
25. Sulawesi Tengah	19.82	80.18
26. Sulawesi Selatan	31.07	68.93
27. Sulawesi Tenggara	21.01	78.99
28. Gorontalo	25.54	74.46
29. Sulawesi Barat	17.97	82.03
30. Maluku	25.33	74.67
31. Maluku Utara	29.31	70.69
32. Irian Jaya Barat	33.13	66.87
33. Papua	21.14	76.86

Source: Statistics Indonesia (2000)

The Indonesian government became aware of the situation and for many years set up assistance programs. The most recent program was the Middle-Term National Development Plan 2005–2009 under the Agenda of Improving Welfare, Agenda III of the National Development Plan. This agenda has led to the creation of several programs that aim to improve the welfare of rural farmers and the poor by developing rural infrastructure, education, health facilities, and services for rural communities.

Furthermore, there are forests in rural Indonesia that are locations for plantation development and forestry industries. By law, a plantation is required to be established only on forestland that has been designated officially as converted for other uses. However, in practice, two powerful factors could undermine the law. First, most conversion forests in Indonesia are available in the relatively undeveloped eastern part of the country; however, most industries prefer to be in the west, closer to a labor force, processing infrastructure, and markets. Second, establishing plantations in such converted forestland is doubly attractive because only after obtaining a land-clearing license can a company clear-cut the area and sell the timber to wood-processing industries. This arrangement may represent a windfall profit over and above the profits expected from future palm oil harvests. As a result, rural areas particularly on the islands of Sumatera, Kalimantan, Sulawesi, and Papua have undergone significant deforestation, with approximately 60 million hectares of forests cleared since 1950. Officially, the country's forest area stands at approximately 105 million hectares (FAO 2001), although numerous sources estimate that forest cover declined to less than 100 million hectares in 1997 (FWI/GFM 2002). The current rate of deforestation is acknowledged officially at approximately two million hectares per annum, which implies that the actual forest cover may well have declined to less than 90 million hectares. Indonesia has almost 10 million hectares of forest plantations, including approximately 3.5 million hectares planted with rubber trees. Until approximately 1990, the involvement of the corporate sector in plantation development was negligible. In contrast, small land holders have always played an important role in the plantation sector, and they established 4.6 million hectares as early as 1969. For a while, because of the financial crisis in 1997, the planting rate declined from 230,000 hectares in 1997 to 78,000 hectares in 2000.

Research conducted by McGee (1987) revealed rural–urban linkages in metropolis areas called JABODETABEK (abbreviation for Jakarta, Bogor, Depok, Tangerang, Bekasi) in Indonesia. Rural–urban linkages exist for flows and exchanges of goods, information, capital, and people. Such linkages have sharpened rural characteristics and have influenced the magnitude of the linkages and the benefits to both rural and urban areas. The mega-urban in JABODETABEK is a model of the socioeconomic space. The following three types of socioeconomic spaces exist.

1. Peri-urban. These areas surround the metropolis and can be reached using daily commuters. Peri-urban areas are marked specifically by a decrease in agricultural activities and a transition of agricultural land use to urban land use.
2. Desa-kota. The term desa-kota is derived from the Indonesian words for country and town, i.e., desa and kota. Desa and kota regions are specified by a mix of agricultural and nonagriculture activities. Typically, a desa-kota region is spread out alongside corridors between cities, is densely populated, and experiences rapid economic growth. The region faces increments of transportation and its infrastructure.
3. The third type of socioeconomic space consists of: (a) rural surrounding secondary and tertiary cities that are densely populated yet have slow economic growth

and (b) frontiers with dispersed populations and obviously low density. This region has a variety of ubiquitous agricultural activities.

The existence of rural transformation mainly in peri-urban and desa-kota corridors raises issues of rapid increases in economic activities that represent shifts from agriculture to nonagriculture; shifts in land use from agricultural to urban activity, such as housing, industrial, and nonagricultural use; increments of population and density; and the ascension of land prices. Such things are not yet handled by appropriate instruments. Hence, as a result, spatial, social, and environmental problems are coming into being.

Furthermore, Fu et al. (1981) constructed a model using observations in rural and urban southeastern countries. This macro-spatial model can describe clearly the characteristics of rural–urban linkages in Indonesia. The model was developed on the basis of the dualism of the northern and southern areas and with consideration of the two sectors, which are modern economy sectors, formal sectors, and traditional economy sectors/informal sectors. Five essential components of the model are world markets, formal sectors, informal sectors, rural sectors with export-oriented activities, and rural sectors with traditional economic activities.

The model explicitly shows the characteristics of the rural–urban linkage among the five components, as depicted in Fig. 2.5. The linkage is asymmetric from the significant gaps in income, welfare, and job opportunities between rural and urban as result of polarization by industry development in urban areas and by penetration of capital and consumer goods as a consequence of a free market. The wage gap increment has pulled migrant flows from rural areas. Then, after being settled in urban areas, migrants typically send remittances to family members remaining in rural areas. This cash transfer and the decreasing trend in agriculture activities in rural areas are among the factors that are pushing a relatively stagnant rural economy.

The linkages between rural and urban areas in Indonesia are significantly influenced by the global economy. During the 1997 economic crisis and the implementation of a free-market policy in Indonesia, the linkages were altered. The crisis has had detrimental impacts on industrial sectors in urban areas but was, conversely, advantageous to agriculture sectors in rural areas because commodities such as chocolate, coffee, and nuts bring benefits to small-medium-sized enterprises in both urban and rural areas. Furthermore, the hegemony and domination of industrial countries have appeared asymmetrically in global markets that, in turn, have disadvantaged economically developing countries.

Moreover, as identified in many cases, the rural–urban linkages tend to be specific and rarely take place in all aspects. Once linkages appear, they need to be cultivated by exploring both the competitive and the comparative advantages of rural and urban areas and the region. Generalization and uniformity of the approach must be ignored; instead, local content and local wisdom are crucial for getting involved.

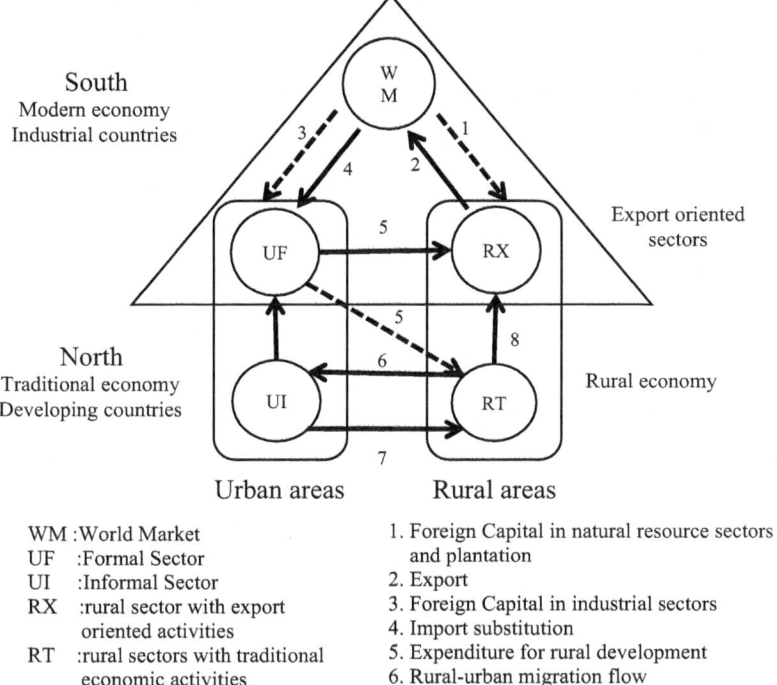

South
Modern economy
Industrial countries

North
Traditional economy
Developing countries

Export oriented
sectors

Rural economy

Urban areas   Rural areas

WM : World Market
UF   : Formal Sector
UI   : Informal Sector
RX   : rural sector with export
         oriented activities
RT   : rural sectors with traditional
         economic activities

1. Foreign Capital in natural resource sectors
   and plantation
2. Export
3. Foreign Capital in industrial sectors
4. Import substitution
5. Expenditure for rural development
6. Rural-urban migration flow
7. Remittance transfer
8. Client-patron relationship

Fig. 2.5 Macro-spatial model of rural–urban linkages (*Source*: Fu et al. 1981)

2.5 Illegal Settlement: A Type of Slum Formation

An illegal or unauthorized settlement refers to a type of slum or, in this case, a shanty or squatter settlement. In addition, this type of settlement is more specifically characterized by the legal aspect, such as housing units that were constructed outside the framework of formal law. This category also includes units built on land for which the property rights are unclear and/or are not sanctioned by law, such as housing units built without a building permit. This feature is commonly observed in many urbanized cities of developing countries and is typically the product of an urgent need for shelter by the urban poor. As a dense settlement comprising communities housed in self-constructed shelters under conditions of informal or traditional land tenure, informal settlements are characterized by a dense proliferation of small, make-shift shelters built from diverse materials, degradation of the local ecosystem, and severe quality of life problems. In Indonesia, these types of settlements often arise on land that poses a flood risk. They are often adjacent to rivers, industrial complexes, and above-ground solid waste disposal sites that pose a major health hazard. Their development is beyond the control of urban governments.

Although the terminology of illegal settlement is not yet widely used, it has appeared, albeit rarely, in some studies. Instead, more popular terminologies, such as "slum," "informal settlement," and "squatter settlement," are preferably used in many studies. Moreover, the existence of marginal settlements in urban areas should be considered not merely from their physical appearance but also from their land status, whether legal or illegal. In addition, in many cases, the land status of marginal settlements is not homogenous but is divided into illegal and legal. Even in some cases, all land ownership in settlements is illegal because the settlement was constructed on land restricted by laws or local ordinances. This type of settlement fully demonstrates the misuse of designated areas through unofficial occupation by low-income groups and is called an illegal settlement. Therefore, clearly, we can specify an illegal settlement as a type of squatter settlement, informal settlement, or slum occupying restricted lands that, hence, has absolutely no legal status regarding land ownership for all settlers. This specification makes an illegal settlement different from any other marginal settlements in urban areas.

In particular, squatter settlements have no legal status of tenure and are a familiar scene in many Indonesia urban and peri-urban areas. Any vacant land, such as riverbanks that are flood-prone areas, hill slopes, areas alongside railways, and even open areas under high-transmission networks, are widely occupied by low-income groups. This phenomenon has been widely observed and identified yet lacks a better understanding. Therefore, urban policy responses often miss the core issues of the phenomenon. In addition, most city authorities are obsessed by city beautification, which provides stimulus for continuously addressing the existence of illegal settlements. Therefore, eviction, demolition, relocation, legalization, and integration are some of the alternative solutions often proposed. The appearance of illegal settlements on restricted areas, such as on riverbank areas within city limits, as found in many cities in developing countries, is a negative effect of urbanization. The urban-poor community has grown rapidly, and many have moved from economically nonviable farming areas to squatter settlements.

In many cases, most of the illegal settlements are usually inhabited by low-income households who seek proximity to the central business district (CBD); hence, they can save on the pecuniary cost of transportation and enjoy urban facilities and amenities. However, as the population has increased, settlements have become denser, and, consequently, the quality of the environment and life within their premises have worsened.

Furthermore, areas massively occupied by human settlements have seen their runoff storage function deteriorate. Moreover, in many cases, social problems such as unhealthy living conditions and poverty have been incurred in illegal settlements. This urban problem needs to be managed to provide a better living environment for city inhabitants. Therefore, many city authorities, particularly in developing countries, are addressing this urban problem. We consider this issue as relevant to our study.

The officially unplanned illegal occupation of urban and peri-urban land for residential purposes is an ongoing phenomenon of Indonesia's towns and cities today. This type of settlement has mushroomed from occupation by the poor who,

Fig. 2.6 Comparison of population in urban, slums, and illegal slums, Indonesia (*Source*: Compiled from data of UN-Habitat 2004; NUSSP 2007)

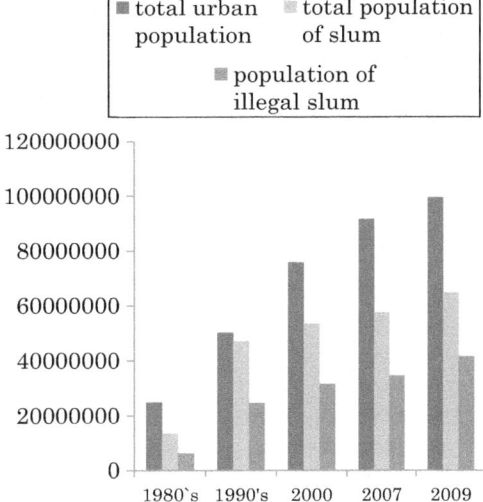

Table 2.9 Size of slums and illegal settlements in Indonesia, 1980–2009

	Size of slum (ha)	Size of illegal settlement (ha)	Percentage %
1980s	9455	4361.41	46.13
1990s	33,034	17,283.39	52.32
2000	37,432	22,088.62	59.01
2007	40,231	24,194.92	60.14
2009	45,324	29,116.14	64.24

Source: Compiled from data of UN-Habitat (2004) and NUSSP (2007)

because of their low income, cannot gain access to formal housing provision facilities. In Indonesia during the 1980s and 1990s, and during the last 9 years, the growth of illegal settlements was in line with an increase in slums. In the 1980s, the urban population living in slum areas was approximately 54% of the total urban population in Indonesia's mega cities. That percentage increased to 69.12% in the 1990s. In line with this increase, the size of illegal settlements in the 1980s and 1990s increased to 46.13% and 52.32%, respectively (see Fig. 2.6). This significance increment cannot be separated from the fact that, during the 1980s and 1990s, rapid urbanization occurred primarily in Indonesia's mega cities, such as Jakarta, Surabaya, Semarang, and Bandung.

Along with the growth of slums in urban areas during the past three decades, occupation areas by illegal settlements increased. In the past decade, approximately 29,116.14 hectares of slum areas within Indonesian cities are considered illegal because of inappropriate occupation in designated areas (see Table 2.9).

An illegal settlement usually occupies vacant land, such as hill slopes, land under high-transmission towers, marginal land on riverbank areas, swamps, land alongside railways, and land at any other location. Of course, locations with a certain function should be restricted by law. However, primarily for many developing countries, the problem is that the law is often enacted long after a settlement has become severely dense; therefore, any effort to implement the law faced difficulties, including resistance from thousands of settlers. In some cases, local authorities might succeed by force to empty the locations; however, given the inconsistencies in urban development, settlements arise again without much to deter them.

Illegal settlements can be eroded away through evictions because local authorities sometimes do not want to take on too much risk by displacing the low-income groups often recognized as the urban poor. The local authority represents the people's political choice and, thus, worries about losing its popularity among the poor. Hence, instead of implementing an eviction policy, local authorities prefer to negotiate a period of letting. Unfortunately, regardless of this period, illegal land transfers continue, and, hence, settlements become denser, and any effort by local authorities to decolonize these areas faces greater difficulties.

Illegal settlements, which are a type of slum, have become an urban problem. Their existence reflects the failure of local and national governments to provide affordable housing for the poor. The situation depicts an indecisive implementation of laws influenced mainly by political and money-oriented interests. It is no wonder that, in some cases, slum organizers have a close connection with certain official authorities who guarantee tolerance. Because illegal settlements are in restricted areas, they have no or limited access to urban infrastructure and facilities, such as clean water networks, electricity, urban sewerage systems, waste disposals, public toilets, and neighboring roads. Hence, as a result, settlements preserve not only a deterioration in the quality of life for its settlers but also environmental degradation if located on water reserves, such as rivers, lakes, ponds, and swamps.

At least until 2007, 17 million people in Indonesian urban areas lived below the poverty line. They occupied 40,000 hectares of land and developed slums in 10,000 locations around the country. Many of the identified locations have no legal status of tenure because they are in prohibited areas that should be maintained as open space given environmental laws and local government ordinances.

Furthermore, the national government of Indonesia through the Neighborhood Upgrading and Shelter Sector Project (NUSSP) has funded approximately 165 billion rupiahs to upgrade 3960 hectares of slums. Since its launch in 2005, NUSSP has absorbed 176.4 billion rupiahs of the national budget and has been implemented in 6143 hectares of slums. It follows that, in 2009, NUSSP has upgraded 2400 hectares of slums in 32 urban areas in Indonesia. Hence, in 2010, the targeted goal that should have been achieved was the amelioration of slums in 100 cities.

2.6   The Study Area

This study analyzed Palangkaraya city, a small yet growing city located on the riverbank of Kahayan in the Central Kalimantan Province in Indonesia. The city is flanked by the Kahayan and Sebangau watersheds, which naturally configure

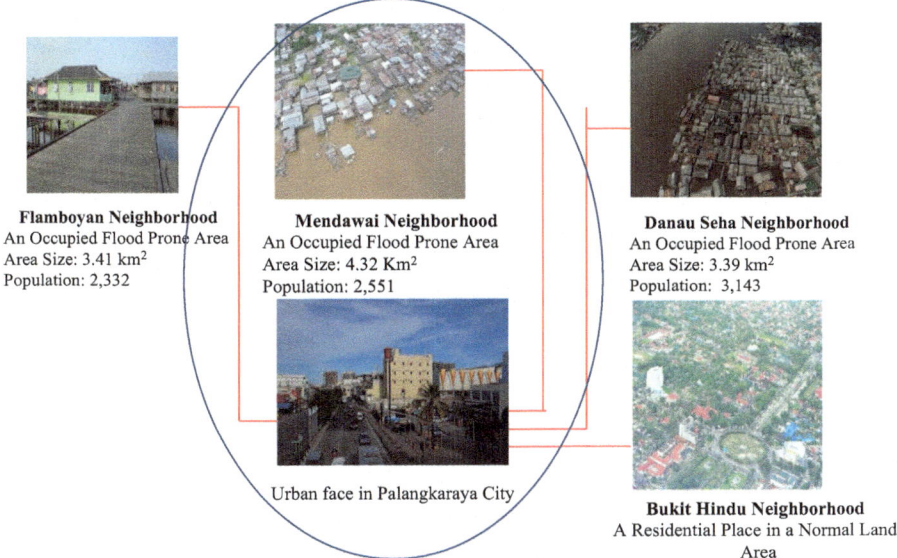

Fig. 2.7 Pictorial diagram of Palangkaraya city (*Source*: Field Survey 2010, Department of Architecture Palangkaraya University)

Palangkaraya city with considerable wetland area. In the city area, the wetland takes various subset forms. One is flood-prone areas. However, despite restrictions attributable to environmental laws, the area is persistently misused for residences. A pictorial diagram of the study area is shown in Fig. 2.7.

2.6.1   Geography and Land Use

The city's geographic position is at $6°40'–7°20'$ east longitude and $1°30'–2°30'$ south latitude. Administratively, Palangkaraya city includes 5 districts consisting of 30 villages. The five districts are Pahandut, Sebangau, JekanRaya, Bukit Batu, and Rakumpit. In addition, the municipality's administrative size is 2678.51 km², and, of its total size, Palangkaraya municipality's land use comprises areas as presented in Table 2.10.

2.6.2   Economic Linkages and Urbanization

Linkages exist between the city and its rural surrounding. These linkages play important roles in local and regional economic development. Rural areas serve as sources of agricultural commodities, raw materials, and labor for the city, whereas

Table 2.10 Land use in
Palangkaraya city

Land use	Size (km^2)
Forest areas	2485.75
Agriculture land	12.65
Settlement areas	45.54
Plantation areas	22.30
River and lake	42.86
Others	69.41
Total size	**2678.51**

Source: BPS Statistic Palangkaraya city (2008)

cities are places of opportunity for rural dwellers, providing markets for agricultural products, services, and housing.

Economic interdependences between urban-based enterprises and rural consumers and between rural producers and urban markets underline their important potential role in processes of rural and urban change in Palangkaraya city.

Furthermore, by using Rutz's index facility in 2000, NUD classified Palangkaraya city as a small city with attributes that categorize it as one level lower than a regional metropolis. This classification is based on the fact that, in 1998, the city had in excess of 150,000 inhabitants and ranked 32nd in terms of the number of facilities, including banks and offices, relative to other cities in Indonesia.

Moreover, although categorized as a small city, urbanization is taking place in Palangkaraya city. The rate of urbanization has varied throughout the decades. The highest rate was during 1990–2000, at 10.32%, as presented in Fig. 2.8.

2.6.3 Existence of Illegal Settlements in Palangkaraya City

Urbanization has contributed to urban problems in Palangkaraya city, such as the appearance of irregularity in land use patterns. As the city has become urbanized, land and housing have become scarce and unaffordable, particularly for low-income groups. For example, a flood-prone area—a type of wetland near a river stream—was unfortunately misused by a low-income group constructing illegal settlements. Without access to urban infrastructures and facilities, health and environmental problems easily arise in settlements.

However, despite such deterioration, low-income groups continue to dwell in these areas. These individuals have adapted to such conditions and can maintain their lower-than-minimum standard of living. In addition, illegal settlements are scattered near a city center, enabling transportation costs to job sites in the CBD to be saved, which may stimulate an increase in settlements.

Because flood-prone areas are alongside riverbanks, illegal settlement formations are adjacent to the river body. During the rainy season, which is from November to March, frequent floods occur that inundate the illegal settlements. However, in response to the floods, instead of moving out of the settlements, the inhabitants

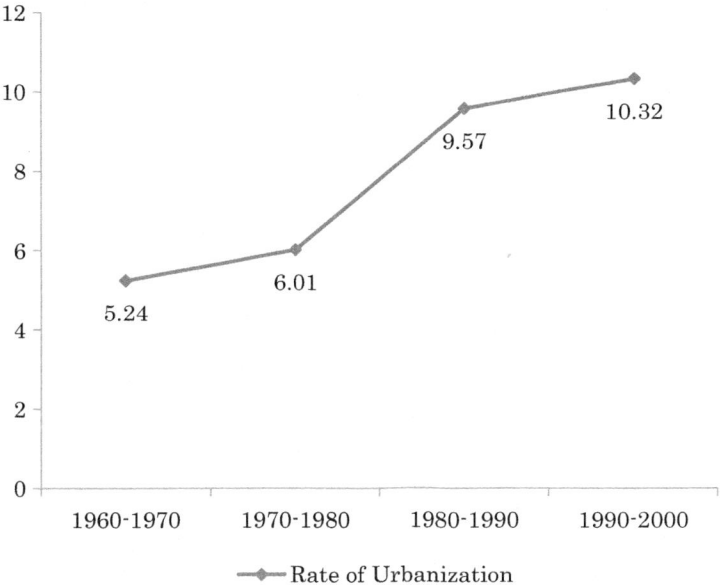

Fig. 2.8 Rate of urbanization in Palangkaraya city 1960–2000 (*Source*: BAPPEDA, Kota, Palangkaraya 2007)

employ various strategies depending on the magnitudes of the floods. For instance, when the water level exceeds a house's floor level, all of the furniture and equipment are removed to a semi attic and people live in rooms above the water. Figure 2.9 indicates the illegal settlement locations in Palangkaraya city.

Actually, the local authority recognized the existence of the settlements as an illegality under PERDA 16/1982. In addition, the municipal authority made many efforts to attempt to resettle the inhabitants at a new location outside the urban area. However, those efforts failed because the inhabitants refused to move. Among the efforts, in 1998, a devastating fire burned almost all of the houses and infrastructure in the Flamboyan neighborhood. Through that event, the municipal authority had a good opportunity to take resettlement action and deflate the area all at once. Taking the opportunity, the municipal authority first sealed the area and established a warning board announcing a ban on redevelopment. Then, the authority constructed new houses near the city boundary. Unfortunately, when the houses were ready, the inhabitants rejected the resettlement simply because it was too far from their job sites. Therefore, instead of accepting the offer, thousands of inhabitants chose to return, and they rebuilt their houses precisely on the previous location. To that fact, the municipal authority succumbed and eventually ignored the flood-prone areas, and the status quo was maintained. Hence, from that time, the settlements were allowed to grow again. Table 2.11 shows the illegal settlements in Palangkaraya city.

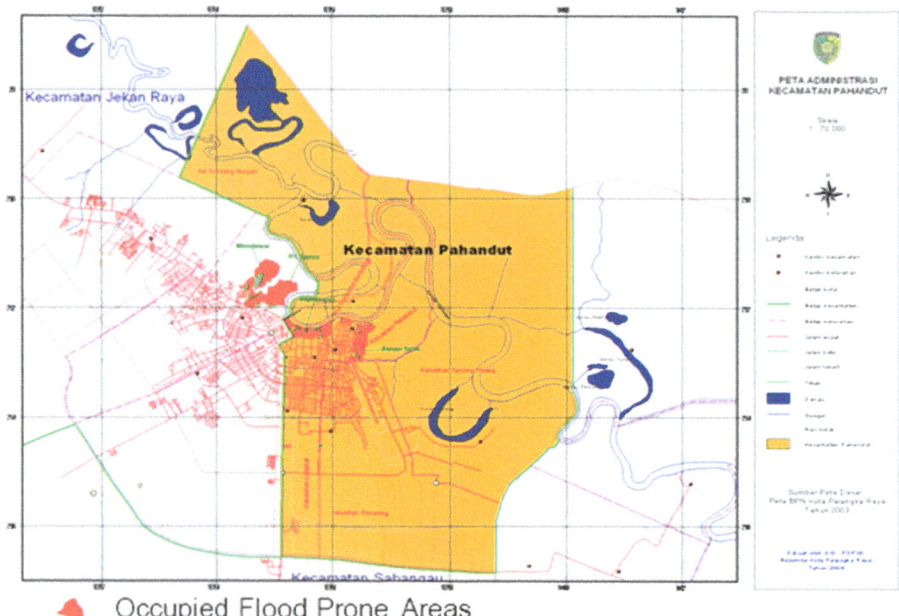

◄ Occupied Flood Prone Areas

Fig. 2.9 Illegal settlement dispersion in Palangkaraya city (*Source*: BAPPEDA, Kota Palangkaraya 2007)

Table 2.11 Illegal settlements in Palangkaraya city

Neighborhood	Size (km^2)	Population	Density (people/km^2)
Danau seha	3.39	3143	927
Flamboyan	3.41	2332	683
Mendawai	4.32	2551	590

Source: Extracted from monographs of kecamatan Pahandut and kecamatan Jekan Raya (2009)

2.6.4 Deforestation in Palangkaraya's Rural Areas

Palangkaraya city is surrounded by several tropical rainforests that are classified as primary forests. These forests are laid in the surrounding rural areas. Figure 2.10 indicates the forest coverage in the Central Kalimantan Province. A little more than half of the total forest area has been converted into large-scale agricultural use. In October 1999, the entire forest was officially listed into three categories: conservation forests at approximately 6.34%, preservation forests at 9.45%, and production forest at 84.21% of the total 10,735,935 hectares.

Sixty-three logging companies hold the legal rights to exploit and manage the production forests. Moreover, 27 forestry industries own timber processing permits. In 2006, log production in the Central Kalimantan Province contributed 12.25% of

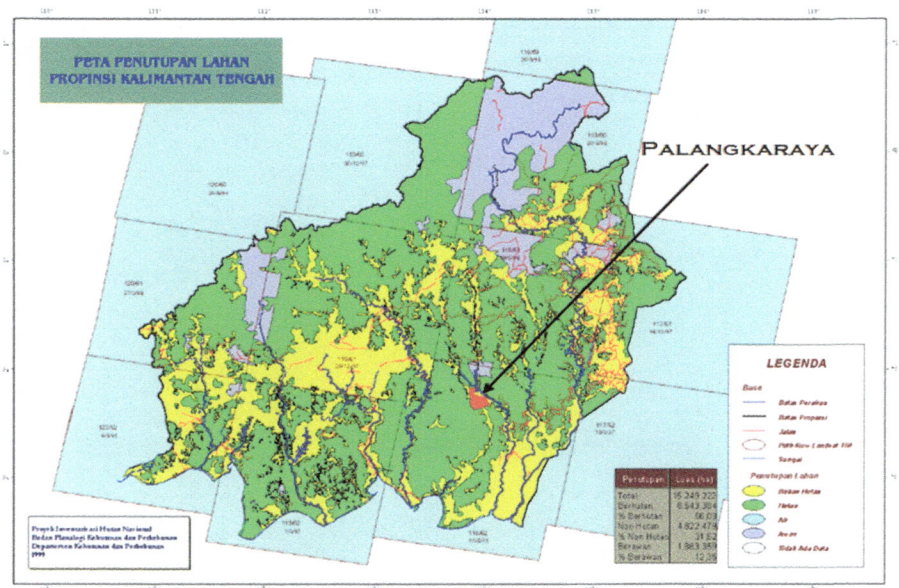

Fig. 2.10 Map of forest coverage in the Central Kalimantan Province 2008 (*Source*: Forestry Planning Agency, Department of Forestry, Republic of Indonesia 2008)

national production, timber production contributed 8.28%, and plywood production contributed 2.06%.

In addition, the deforestation rate in the surrounding forests during the last 12 years was recorded at approximately 138,208 hectares/year (Forestry Planning Agency, Department of Forestry, Republic of Indonesia, 2008).

2.6.5 Flood Occurrences

Because the existence of the forests was largely eroded, the level of the water that was inundating the riverbank areas began to increase. Therefore, as observed, since the last decade, devastating floods could routinely occur every year. Runoff has turned into a permanent threat to any illegal settlements in the flood-prone areas, and such a condition did not occur previously in the cities in the Central Kalimantan Province.

When the water inundation level increases to higher than the normal limit, it then becomes a hazard to any riverbank settlement in the urban areas. The damage cannot be counted because many assets, primarily durable ones such as houses and household goods perish. That casualties also occur create definite inestimable losses. Furthermore, wooden construction is limited in durability when faced with the brunt of floods over a long period. The lateral force of the flood's current collapses

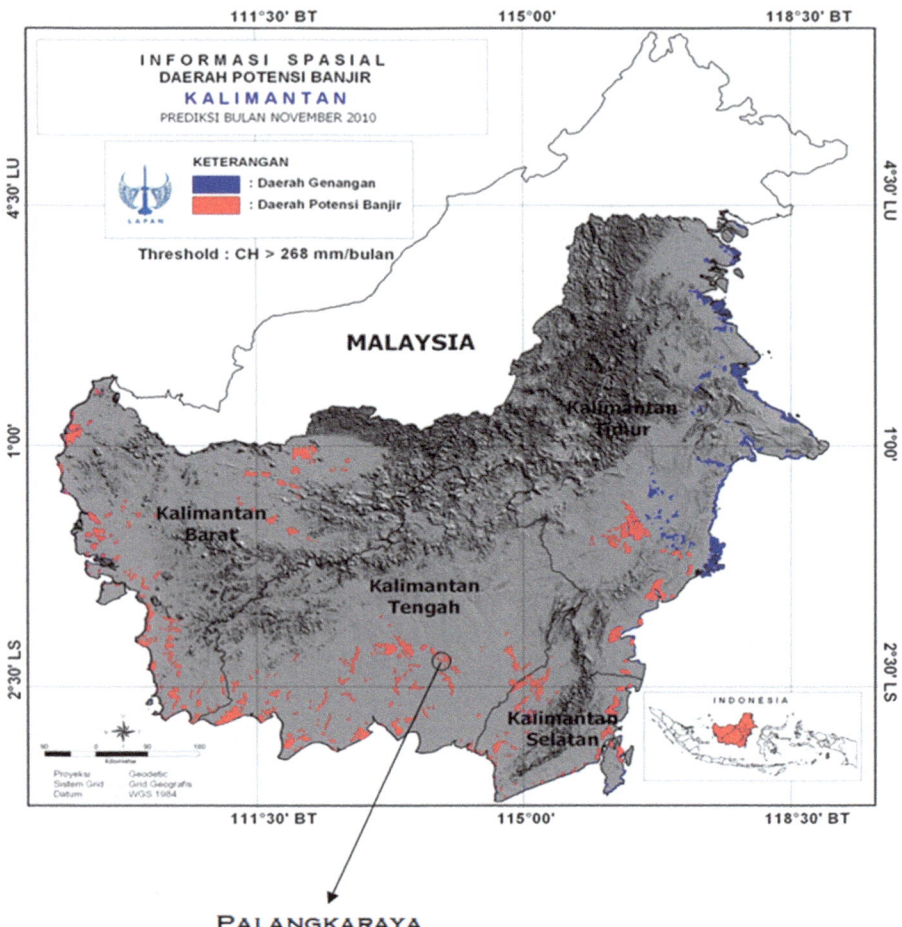

Fig. 2.11 Potential flood areas in Kalimantan Region 2010 (*Source*: LAPAN, Indonesia 2010)

the construction and then sweeps it away. Therefore, without a doubt, settlers living in areas on riverbanks face a serious risk, in this case the obliteration of assets. In such a circumstance, stimulated by global climate change and compounded by uncontrollable massive deforestation in many water catchment areas, many river-bank settlements in the cities of the Central Kalimantan Province, Indonesia, currently face the potential risk of flood. Figure 2.11 indicates the potential flood areas in the Kalimantan region. As reported, recent floods have severely inundated 27 neighborhoods in eight cities of the Central Kalimantan Province during floods from 2000 to 2010. These floods have severely affected many household assets and urban infrastructure. In addition, the damages were so significant that they were even almost uncountable at the time.

2.7 Urban Economics Theories

The existence of illegal settlements in Palangkaraya city, Indonesia, is analyzed by applying urban economics approaches. This section is aimed at elaborating on urban economics theories, including modern urban land use theories, to provide an appropriate theoretical foundation for this study.

2.7.1 Theoretical Considerations

Numerous studies exist on the urban phenomena, such as slums, informal settlements, squatter settlements, shantytowns, and others, from the urban economics point of view. Apparently, these studies have yielded mainstream theories of urban economics. Hence, by applying these theories, including their approaches and methods, one can analyze the various urban phenomena. Moreover, as shown in several prominent studies, the urban economics approaches could also be employed in urban planning processes because these processes require multidimensions ranging from social, economic, and environment dimensions. Henceforth, as such, the scientific approach is employed in urban economics studies and, hence, is then applied in an urban planning process. Therefore, such an attempt could be regarded as systematic and analytical in an urban planning process aimed at shaping the future of urban areas.

A city must be planned based on a planning process. City and urban plans are needed to shape a city for future vibrant economic growth, long-life welfare, and a better environment. Previously, for decades, the urban planning practice was about how to make public or political decisions using more rationality (Altshuler 1965; Blowers 1986; Friedmann 1987). Furthermore, in modernists' planning, rational-base planning was perceived as efficient because it accommodates selectively rational actions that aimed to maximize the attainments at the end.

Conversely, in postmodernist planning, the knowledge foundation of practice and theory should be considered. The argument is that fragmented power, distrust of governments and experts, and incommensurable discourses exist in the postmodern era. Modernist planning seeks to identify a relationship between means and ends in society. Unfortunately, the relationship actually requests broader justifications than mere self-interest. Hence, the modernist planning practice is not suitable for those realms in urban spaces today. Therefore, urban planning needs a breakthrough in approaching specific urban problems, such as the birth of slums, which is a typical phenomenon in the urban spaces of developing countries. Therefore, the replication of urban planning practices as implemented in developed countries might not be suitable for developing countries.

Some works of leading scholars, such as von Thünen (1826), Walras (1874), Keynes (1936, 1964), Alonzo (1964), Solow (1973), Muth (1969), Mills (1967, 1972a, b), Richardson (1977), and Fujita (1989), are thoroughly referenced in this study. Subsequently, studies on slums and illegal settlements by Jimenez (1984), Friedman et al. (1988), Payne (1989), and Kapoor and Blanc (2008), as well as the model of Lanjouw and Levy (2002), are referenced.

Herewith, among other researchers who examined informal settlements from a spatial economics point of view, Payne (1989) examined the production and consumption process in informal lands and housing markets. Other studies include Jimenez (1984) and Friedman et al. (1988), who examined the estimation of price or rent differentials in both formal and informal settlements. These differentials are attributed to the risk of eviction in informal settlements. A model of Lanjouw and Levy (2002) showed that the incompleteness of housing markets arises from the absence of land tenure in informal settlements. Their model focused on the economical interactions in informal settlements between landlords and renters. Therefore, their findings are quite convincing that an urban economics approach that examines the rational behavior of economic agents in the city to generate land use patterns and urban structures could possibly be used to analyze such slum phenomena within an urban area.

During the past several decades, many countries around the globe have experienced rapid urbanization with the result that a large proportion of the world's population was attracted to living in cities. As people flocked to cities, the consequences of urban problems were revealed. Many scientists made efforts to develop a better understanding of those urban problems, and such tireless efforts boosted the development of a new branch of economics—urban economics—of which the modern urban land use theory was a part.

Urban economics is a new field that was triggered by the endeavors of scientists who attempted to develop a better understanding of cities from an economics point of view. During the past several decades, many cities around the world were facing rapid urbanization. City areas were unexpectedly flooded by migrants who sought employment and better urban facilities and amenities. Because the increment of the population was not fully anticipated by most authorities given the limitations in city financing and capacity, urban problems occurred in the areas of social, land and housing, and environmental and health in cities. Urban economics aims to investigate these phenomena and to find their relationships, among others, driven by economic activities among economic agents in the city.

Urban economics is a relatively young field of economics and hardly existed before the 1960s, except in real estate and land economics (Richardson 1977). This field has been developed by many general economic theorists who derived analytical results on urban spatial environments. The urban economics approach involves mainstream methodologies and concepts in economic theories to analyze urban problems. The focus is on economic behavior over space rather than through time.

Urban economics models seek to explain household behavior in consuming goods and lands in city areas, the countryside, and regions, enabling land use patterns to be determined. The concept of the urban economics model has been developed over time in economics both at a theoretical level and as a tool for empirical analysis. Urban economic models have proven to be relevant and useful for understanding economic interactions between markets and agents. In particular, in the urban economics field, Alonzo (1964), Solow (1973), Muth (1969), Mills (1967), Fujita (1989), and Anas et al. (1998) largely applied a general equilibrium analysis when seeking an explanation for land use patterns and housing prices in cities.

Moreover, land use patterns as a foundation for urban problems are determined through a complex set of decisions made by households and firms. Three basic factors—accessibility, space, and environmental amenities—must be considered in tradeoff problems faced by households and firms in a city.

Lucas and Rossi-Hansberg (2002) indicated an endogenous land use pattern over a plane city, inspired by the work of Fujita and Ogawa (1982); however, for simplification, the commodity market is neglected. Another exceptional urban economics study is by Anas et al. (1998), who provided a good discussion on the formation of urban configurations.

Moreover, Miyata (2009) showed a two-dimensional urban economics model that internalizes commodity and labor flows and transport networks. Differing from Beckmann and Puu (1985), Miyata introduced bid rent functions for both firms and households. Furthermore, by applying the theory of partial differential equations (Courant and Hilbert 1953, 1962), including the asymptotic expansion method (Hormander 1990; Duistermaat 1996), Miyata achieved rigorous modifications to the results of Beckmann and Puu (1985).

Following these previous studies, Permana and Miyata (2012) then started the initial development of urban economic models. The preliminary model incorporated flood damage rates on household assets, yielding a reverse result of the formation of land use patterns in a city. This new finding never appears in the traditional urban economic models. Subsequently, the initial model was integrated into a two-dimensional spatial model focusing on commodity and labor flows by applying the achievement of Miyata (2009).

2.7.2 The Residential Choice Model

As observed, the movement of people from rural to urban areas contributes to the increments of density in urban areas. Each household that moves to city areas faces a complex set of decisions regarding where in the city to reside. These households must think about the tradeoffs that can be made among accessibility, space, and environmental amenities. These amenities must be weighed and matched with budget and time constraints. Because a tradeoff has some constraints, households need to make sacrifices. For instance, spacious housing is desired by most city inhabitants but often comes with less accessibility. The question is whether the household prefers a small living space with more accessibility or the reverse.

Modern research on housing choice began with the study of Alonzo (1964), who considered a city in which employment opportunities are located as a single city trough time center. In Alonzo, the residential choice of households is based on maximizing the utility function, which depends on expenditures on goods, lot size, and distance to the city center. Furthermore, Lowry (1964) applied the gravity model to the result of residential location modeling. Specifically, Lowry assumed that retail trade and services are located in relation to residential demand and that households are located in relation to combined retail and basic employment. Workers are hypothesized to have a trip home from work and are distributed to available residential sites according to the gravity model, which attenuates their trip over an increasing distance.

Another stream of the research on modeling residential choice location is based on discrete choice theory. In the context of a residential location, the consumption decision is a discrete choice between alternative households or a neighborhood.

To understand a household's residential choice decision, a basic residential choice model formulated by Fujita (1989) was studied. This basic model develops an understanding in particular about the tradeoff between accessibility and space. The model is developed using a set of assumptions:

1. The city is assumed to have only a single center, the CBD, in which all employment is located.
2. The city has no congestion, and the only travel is by workers who commute from residential areas to the CBD.
3. The city has no variances in geographical features. It is a plain city and all land is assumed to be ready for residential use.

As usual, the household maximizes its utility subject to a budget constraint on the basis of the consumption of goods and land. The household obtains a fixed income per unit time and spends it on goods, land, and transportation. Suppose the household is located at a distance from the CBD and has to pay land rent at the location. Furthermore, transportation must be paid for from the household budget; hence, the budget constraint is given by

$$z + R(t)s = y - k(t) \qquad (2.1)$$

By solving the maximization problem, the household's residential decision could be ascertained in a straightforward manner.

2.7.3   The Bid Rent Concept

The bid rent function approach was first used by von Thünen (1826) in his agricultural land use model, which was a cornerstone of land use theory. Subsequently, the bid rent function approach was extended by Alonzo (1964) to the urban context. This approach has the same essence as the indirect utility function approach, which was introduced into the urban land use model by Solow (1973).

Fujita (1989) introduced the concept of bid rent that mimics a von Thünen model. He showed that by employing the bid rent function approach, urban economics models can be more rigorously developed than previous models, hence, providing deep explanations of urban land use.

Fujita (1989) considered land consumption and initially makes the assumption that land is a featureless plain and its typology is not considered as a factor input in the utility function. Hence, land use patterns in the city can be determined for high-income households that can offer higher bid rent than low-income households that populate residential areas near the city center.

By definition, the bid rent is the maximum rent per unit of land that a representative household is able to pay for residing at a distance while enjoying a fixed utility level. Using this approach, the residential choice by a household is determined by the bid rent, which can be obtained when $(y - kt - z)/s$ is maximized subject to the utility constraint. In a graphical approach, the bid rent is given by the slope of the budget line at a distance, which is just tangent to the utility indifference curve.

The bid rent approach was first introduced into an agricultural land use model by von Thünen (1826). He defined land rent as revenue minus cost, and cost was divided between production and transportation costs. One implication of his model is that an increase in distance increased transportation costs and, as a result, land rent decreased.

Moreover, Alonzo (1964) introduced the concept of a bid rent function originally called the bid-price curve. He defined the bid rent function of a household as the set of land rents that households are willing to pay at various distances from the city center to maintain the same level of utility everywhere to make households indifferent among locations.

Recalling Fujita's definition, the bid rent function is a function of income and utility. If income increases, then the ability of households to pay rent (bid rent) increases. Income is obtained as laborers endow working time and supply it to firms. This income will be proportionally allocated to a consumption bundle that consists of goods and land. A certain allocation is for consuming goods and the rest is for land. Through an appropriate choice, the maximum ability to pay land rent is derived. As specified by Fujita (1989), the bid rent is mathematically expressed as follows:

$$r(t, u) = \max_{\{z,s\}} \left\{ \frac{y - kt - z}{s} \mid u(z, s) = u \right\} \qquad (2.2)$$

The bid rent is a conceptual device that describes the ability of a representative household to pay for land under a fixed utility level. The bid rent is the maximum rent per unit of land that the household can pay for living at a distance t and enjoying a fixed utility level u. Each household achieves its maximum bid rent through the appropriate choice of a consumption bundle (goods and lands).

Monocentric cities have been largely admitted as the mainstay of the land use theory for decades. In this model, the city is viewed as a circular residential area surrounding a CBD in which all employment is located. Because households are identical, they are assumed to make residential decisions that give the tradeoff between commuting cost and the willingness to have housing space (Anas 1990).

People who live in city areas are assumed to consume goods and land to live. Income is a constraint of consumption and is calculated as net income after deducting transportation expenditures. The more that people consume such amounts of a good, the less remaining income they have to allocate to land rent. Hence, the ability to pay for land is reduced because most of the money went to consuming goods rather than to consuming land. The ability to pay for land in each location under each fixed utility level is called bid rent (Fujita 1989).

2.7.4 Flood Damage Estimation

Fujita's theory on bid rent is based on the assumption that land is homogeneous. Therefore, applying his model to analyze a city such as Palangkaraya, in which heterogeneous urban land quality exists, is inappropriate. Approximately 11% of the total size of Palangkaraya city is wetland areas. Some of these areas are in urban areas alongside the Kahayan riverbank, which is permanently prone to runoff, particularly during the rainy season. Although the flood-prone area is a high-risk site for residential use, low-income households tend to consciously occupy these areas and take risks regarding their assets.

Therefore, to properly analyze such a city with a land quality combination comprised of normal and wetland areas, we need to consider the risk of floods in households' residential decisions.

A few economic analyses exist on flood measurements. However, in this case, studies by Holway and Burby (1990), MacDonald et al. (1987), and Shilling et al. (1985) are highlighted. Their studies employ the hedonic land price approach, which represents flood hazards using a dummy variable.

Furthermore, different from previous studies, Miyata and Abe (1991) introduced a specific variable: annual expected flood water depth. This variable represents a flood prevention measurement. Instead of utilizing data on past floods, which are occasionally inconsistent and not well-managed—possibly causing bias—Miyata and Abe introduced annual expected flood water depth. This attempt could more simply estimate the nature of flooding than previously, while taking into account accuracy.

Furthermore, Permana and Miyata (2012) employed the concept of the annual expected flood water depth to measure damages from floods to household assets. Here, a household's assets are durable goods, such as houses, cars, appliances, and others.

A household asset function is defined as an increasing function of income; hence, more income means that households own more assets, and this definition may intuitively reflect a real-life fact. The idea is that because floods occur stochastically, a bias may exist if the likelihood of flood occurrences is estimated using a specific case from the historical flood data records. Therefore, they excluded the arbitrariness in selecting specific past flood data. The expected flood damage rate (EFDR) on household assets is estimated by calculating the damage rate on these assets that correspond to flood volume and grid square and then by computing probable mean flood volume values. The values of the variable range from 0 to 1. If the value is 0, then no damage to the household's assets occurs from floods; conversely, if the value is 1, then the flood completely damages the household's assets.

References

Alonzo, W. (1964). *Location and land use*. Cambridge: Harvard University Press.
Altshuler, A. (1965). *The city planning process: A political analysis*. Ithaca: Cornell University Press.
Anas, A. (1990). Taste heterogeneity and urban spatial structure: The logit model and monocentric theory reconsidered. *Journal of Urban Economics, 28*(3), 318–335.
Anas, A., Arnott, R., & Small, K. (1998). Urban spatial structure. *Journal of Economic Literature, 36*(3), 1426–1464.
Anderson, N. (1959). *The urban community: A world perspective*. New York: Holt, Rinehart & Winston.
Badan Pusat Statistik (BPS) Kota Palangka Raya, & (BAPPEDA), Badan Perencanaan Pembangunan Daerah Kota Palangka Raya. (2007). Kota Palangka Raya dalam Angka (Palangka Raya City in Figures). Palangkaraya: Badan Pusat Statistik Kota Palangka Raya. Retrieved May 1, 2014, from https://palangkakota.bps.go.id/webbeta/website/pdf_publikasi/Palangka-Raya-Dalam-Angka-2007.pdf
Beckmann, M. J., & Puu, T. (1985). *Spatial economics*. Amsterdam: North-Holland.
Blowers, A. (1986). Town planning – Paradoxes and prospects. *The Planner, 72*, 82–96.
Central Bureau of Statistics (CBS). (1989). *Housing construction statistics in Indonesia 1988*. Jakarta: CBS.
CiptaKarya, Direktorat Jenderal. (2007) Program Peningkatan Kualitan Lingkungan Pemukiman Kumuh (NUSSP). Pekerjaan Umum Dan Perumahan Rakyat Republik Indonesia.
Courant, R., & Hilbert, D. (1953). *Methods of mathematical physics, I*. New York: Interscience Publishers, Inc..
Courant, R., & Hilbert, D. (1962). *Methods of mathematical physics* (Vol. II). New York: Interscience Publishers, Inc..
Davis, M. (2006), Planet of slums,. Verso.
Duistermaat, J. J. (2011[1996]). *Fourier integral operators* (Modern Birkhäuser Classics). New York: Birkhäuser/Springer.
Field Survey of Palangkaraya City (2010). Department of Architecture, Palangkaraya University. Retrieved from http://www.upr.ac.id
Firman, T. (2004). New town development in Jakarta Metropolitan Region: A perspective of spatial segregation. *Habitat International, 28*(3), 349–368.
Firoz, A. B. M. (2004). *Urban growth dynamics of Khulna City*. Unpublished BURP Thesis, Urban and Rural Planning Discipline. (pp. 27–32).Khulna: Khulna University.
Food and Agriculture Organization of the United Nations. (2001). *State of the world's forests*.
Friedman, J. (1987). *Planning in the public domain: From knowledge to action*. Princeton: Princeton University Press.
Friedman, J., Jimenez, E., & Mayo, S. K. (1988). The demand for tenure security in developing countries. *Journal of Development Economics, 29*(2), 185–198.
Fu-Chen, F., Edralin, J. S., & Dung, N. T. (Eds.). (1981). *Rural-Urban relations and regional development, Regional Development Series; v. 5. Singapore*. Nagoya: Maruzen Asia for United Nations Centre for Regional Development.
Fujita, M. (1989). *Urban economic theory. Land use and city size*. Cambridge: Cambridge University Press.

Fujita, M., & Ogawa, H. (1982). Multiple equilibria and structural transition of non-monocentric urban configurations. *Regional Science and Urban Economics, 12*, 161–196.

FWI/GFM. (2002). *The state of the forest: Indonesia*. Bogor/Washington, DC: Forest Watch Indonesia/Global Forest Watch.

Holway, J. M., & Burby, R. J. (1990). The effects of floodplain development controls on residential land values. *Land Economics, 66*(3), 259–271.

Hormander, L. (1990). *An introduction to complex analysis in several variables* (3rd ed.). Amsterdam: North-Holland Mathematical Library.

Jimenez, E. (1984). Tenure security and urban squatting. *Review of Economics and Statistics, 66*(4), 556–562.

Kapoor, M., & Blanc, D. (2008). Measuring risk on investment in informal (illegal) housing: Theory and evidence from Pune, India. *Regional Science and Urban Economics, 38*(4), 311–329.

Keynes, J. M. (1936[1964]). *The general theory of employment, interest, and money*. New York: Harcourt Brace Jovanovich.

Lanjouw, J. O., & Levy, P. (2002). Untitled: A study of formal and informal property rights in urban Ecuador. *The Economic Journal, 112*(482), 986–1019.

Lowry, I. S. (1964). *A model of metropolis*. Santa Monica: RM-4035-RC, Rand Corporation.

Lucus, R. E., & Rossi-Hansberg, E. (2002). On the internal structure of cities. *Econometrica, 70*, 1445–1476.

MacDonald, D., Murdoch, J. C., & White, H. L. (1987). Uncertain hazards, insurance, and consumer choice: Evidence from housing markets. *Land Economics, 63*(4), 361–371.

Map of Forest Coverage in Central Kalimantan Province. (2008). Forestry Planning Agency, Department of Forestry Republic of Indonesia. Retrieved from: http://fwi.or.id/wp-content/uploads/2013/02/PHKI_2000-2009_FWI_low-res.pdf

McGee, T. G. (1987). *Urbanization or Kotadesasi-The emergence of new regions of economic interaction in Asia*, Working paper. Honolulu: Environment and Policy Institute, East West Center.

Mills, E. S. (1967). An aggregative model of resource allocation in a metropolitan area. *American Economic Review, 57*, 197–210.

Mills, E. S. (1972a). *Studies in the structure of the urban economy*. Baltimore: Johns Hopkins University Press.

Mills, E. S. (1972b). *Urban economics*. Glenview: Scott Foresman.

Miyata, Y. (2009). Integrating commodity and labor flows into monocentric city over a two dimensional continuous space. *Studies in Regional Science, 39*(3), 631–658.

Miyata, Y., & Abe, H. (1991). Evaluating the impacts of the flood control project using the land price function. *Journal of the City Planning Institute of Japan, 26*, 109–114. in Japanese.

Muth, R. F. (1969). *Cities and Housing*. Chicago/London: University of Chicago Press.

Pahandut dalam Angka. (2009). Monograph of Kecamatan Pahandut and Kecamatan Jekan Raya. Retrieved from: https://palangkakota.bps.go.id/webbeta/website/pdf_publikasi/Pahandut-Dalam-Angka-2009.pdf

Payne, G. (1989). *Informal housing and land subdivisions in third world cities: A review of the literature*. Oxford: Oxford Polytechnic (now Oxford Brookes University).

Permana, I., & Miyata, Y. (2012). *The general equilibrium model of illegal settlements in Palangkaraya City, Indonesia: Numerical simulations*. The 52nd ERSA Congress, Bratislava, Slovakia, 2012.

Population Reference Bureau. (2006, May 1). *World population data sheet*. Washington, DC: The Bureau. http://www.prb.org/pdf06/06worlddatasheet.pdf

Potential Flood Areas in Kalimantan Region. (2010). Lembaga Penerbangan dan Antariksa Nasional. Indonesia. Retrieved from: http://pusfatja.lapan.go.id/index.php/home

Richardson, H. W. (1977). *The new urban economics: And alternatives*. London: Pion.

Shilling, J. D., Benjamin, J. D., & Sirmans, C. F. (1985). Adjusting comparable sales for floodplain location. *Appraisal Journal, 53*(3), 429–436.

Solow, R. M. (1973). On equilibrium models of urban locations. In J. M. Parkin (Ed.), *Essays in modern economics* (pp. 2–16). London: Longman.

Suhandjaja, A. (1991). "Indonesia", in AsDB/EDI, The urban poor and basic infrastructure services in Asia and the Pacific, Volume II, Manila, the Philippines.

The Urban Institute/Hasfarm Dian Konsultan. (1989, March). *Urban housing studies* (Draft Final Report). Jakarta.

UNESCAP. (2000). *State of the environment in Asia and the Pacific*. Bangkok: UNESCAP.

United Nations. (1993). *World urbanization prospects 1992: Estimates and projections of urban and rural populations and of urban agglomerations*. New York: Department of Economic and Social Information and Policy Analysis, ST/ESA/SER, A/136, United Nations.

United Nations. (2004). *World urbanization prospects: The 2003 revision*. New York: Department of Economic and Social Affairs/Population Division, ESA/P/WP.190.

United Nations Human Settlements Programme (UN-HABITAT). (2001). *Cities in a globalizing world – Global report on human settlements 2001*. UN-Habitat.

United Nations Human Settlements Programme (UN-HABITAT). (2004). *The state of the world's cities 2004/2005 globalization and urban culture*. UN-Habitat.

United Nations Human Settlements Programme (UN-HABITAT). (2010). *State of the world's cities 2010/11 cities for all: Bridging the urban divide*. Routledge.

von Thünen, J. H. (1826). Der Isolierte Staat in Beziehung auf Landwirtschaft und Nationalekonomie, Hamburg.

Walras, L. (1874). *Elements of pure economics: Or the theory of social wealth*. Homewood: Richard Irwin. (1954 translation of 1926 edition).

Chapter 3
Theoretical Development of the Partial Equilibrium Model

3.1 Introduction

The partial equilibrium is a type of economic equilibrium model commonly used to analyze cities and urban areas from an urban economics point of view. In a partial equilibrium model, clearance on the market of certain specific goods is obtained independently from prices and quantities demanded and supplied in other markets. In other words, the prices of all substitutes and complements, as well as consumers' income levels, are constant. This constancy enables a dynamic process that allows prices to be adjusted until supply equals demand. This powerfully simple technique allows one to study equilibrium, efficiency, and comparative statics. The stringency of the simplifying assumptions inherent in this approach makes the model produce results that do not effectively reflect real-world economic phenomena, although seemingly precise.

This chapter follows the Fujita formulation but significantly differs in the following points. First, land qualities indexed by values of the EFDR to household assets are introduced. The EFDR is an explanatory variable that represents expected damage by flood events. This attempt has yet to be considered in Fujita's model. Second, the asset function, which is an increasing function of a household's income that measures the household's assets in the city, is introduced. Then, by applying the bid rent approach, which is conceptually much richer than the basic model of residential choice, and by conducting problem maximization subject to a utility function that incorporates the expected damage rate and the asset function, a new type of bid rent function and bid max lot size is formulated.

© Springer Nature Singapore Pte Ltd. 2018
Y. Miyata et al., *Environmental and Natural Disaster Resilience of Indonesia*,
New Frontiers in Regional Science: Asian Perspectives 23,
https://doi.org/10.1007/978-981-10-8210-8_3

3.2 The Model

This theoretical model can be distinguished from others in the following manner.

1. Land quality is considered. Normal land and flood-prone areas exist in the city. Normal land areas face no flood risk, whereas flood-prone areas face the risk of floods.
2. The utility functions used in this study incorporate expected flood damage.
3. To take into account the expected flood damage, we consider the asset function in each household. The asset function is assumed to be an increasing function of income, hence describing that a flood event possibly causes greater losses for households with more assets and, conversely, lesser losses for households with fewer assets. This fact influences the offer of the bid rent of households in the city.

3.2.1 Shape of the City

The city is located near a river stream. The region is influenced by a tropical climate that assures high precipitation. Along with massive deforestation activity at the upper river, periodic runoff water inundates areas alongside the river during the rainy season. The city has a CBD where firms, shops, and markets are located. Residential areas are built to surround the CBD. Also surrounding the CBD are flood-prone areas. The distance to the CBD for each area is different, but the areas are considerably close enough to the city center. Some of the flood-prone areas have been illegally occupied by thousands of houses. Agricultural land is located just outside the city area. For convenience for the subsequent analysis, the shape of the city is graphically presented as shown in Fig. 3.1.

3.2.2 Main Assumptions in the Model

The model of this study is based on the following assumptions.

1. The study area is assumed to be a monocentric city. All the production activities are in the CBD.

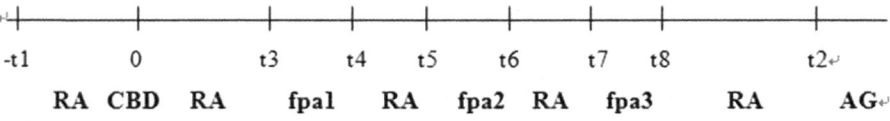

Fig. 3.1 Shape of the city
where
CBD central business district, *Fpa* flood-prone area, *RA* residential area *AG* agriculture land

2. Two types of households exist in the city. They are high-income and low-income households. The households consume goods and land. The commodity is assumed to be the numeraire.
3. The city is closed for the high-income group but open for the low-income group. Thus, the number of high-income households is fixed, whereas that of low-income households is internally determined by the supreme utility level.
4. The incomes of the two types of households are exogenously given. The incomes of the households in the two groups are different but equal in the same group.
5. Two types of land exist in the city. The normal land areas face no flood risk, whereas the flood-prone areas face flood risk.

3.2.3 Expected Flood Damage Rate

Because the city faces stochastic flood occurrences, a possible bias may exist when estimating the damage rate from a flood using the available data. Instead, the EFDR on a household's assets is employed as follows:

$$\int_0^\infty P(Q)d(Q)A(y_i)dQ = cy_i^{\gamma_i} \tag{3.1}$$

where

c: expected damage rate on a household asset

$c = 0$ if a household lives in a normal land area and $c > 1$ if a household lives in a flood-prone area

$P(Q)$: probability of occurrence of the volume of flood flow Q

$d(Q)$: correspondence of damage rate

Because the city is located on a river basin and massive deforestation has occurred at the upper river, the city could experience severe floods, particularly during the rainy season. The runoff often inundates occupied flood-prone areas along the riverbanks. Floods can damage the assets of households that dwell on the riverbank. Heavy floods can severely damage durable goods and houses; thus, floods are a real threat to household assets. To analyze such flood-prone areas, we introduce an asset function. The amount and value of each household's assets may depend on income. In general, high-income households have more assets than low-income households. Depending on the type of assets, they may have twice the value or, more, from income. Therefore, the asset function can be considered an increasing the function of income. The risk of high-income households facing asset-related losses during destructive flood events is higher than that of low-income households that have small amounts of assets only. The asset function is specified as follows:

$$A_i(y_i) \equiv y_i^{\gamma_i} \ (\gamma_i > 1) \tag{3.2}$$

3.2.4   Maximization Problem

Land quality indexed by the value of the expected flood damage on household assets in a household utility function is taken into account; hence, the utility function of both types of households in the city is assumed in the following formula:

$$u_i(z_i, s_i, cy_i^\gamma) = \frac{1}{1 + c(t)y_i^\gamma} z_i(t)^{\alpha_i} s_i(t)^{\beta_i} \ (\alpha_i + \beta_i = 1) \tag{3.3}$$

where

$i = 1$ for a high-income household and $i = 2$ for a low-income household
$u_i(t)$: utility function of households at location t
y_i household income of each type of household
$z_i(t)$: consumption of goods by households at location t
$s_i(t)$: land consumption by households at location t
α_i and β_i: elasticity parameters
$c(t)$: expected damage rate on household assets at location t

The bid rent function for both types of households is specified as follows:

$$r_i(t) = \max_{\{z_i, s_i\}} \frac{y_i - z_i(t) - kt}{s_i(t)} \tag{3.4}$$

subject to

$$u_i(t) = u_i^* \tag{3.5}$$

where

$r_i(t)$: bid rent of households at location t
y_i: income of households (exogenous variable)
$s_i(t)$: lot size of households at location t
u_i^*: equilibrium utility level

3.2.5   Necessary Conditions in the Model

To solve maximization problems (3.4) and (3.5), we consider the following expenditure function:

$$E_i(t) = \min_{\{z_i, s_i\}} z_i(t) + r_i(t)s_i(t) \tag{3.6}$$

subject to

$$u_i^* = \frac{1}{1 + c(t)y_i^{\gamma}} z_i(t)^{\alpha_i} s_i(t)^{\beta_i} \tag{3.7}$$

To solve minimization problems (3.6) and (3.7), we call on the Lagrange multiplier as follows:

$$L = z_i(t) + r_i(t)s_i(t) + \lambda \left(u_i^* - \frac{z_i(t)^{\alpha_i} s_i(t)^{\beta_i}}{1 + c(t)y_i^{\gamma}} \right) \tag{3.8}$$

The necessary conditions for the minimization in (3.6) to (3.7) are summarized as follows:

$$\frac{\partial L}{\partial z_i(t)} = 1 - \lambda \frac{\alpha_i z_i(t)^{\alpha_i - 1} s_i(t)^{\beta_i}}{1 + c(t)y_i^{\gamma}} = 0 \tag{3.9}$$

$$\frac{\partial L}{\partial s_i(t)} = r_i(t) - \lambda \frac{\beta_i z_i(t)^{\alpha_i} s_i(t)^{\beta_i - 1}}{1 + c(t)y_i^{\gamma}} = 0 \tag{3.10}$$

These conditions are arranged by dividing Eq. (3.9) into Eq. (3.10) to obtain

$$\frac{1}{r_i(t)} = \frac{\alpha_i}{\beta_i} \frac{s_i(t)}{z_i(t)} \tag{3.11}$$

Rearranging Eq. (3.11) yields

$$s_i(t) = \frac{\beta_i}{\alpha_i} \frac{z_i(t)}{r_i(t)} \tag{3.12}$$

Substituting Eq. (3.12) into Eq. (3.7) results in the following:

$$u_i^* = \frac{1}{1 + c(t)y_i^{\gamma}} z_i(t)^{\alpha_i} \left(\frac{\beta_i}{\alpha_i} \right)^{\beta_i} \left(\frac{z_i(t)}{r_i(t)} \right)^{\beta_i} \tag{3.13}$$

Then compensated demand for goods and land are obtained as follows:

$$z_i(t) = (1 + c(t)y_i^{\gamma}) \left(\frac{\alpha_i}{\beta_i} \right)^{\beta_i} r_i(t)^{\beta_i} u_i^* \tag{3.14}$$

$$s_i(t) = (1 + c(t)y_i^{\gamma}) \left(\frac{\beta_i}{\alpha_i} \right)^{\alpha_i} \left(\frac{1}{r_i(t)} \right)^{\alpha_i} u_i^* \tag{3.15}$$

3.2.6   Bid Rent Function and Bid Max Lot Size Function

To obtain the bid rent function and the bid max lot size function, Eqs. (3.14) and (3.15) are substituted into Eq. (3.6) to yield

$$E_i = \left(\frac{1}{\alpha_i}\right)\left(\frac{\alpha_i}{\beta_i}\right)^{\beta_i}(1 + c(t)y_i^\gamma)r_i(t)^{\beta_i}u_i^* \tag{3.16}$$

Because $E_i = y_i - kt$, we have

$$y_i - kt = \left(\frac{1}{\alpha_i}\right)\left(\frac{\alpha_i}{\beta_i}\right)^{\beta_i}(1 + c(t)y_i^\gamma)r_i(t)^{\beta_i}u_i^* \tag{3.17}$$

Rearranging Eq. (3.17) derives the bid rent function in representative households as follows:

$$r_i(t) = \beta_i(\alpha_i)^{\frac{\alpha_i}{\beta_i}}\left(\frac{y_i - kt}{(1 + c(t)y_i^\gamma)u_i^*}\right)^{\frac{1}{\beta_i}} \tag{3.18}$$

By substituting Eq. (3.18) into Eqs. (3.14) and (3.15), we obtain the demand for goods and the bid max lot size as follows:

$$z_i(t) = \alpha_i(y_i - kt) \tag{3.19}$$

$$s_i(t) = \left(\frac{1}{\alpha_i(y_i - kt)}\right)^{\frac{\alpha_i}{\beta_i}}(1 + c(t)y_i^\gamma)^{\frac{1}{\beta_i}}\left(u_i^*\right)^{\frac{1}{\beta_i}} \tag{3.20}$$

Conducting a partial differentiation with respect to y_i and u_i^* and, we obtain the following inequalities:

$$\frac{\partial r_1}{\partial y_1} < 0, \ \frac{\partial r_1}{\partial u_1^*} < 0 \qquad t \in [t_3, t_4] \cup [t_5, t_6] \cup [t_7, t_8] \tag{3.21}$$

$$\frac{\partial r_1}{\partial y_1} > 0 \qquad t \notin [t_3, t_4] \cup [t_5, t_6] \cup [t_7, t_8] \tag{3.22}$$

The model indicates that the bid rent of a high-income household in flood-prone areas is negatively affected by the expected damage to assets from a flood. The magnitude of the bid rent is higher than that in Eq. (3.18). As a result, the bid rent of a high-income household is lower than that of a low-income household in the flood-prone areas. This result should be highlighted to show the reverse conclusion for normal land areas.

The next implication of the model is that, for normal land for which the expected damage rate on a household's asset takes the value of 0 ($c = 0$), the bid rent of the representative high-income household is higher than that of the low-income household; hence, the high-income households reside on normal land. Conversely, in flood-prone areas in which the expected damage rate on a household's assets takes a value greater than 0 $(c > 0)$, the bid rent of a representative high-income household is lower than that of a low-income household. Therefore, the flood-prone areas are populated by low-income households. We assume that the expected damage rate is constant in the flood-prone area.

$$c(t) = c_{34} \quad t \in [t_3, t_4]$$
$$c(t) = c_{56} \quad t \in [t_5, t_6]$$
$$c(t) = c_{78} \quad t \in [t_7, t_8]$$

3.2.7 City Boundary

The city boundary is determined by the intersection between the slope of the bid rent and the constant line of agricultural land rent. This boundary is expressed by Eq. (3.23), assuming the fringe areas are populated by high-income households.

$$r_1(-t_1) = rA \tag{3.23}$$

Thus, the following equation is obtained:

$$\beta_1(\alpha_1)^{\frac{\alpha_1}{\beta_1}} \left(\frac{y_1 - kt}{u_1^*} \right)^{\frac{1}{\beta_1}} = rA \tag{3.24}$$

Solving Eq. (3.24), we determine the city boundaries in the left- and right-hand sides in the city as follows:

$$t_1 = \frac{1}{k} \left\{ y_1 - \left(\frac{rA}{\beta_1(\alpha_1)^{\frac{\alpha_1}{\beta_1}}} \right)^{\beta_1} u_1^* \right\} \tag{3.25}$$

$$t_2 = \frac{1}{k} \left\{ y_1 - \left(\frac{rA}{\beta_1(\alpha_1)^{\frac{\alpha_1}{\beta_1}}} \right)^{\beta_1} u_1^* \right\} \tag{3.26}$$

Once t_1 and t_2 are determined, land to the right-hand side of t_1 and that to the left-hand side of t_2 is used for housing, whereas land to the left-hand side of t_1 and that to the right-hand side of t_2 is used for agriculture.

3.2.8 The Population

The population is calculated as the integration of the density in each location. Because the density is a reciprocal of lot size, the population on normal land is determined as follows:

$$\int_{-t_1}^{0} \frac{1}{s_1} dt + \int_{0}^{t_3} \frac{1}{s_1} dt + \int_{t_4}^{t_5} \frac{1}{s_1} dt + \int_{t_6}^{t_7} \frac{1}{s_1} dt + \int_{t_8}^{t_2} \frac{1}{s_1} dt = N_1 \qquad (3.27)$$

Each term in Eq. (3.27) is calculated as follows:

$$\int_{-t_1}^{0} \frac{1}{s_1} dt = \int_{0}^{t_1} \frac{1}{s_1} dt = \int_{0}^{t_1} (\alpha_1(y_1 - kt))^{\frac{\alpha_1}{\beta_1}} (u_1^*)^{\frac{-1}{\beta_1}} dt$$
$$= \frac{1}{k} (\alpha_1)^{\frac{\alpha_1}{\beta_1}} \beta_1 (y_1)^{\frac{1}{\beta_1}} (u_1^*)^{\frac{-1}{\beta_1}} - \frac{rA}{k} = f(0) (u_1^*)^{\frac{-1}{\beta_1}} - \frac{rA}{k} \qquad (3.28)$$

$$\int_{0}^{t_3} \frac{1}{s_1} dt = f(0) (u_1^*)^{\frac{-1}{\beta_1}} - f(t_3) (u_1^*)^{\frac{-1}{\beta_1}} \qquad (3.29)$$

$$\int_{t_4}^{t_5} \frac{1}{s_1} dt = f(t_4) (u_1^*)^{\frac{-1}{\beta_1}} - f(t_5) (u_1^*)^{\frac{-1}{\beta_1}} \qquad (3.30)$$

$$\int_{t_6}^{t_7} \frac{1}{s_1} dt = f(t_6) (u_1^*)^{\frac{-1}{\beta_1}} - f(t_7) (u_1^*)^{\frac{-1}{\beta_1}} \qquad (3.31)$$

$$\int_{t_8}^{t_2} \frac{1}{s_1} dt = f(t_8) (u_1^*)^{\frac{-1}{\beta_1}} - \frac{rA}{k} \qquad (3.32)$$

where

$$f(x) = \frac{1}{k} (\alpha_1)^{\frac{\alpha_1}{\beta_1}} \beta_1 (y_1 - kx)^{\frac{1}{\beta_1}}$$

Substituting Eqs. (3.28), (3.29), (3.30), (3.31), and (3.32) into Eq. (3.27) results in the number of high-income households in the city as follows:

$$N_1 = \{2f(0) - f(t_3) + f(t_4) - f(t_5) + f(t_6) - f(t_7) + f(t_8)\} (u_1^*)^{\frac{-1}{\beta_1}}$$
$$- 2\frac{rA}{k} \qquad (3.33)$$

Finally, the equilibrium utility level in a high-income household is derived as follows:

$$u_1^* = \{2f(0) - f(t_3) + f(t_4) - f(t_5) + f(t_6) - f(t_7) + f(t_8)\}^{\beta_1} \left(N_1 + 2\frac{rA}{k}\right)^{-\beta_1}$$

$$(3.34)$$

The population in the flood-prone areas is counted as follows:

$$\int_{t_3}^{t_4} \frac{1}{s_2} dt + \int_{t_5}^{t_6} \frac{1}{s_2} dt + \int_{t_7}^{t_8} \frac{1}{s_2} dt = N_2 \qquad (3.35)$$

$$\int_{t_3}^{t_4} \frac{1}{s_2} dt = \int_{t_3}^{t_4} (\alpha_2(y_2 - kt))^{\frac{\alpha_2}{\beta_2}} (1 + c_{34}y_2^{\gamma})^{\frac{-1}{\beta_2}} (u_2^*)^{\frac{-1}{\beta_2}} dt$$

$$= (g(t_3) - g(t_4))(1 + c_{34}y_2^{\gamma})^{\frac{-1}{\beta_2}} (u_2^*)^{\frac{-1}{\beta_2}} \qquad (3.36)$$

where

$$g(x) = \frac{\beta_2}{\alpha_2 k} \left(\alpha_2(y_2 - kx)\right)^{\frac{1}{\beta_2}}$$

$$\int_{t_5}^{t_6} \frac{1}{s_2} dt = (g(t_5) - g(t_6))(1 + c_{56}y_2^{\gamma})^{\frac{-1}{\beta_2}} (u_2^*)^{\frac{-1}{\beta_2}} \qquad (3.37)$$

$$\int_{t_7}^{t_8} \frac{1}{s_2} dt = (g(t_7) - g(t_8))(1 + c_{78}y_2^{\gamma})^{\frac{-1}{\beta_2}} (u_2^*)^{\frac{-1}{\beta_2}} \qquad (3.38)$$

Substituting Eqs. (3.36), (3.37), and (3.38) into Eq. (3.35) results in the number of low-income households in flood-prone areas as follows:

$$N_2 = \left\{ \{g(t_3) - g(t_4)\}(1 + c_{34}y_2^{\gamma})^{\frac{-1}{\beta_2}} + \{g(t_5) - g(t_6)\}(1 + c_{56}y_2^{\gamma})^{\frac{-1}{\beta_2}} \right.$$
$$\left. + g(t_7) - g(t_8)(1 + c_{78}y_2^{\gamma})^{\frac{-1}{\beta_2}} \right\} (u_2^*)^{\frac{-1}{\beta_2}} \qquad (3.39)$$

3.3   Numerical Simulation

The following section presents a numerical simulation using statistical data and field survey data on Palangkaraya city.

3.3.1 Statistical Data

Lack of appropriate data as a result of weaknesses in data collection and data management by governmental institutions is a barrier for the following numerical simulation; however, statistical data from Statistics Indonesia 2007 on Gross Domestic Product Account 2005–2007 and Average Expenditure per capita per month by commodity group can be used to estimate some parameters, particularly the elasticity parameters α and β. Furthermore, other 2007 statistical data on figures at the provincial and city levels from Statistics Indonesia on the Central Kalimantan Province and Palangkaraya city were mainly used in this simulation. Although some of the data at the provincial and city levels are different, the gap can be minimized using a data adjustment technique. As shown in Table 3.1, the following brief statistical data on Palangkaraya city have been adjusted.

Furthermore, given a lack of statistical data from official institutions regarding illegal settlements in flood-prone areas, we use a field survey data collected in 2007 by the Department of Architecture at Palangkaraya University. Henceforth, data on physical size, population, and density of illegal settlements are presented in Table 3.2.

The field survey data also present the annual income of the sample households for both the normal land and the flood-prone areas in the city, including the representative average residence distance to the CBD, as shown in Table 3.3.

For the numerical simulation, three model parameters must be estimated. They are parameters α and β in the utility function and parameter γ in the asset function. Simply, we estimate parameters α and β by taking into account total national income, which is the sum of GDP reduced by net factor income from the rest of the world,

Table 3.1 Statistical data on Palangkaraya city

Population	188,816 (2007)
Size	2678.51 km^2
Population density	70.23 people/km^2
Swamp areas including flood pone areas	40.003 km^2
Normal land	2278.48 km^2
Occupied flood pone areas	11.12 km^2

Source: Extracted from Palangkaraya in Figures, BPS kota Palangkaraya (2007) and Kalimantan Tengah in Figures (2007)

Table 3.2 Size, population, and density of illegal settlements in flood-prone areas

Neighborhood	Size (km^2)	Population	Density (people/km^2)
Danau seha	3.39	3143	927
Flamboyan	3.41	2332	683
Mendawai	4.32	2551	590

Source: Field Survey by Department of Architecture UNPAR, September (2007)

Table 3.3 Field survey data on representative households' annual income and distance of residences to the CBD in Palangkaraya city

Land quality	Linear position	Representative distance to the CBD (km)		Average annual income of sample households	
		The nearest (km)	The farthest (km)	High-income household (Rp)	Low-income household (Rp)
The normal land	$0-t_3$	0	3	34,230,331	
	t_4-t_5	5	7	34,228,233	
	t_6-t_7	9	11	32,229,344	
	t_8-t_2	14	20	34,230,561	
	$0-t_2$	0	20	34,230,223	
The flood-prone area	t_3-t_4	3	5		12,304,881
	t_5-t_6	7	9		12,304,443
	t_7-t_8	11	14		12,304,532

Source: Field Survey by Department of Architecture UNPAR, September (2007)

reduced by net indirect taxes and fixed capital consumption. The total national income equals total national consumption, which includes total household consumption. Table 3.4 shows the gross domestic product account of Indonesia.

Meanwhile, the number of low-income households in the entire country is calculated using the percentage of the population who live below the poverty line as claimed by the national government, or 16.58% on average in 2010, as shown in Table 3.5.

Household income is distributed proportionally into two types of households: high-income and low-income households. Low-income households represent a group of households that earn less than USD 1 per day, whereas the rest of the group is classified as high-income households that obviously earn more than USD 1 per day. Table 3.6 shows the regional income of households.

Then, parameter α in the utility function of both households can be calculated as follows:

$$\alpha_1 = \frac{px_1}{y_1} \text{ and } \alpha_2 = \frac{px_2}{y_2}$$

where

α_1, α_2: elasticity parameters
p: price of consumption goods
x_1, x_2: consumption goods by high-income and low-income households
w_1, w_2: wages of high-income and low-income households

and because

$\alpha + \beta = 1$.

Then, once parameter α is estimated, parameter β can be determined. Furthermore, parameter γ in the asset function is difficult to estimate given a lack of

Table 3.4 Gross domestic product account of Indonesia, 2005–2010

Item	2005	2006	2007	2008	2009	2010
(1)	(2)	(3)	(4)	(5)	(6)	(7)
1 Private final consumption expenditure	1785.40	2092.70	2511.20	2622.30	2721.40	2853.50
2 General government final consumption expenditure	224.50	288.90	329.10	331.20	334.67	337.62
3 Gross domestic fixed capital formation	655.30	805.30	983.90	994.20	998.12	1083.50
4 Change in inventories	39.60	42.20	0.70	0.82	0.94	0.99
5 Statistical discrepancy	−47.00	−69.10	−27.50	−30.60	−31.50	−31.90
6 Export of goods and services	945.80	1036.50	1161.40	1171.50	1832.20	1932.60
7 (Less) import of goods and services	830.40	855.80	1002	1050	1077	1087
Gross domestic product (GDP)	**2773.20**	**3340.70**	**3956.80**	**4039.42**	**4778.83**	**5089.31**
8 Net factor income from the rest of the world	−135.50	−142.90	−156.60	−166.80	−177.80	−182.43
Gross national product (GNP)	**2637.70**	**3197.80**	**3800.20**	**3872.62**	**4601.03**	**4906.88**
9 (Less) net indirect taxes	53.30	98.70	112.80	119.50	121.40	125.90
10 (Less) consumption of fixed capital	138.10	166.00	197.20	201.40	210.50	212.70
National income	**2446.30**	**2933.10**	**3490.20**	**3551.72**	**4269.13**	**4568.28**

Source: BPS (Statistics Indonesia) (2011)

appropriate statistical data provided by the local government. However, by using the field survey data, parameter γ can be estimated using the following equations:

$$\ln A_1 = \gamma_1 + \ln y_1$$
$$\gamma_1 = \ln A_1 - \ln y_1$$

and

$$\ln A_2 = \gamma_2 + \ln y_2$$
$$\gamma_2 = \ln A_2 - \ln y_2$$

As a result, Table 3.7 presents parameters α, β, and γ.

Table 3.5 Population of Indonesia, 2005–2010

Year	Population in million	Percent change (%)
2005	219.852	
2006	222.747	1.32
2007	225.642	1.30
2008	228.523	1.28
2009	231.370	1.25
2010	237.641	2.71
Average number of population	**227.6291667**	**1.31**
Year	Number of low-income households	
2005	36.4514616	
2006	36.9314526	
2007	37.4114436	
2008	37.8891134	
2009	38.3611460	
2010	39.4008778	
Average number of LIH	**37.74091583**	
Percentage	**16.58**	

Source: Compiled from BPS (Statistics Indonesia) (2011)

3.3.2 Agricultural Land Rent

Agricultural land rent is treated as an exogenous variable. However, an approach to calculate this rent is from the model by Soekartawi (2007). According to this model, agricultural rent simply equals revenue from an agricultural product minus profits, minus the cost of production, minus the depreciation value, and minus the capital interest rate.

Then, by inputting selected agricultural data from Statistics Indonesia on the Central Kalimantan Province and Palangkaraya city, 2007, the agricultural land rent can be determined and then exogenously given.

3.3.3 Estimating Expected Flood Damage Rate on Household Assets

Because floods occur stochastically, selecting the floods that cause damage to household assets might be very difficult. Therefore, instead of retrieving the difficulty by arbitrarily selecting specific past floods, we use the EFDR expressed as the damage caused by particular floods. Then, we calculate the probability of the water discharge exceeding the average in cubic meters per second, as presented in Table 3.8.

Table 3.6 Regional income of households, 2005–2010

Year	National income	Income per capita		Number of population	
		HIH	LIH	HIH	LIH
2005	2.4463×10^{16}	89,154,968.37	22,115,340.75	183,400,538.40	36,451,461.60
2006	2.9331×10^{16}	105,506,996.99	26,171,544.14	185,815,547.40	36,931,452.60
2007	3.4902×10^{16}	123,935,758.60	30,742,891.65	188,230,556.40	37,411,443.60
2008	3.55172×10^{16}	124,530,307.30	30,890,372.46	190,633,886.60	37,889,113.40
2009	4.26913×10^{16}	147,842,258.68	36,673,019.88	193,008,854.00	38,361,146.00
2010	4.56828×10^{16}	154,027,263.41	38,207,241.58	198,240,122.20	39,400,877.80
Average	**3.54312E + 16**	**124,166,258.89**	**30,800,068.41**	**189,888,250.83**	**37,740,915.83**

Source: Compiled from BPS (Statistics Indonesia) (2011)

Table 3.7 Elasticity parameters in high-income and low-income households

	Parameter α	Parameter β	Parameter γ
High-income households	0.62	0.38	1.49
Low-income households	0.73	0.27	1.13

Table 3.8 Volume of discharge and probability of exceeding

	Case 1	Case 2	Case 3	Case 4	Case 5
Volume of discharge (m³/s)	69.70785717	84.45	235.12	500	715
Return period (T) year	1	5	17	20	30
Probability of exceeding	1	0.2	0.058823529	0.005	0.001398601

Table 3.9 Expected flood damage rate (EFDR)

Flood occurrences of water discharge (m³/s)	Probability of exceeding	Damage rate to household assets (%)	Pxd
69.7	1	60	0.6
84.45	0.2	65	0.13
235.12	0.058823529	85	0.05
500	0.05	90	0.045
715	0.033333333	99	0.03304
The EFDR			**0.85804**

The procedure for calculating the damage rate to household assets was determined as follows:

$$\text{Household Assets} = \text{House Assets} + \text{Furniture Assets}$$

House assets were taken from the data on prices per unit area as represented in the land and building tax imposition base per unit area (NJOP, Nilai Jual Obyek Pajak), as summarized by the Palangkaraya city tax office (2010). The data on household furniture assets were taken from the national median of the valuation per household in Indonesia in 2010, which is 29,491,874 rupiah or USD 3210 per household:

$$\text{Damage rate to household assets} = (\text{Household assets damage}/\text{Household assets}) \times 100\%$$

Household asset damage was calculated by multiplying household assets by the damage rate as a function of water depth. The damage rate was obtained directly from the empirical data of the Palangkaraya Public Work Agency (PPWA 2010).

Then, the EFDR is calculated as the sum of the possibility of exceeding multiplied by each damage rate to household assets. The result is presented in Table 3.9 and in Fig. 3.2

Here, five flood occurrence cases were taken. The minimum water discharge that could exceed the river height and, hence, damage household assets in the flood-prone areas is 69.7 m³/s. Because this discharge occurs annually, the probability of

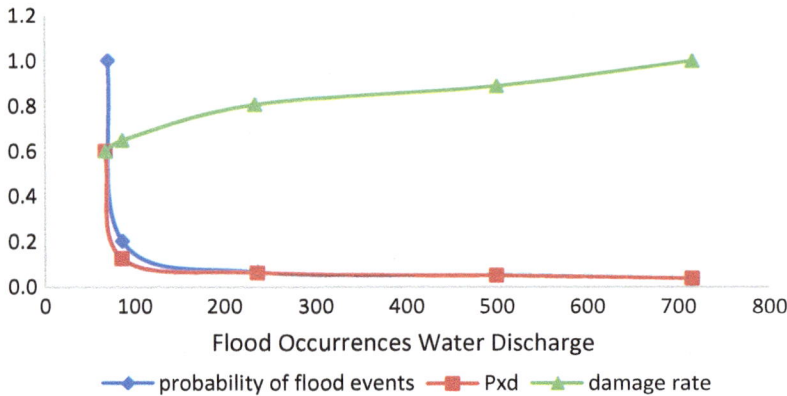

Fig. 3.2 Expected damage rate to household assets

exceeding will obviously be 1 (one time per year). The most devastating scenario is a flood with 715 m^3/s water discharge; however, the return period of the flood occurrence with such a water discharge is 30 years, indicating a possibility of exceeding 0.03.

3.3.4 Results

The bid rents of the representative high-income households on normal land in the area 0–t_3, t_4–t_5, t_6–t_7, and t_8–t_2 are 7,304,430.21 rupiahs, 6,797,398.18 rupiahs, 6,258,676.65 rupiahs, and 5,212,923.08 rupiahs, respectively, which are absolutely higher than those of the low-income households. The high-income households could earn higher wages than the low-income households, and, under the fixed utility level, the high-income households are able to pay higher land rent than low-income households.

Furthermore, the bid rents of the high-income households in the flood-prone areas in the areas $t_3 - t_4$, $t_5 - t_6$, and $t_7 - t_8$ are 0.000147755 rupiahs, 0.000137082 rupiahs, and 0.000125475 rupiahs, respectively, which are slightly lower than those of the low-income households. Given their high incomes, the high-income households could own more valuable assets than the low-income households. Assets consisting of housing units and durable goods are vulnerable to floods. Hence, in extreme floods, the high-income households face greater losses than the low-income households. Therefore, the bid rent of the high-income households becomes lower than that of the low-income households. Moreover, because the low-income households can bid higher than the high-income households, the flood-prone areas are then populated by the low-income households. The result is shown, graphically, in Fig. 3.3.

(a)

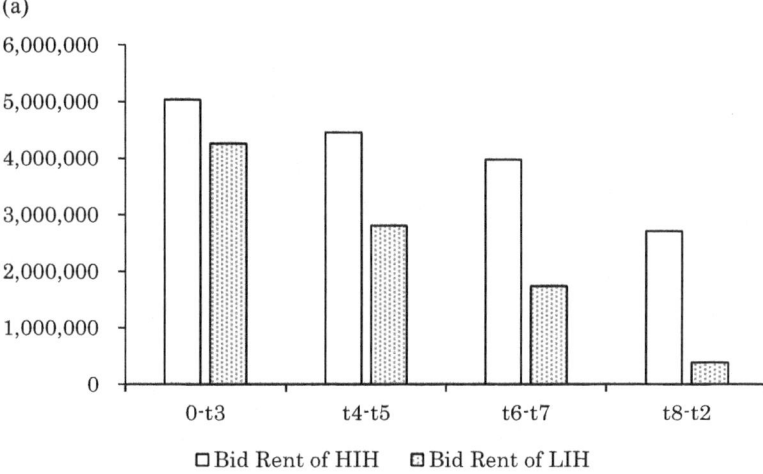

☐ Bid Rent of HIH ☒ Bid Rent of LIH

(b)

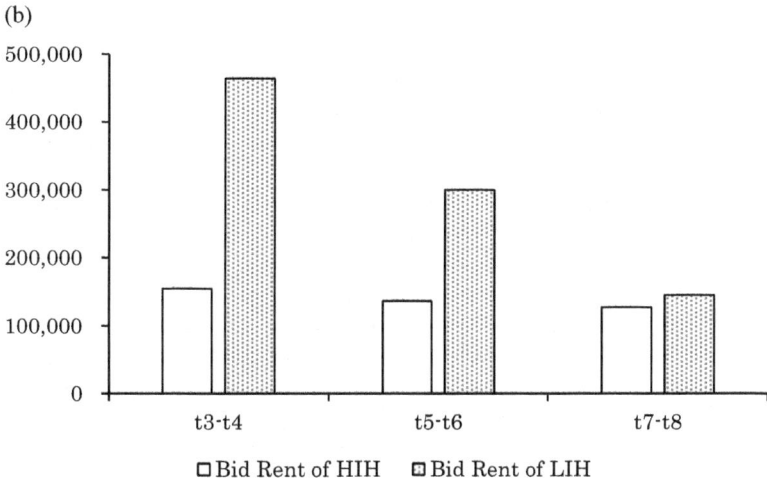

☐ Bid Rent of HIH ☒ Bid Rent of LIH

Fig. 3.3 Estimation of bid rent of representative high-income households and low-income house-holds in Palangkaraya city. (**a**) The bid rent in the normal land. (**b**) The bid rent in the flood prone areas

To draw all the bid rents in the city, we add more representative households from the targeted areas; however, the number is strictly set in equal proportion in both types of households. Then, the bid rent curve of both types of households in the entire city is depicted differently relative to other bid rent curves that show that the bid rent of the representative high-income households is lower in the flood-prone areas than that of the low-income households. The total bid rent in Palangkaraya city is presented as shown in Fig. 3.4.

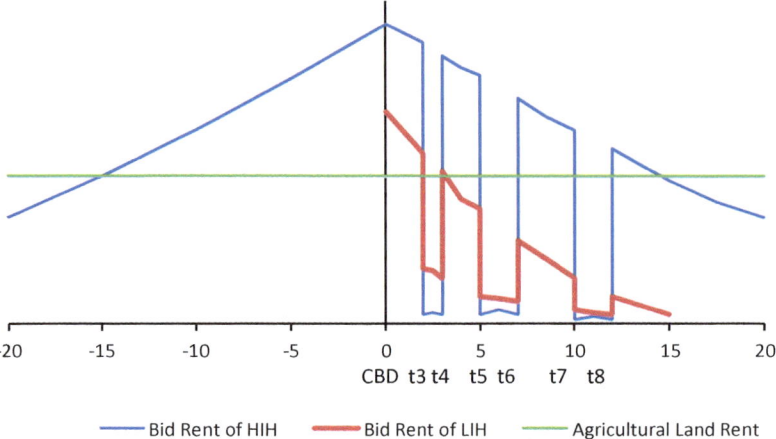

Fig. 3.4 Bid rent curves in Palangkaraya city

3.4 Concluding Remarks

This study applied a new urban economics approach to analyze illegal settlements in flood-prone areas within a city that faces considerable stochastic flood occurrences as a natural environment being deteriorated by human activities. Our model incorporated the expected flood damage on household assets to derive a different type of bid rent function and bid max lot size function that could systematically explain the appearance of illegal settlements in flood-prone areas. The bid rent of high-income households in flood-prone areas becomes lower than that of low-income households. This result is highlighted as being significantly different from that in the previous literature.

Assets owned by each household are the key determinant that influences the bid rents in the flood-prone areas. Because assets are assumed to be an increasing function of income, those owned by the high-income households are much higher than those owned by the low-income households. Hence, the representative individual of high-income households has more to lose with respect to their assets than low-income households in flood occurrences. This results in the fact that the bid rent offered by each high-income group becomes lower than that offered by each low-income household.

The land use pattern in the city is assumed to be determined by the bid rents of both the high-income and low-income households. On normal land, where no flood risk exists, the bid rent offered by the high-income households is higher than that offered by the low-income households. Hence, the normal land areas are used by the high-income households. Conversely, in the flood-prone areas, because the bid rent offered by the representative individual of the high-income households is lower than that of the low-income households, flood-prone areas are occupied and populated by the low-income households.

References

Soekartawi, S. (2007). Beberapa Hal Yang Perlu Diperhatikan Dalam Melakukan Analisis Sistem Agroindustri Terpadu. *Agribusiness and Agricultural Economic Journal, 1*(2), 31–47.

Badan Pusat Statistik (BPS) Kota Palangka Raya, & (BAPPEDA), Badan Perencanaan Pembangunan Daerah Kota Palangka Raya. (2007). *Kota Palangka Raya dalam Angka* (Palangka Raya City in figures). Palangkaraya: Badan Pusat Statistik Kota Palangka Raya. Retrieved from https://palangkakota.bps.go.id/webbeta/website/pdf_publikasi/Palangka-Raya-Dalam-Angka-2007.pdf (2014.6.1).

Badan Pusat Statistik (BPS) Indonesia. (2011). *Produk Domestik Bruto Indonesia Menurut Penggunaan Tahun 2005–2010.* Jakarta: Badan Pusat Statistik Indonesia. Retrieved from https://www.bps.go.id/index.php (2014.6.1).

Representative Households' Annual Income And Distance Of Residences To The CBD In Palangkaraya City. (2007, September). *Field survey by Department of Architecture UNPAR.* Retrieved from http://www.upr.ac.id (2014.6.1).

Badan Pusat Statistik (BPS) Provinsi Kalimantan Tengah. (2007). *Kalimantan Tengah dalam Angka* (Kalimantan Tengah in figures). Palangkaraya: Badan Pusat Statistik Provinsi Kalimantan Tengah. Retrieved from http://kalteng.bps.go.id/webbeta/websiteV2/pdf_publikasi/Kalimantan-Tengah-Dalam-Angka-2007.pdf

Chapter 4
General Equilibrium Analysis

4.1 Introduction

In Chap. 3, a partial equilibrium urban economics model was constructed, hence explaining the existence of illegal settlements in the flood-prone areas in Palangkaraya City in the Central Kalimantan Province. The model employed the EFDR on household assets, hence constituting land quality in the city. Applying the model leads to the conclusion that, in the flood-prone areas, the bid rent of high-income households can become lower than that of low-income households. Nevertheless, the partial equilibrium model is slightly lacking in reality because income is assumed to be exogenously given. In contrast, a general equilibrium model takes into account firms at which the households can endow available working time to obtain income. For that matter, income can be endogenously determined.

The general equilibrium model seeks to explain the behavior of supply, demand, and prices in an entire economy with several or many markets by seeking to prove that equilibrium prices for goods exist and that all prices are at equilibrium. As with all models, this model is an abstraction from a real economy; it is proposed to be a useful model by considering both equilibrium prices as long-term and actual prices as deviations from equilibrium. Broadly, general equilibrium attempts to provide an understanding of the entire economy using a "bottom–up" approach starting with individual markets and agents.

This chapter discusses a general equilibrium analysis that takes into account firms in the CBD, thus, internalizing the income of both types of households. Each household optimizes its bid rent constrained by a fixed utility level. By incorporating the expected damage rate on a household's assets, a new bid rent function and a bid max lot size function are obtained (Fig. 4.1).

© Springer Nature Singapore Pte Ltd. 2018
Y. Miyata et al., *Environmental and Natural Disaster Resilience of Indonesia*,
New Frontiers in Regional Science: Asian Perspectives 23,
https://doi.org/10.1007/978-981-10-8210-8_4

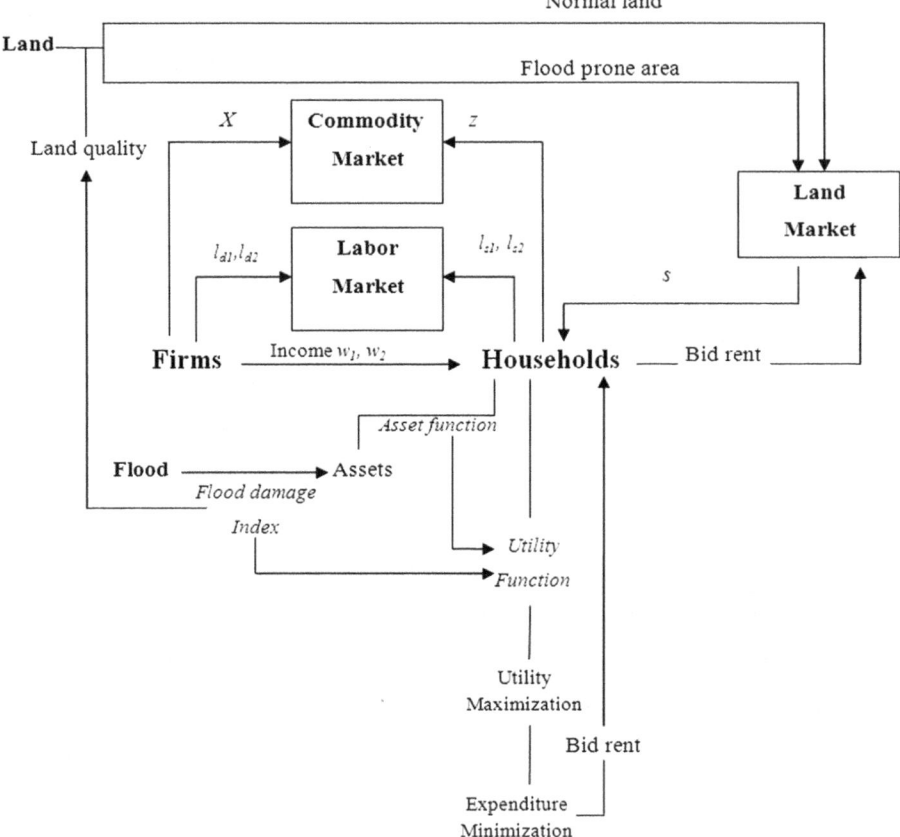

Fig. 4.1 Model Structure

4.2   The Model

We construct a general equilibrium model following standard urban economics using the bid rent function approach. However, our model can be distinguished from Fujita's model and other urban economics model in the following manner:

1. Our model takes into account land quality in a city area, namely, normal land and flood-prone areas. The normal land areas face no flood risk, whereas the flood-prone areas face stochastic flood occurrences. This assumption has yet to be discussed in Fujita's model.
2. The expected flood damage on a household's assets is introduced in our model to estimate the damages caused by stochastic flood events. Moreover, household assets are by definition introduced as an increasing function of income. Hence, the expected flood damage and asset function, which is defined as an increasing function of income,

measure land quality that must be considered in the utility maximization problem, yielding different types of bid rent functions and bid max lot size functions.

The model under study is based on the following assumptions:

1. The study area is assumed to be a monocentric city. All the firms are in the CBD and are assumed to be homogeneous, producing a single type of commodity.
2. Two types of households exist in the city: high income and low income. The households consume goods and acquire land. The commodity is assumed to be the numeraire.
3. The city is closed for the high-income group but open for the low-income group. Thus, the number of high-income households is fixed, whereas that of low-income households is internally determined depending on the supreme utility level.
4. Two types of land exist in the city. The normal land areas are assumed to face no flood risk, whereas the flood-prone areas face flood risk with probability of occurrence.

4.2.1 Geographical Location of the City

Geographically, the city is in a tropical region characterized by high evaporation, high humidity, and high precipitation. Furthermore, river basin systems, deforestations, and flood occurrences exist in the region. Hence, most of the cities and settlements in naturally configured flood-prone areas are located alongside river bodies. In fact, some of the flood-prone areas have been occupied and converted for residential use without the clearance of property rights and building permits. The city has a CBD, which is where all the firms are located. Surrounding the CBD are residential areas constructed on both normal land and flood-prone areas. The distance to the CBD for each of the areas is different, but they are considerably close enough to the city center. Agricultural land is located just outside the city area.

4.2.2 Firms

All of the firms are assumed to be in the CBD. Each firm produces a single type of commodity. Then, firms' production function may be written as follows:

$$X = (N_1)^\theta \left\{ \zeta^{\frac{1}{\sigma}} l d_1^{\frac{\sigma-1}{\sigma}} + (1-\zeta)^{\frac{1}{\sigma}} l d_2^{\frac{\sigma-1}{\sigma}} \right\}^{\frac{\sigma}{\sigma-1}} \quad (0 < \sigma < 1) \tag{4.1}$$

where:

X: output of a firm
N_1: number of high-income households

ld_1: demand for skilled labor
ld_2: demand for unskilled labor
ζ: share parameter
σ: elasticity parameter
θ: elasticity parameter

Each firm is a price taker for commodities and production factors. Given the linear homogeneity of one degree in each firm's technology, the equilibrium profit in each firm becomes zero. To obtain the conditional demand for labor in a firm, we consider the following cost function:

$$C = \min_{\{ld_1, ld_2\}} w_1 ld_1 + w_2 ld_2 \tag{4.2}$$

subject to

$$X = f(ld_1, ld_2) \tag{4.3}$$

Then, the conditional demands for labor in each type of household are obtained as follows:

$$ld_1 = \frac{\zeta X}{w_1^\sigma N_1^\theta \left(\zeta w_1^{1-\sigma} + (1-\zeta)w_2^{1-\sigma}\right)^{\frac{\sigma}{\sigma-1}}} \tag{4.4}$$

$$ld_2 = \frac{(1-\zeta)X}{w_2^\sigma N_1^\theta \left(\zeta w_1^{1-\sigma} + (1-\zeta)w_2^{1-\sigma}\right)^{\frac{\sigma}{\sigma-1}}} \tag{4.5}$$

Both types of households elastically supply labor ld_1, ld_2 to the representative firm, obtaining income w_1, w_2. Here, the representative high-skilled labor of the high-income group earns relatively a higher wage rate than that of the representative low-skilled labor of the low-income group. Then, the inequality is written as follows:

$$w_1 > w_2 \tag{4.6}$$

4.2.3 Households

Because the city area faces frequent flood occurrences, we consider flood damage to the assets of each type of household. The amount and value of the assets may depend on income. Assets may have values that are twice that of income depending on the type of asset. Therefore, the asset function can be considered an increasing function of income. We define the asset function as follows:

$$A_i(t) \equiv (w_i)^\gamma \qquad (\gamma > 1) \tag{4.7}$$

where:

w_i: household income
γ: elasticity parameter

Because floods occur stochastically, to avoid such a possible bias, we estimate the flood damage on a household's asset using an index that expresses the damage rate of stochastic flood occurrences instead of past-recorded flood occurrences as a data source. Then, the EFDR on a household's asset is introduced as follows:

$$c(t) \equiv \int_0^\infty P(Q(t))c(Q(t))\, dQ(t) \tag{4.8}$$

where:

$c(t)$: expected damage rate on household assets at location $Q(t)$
$P(Q(t))$: probability density function of flood volume $Q(t)$
$c(Q(t))$: damage rate on household assets when flood volume is $Q(t)$

We incorporate the asset function and the expected damage rate on household assets into the utility functions for the two types of households. Then, the household utility function at location t is assumed to be expressed as follows:

$$u_i\big(z_i(t), s_{Hi}(t)\big) \equiv \frac{z_i(t)^{\alpha_i} s_{Hi}(t)^{\beta_i}}{1 + c(t)A_i(t)} \qquad (\alpha_i + \beta_i = 1) \tag{4.9}$$

for $t \notin [t_3, t_4] \cup [t_5, t_6] \cup [t_7, t_8]$ and $t \in [t_3, t_4] \cup [t_5, t_6] \cup [t_7, t_8]$

where:

$i = 1$ for a high-income household and $i = 2$ for a low-income household
$u_i(z_i(t), s_{Hi}(t))$: household utility function at location t
$z_i(t)$: household consumption at location t
$s_{Hi}(t)$: household land at location t
$c(t)$:damage rate by flood $c(t) = 0$ on normal land and $0 < c(t) < 1$ in flood-prone
     areas
α_i and β_i: elasticity parameters in the utility function
$A_i(t)$: household assets at location t

Both types of households endow available working time ls_1, ls_2 to firms to obtain income of w_1, w_2. In a household's locational equilibrium, the household utility level takes the same value, u_i^*, irrespective of the household's place of residence. Therefore, the household bid rent function is specified as follows:

$$r_{Hi}(t) = \max_{\{z_i, s_{Hi}\}} \frac{w_i - z_i(t) - kt}{s_{Hi}(t)} \tag{4.10}$$

subject to

$$u_i(t) = u_i^* \tag{4.11}$$

where:

$r_{Hi}(t)$: a household's bid rent at location t
$i = 1$ for a high-income household and $i = 2$ for a low-income household
w_i: household income of each type of household
$s_{Hi}(t)$: a household's land at location t
u_i^*: a household's utility level
k: cost of transportation
t: distance from the CBD

To solve the maximization problems (4.10) and (4.11), we consider the following expenditure function:

$$E_i(t) = \min_{\{z_i, s_{Hi}\}} z_i(t) + r_{Hi}(t) s_{Hi}(t) \tag{4.12}$$

subject to

$$u_i^* = \frac{z_i(t)^{\alpha_i} s_{Hi}(t)^{\beta_i}}{1 + c(t)(w_i)^{\gamma}} \tag{4.13}$$

Then, the compensated demand functions for consumption and land are obtained as follows:

$$z_i(t) = [1 + c(t)w_i^{\gamma}] \left(\frac{\alpha_i}{\beta_i}\right)^{\beta_i} r_{Hi}(t)^{\beta_i} u_i^* \tag{4.14}$$

$$s_{Hi}(t) = [1 + c(t)w_i^{\gamma}] \left(\frac{\beta_i}{\alpha_i}\right)^{\alpha_i} \left(\frac{1}{r_{Hi}(t)}\right)^{\alpha_i} u_i^* \tag{4.15}$$

Therefore, the expenditure function is solved as follows:

$$E_i(t) = [1 + c(t)w_i^{\gamma}] \left(\frac{\alpha_i}{\beta_i}\right)^{\beta_i} r_{Hi}(t)^{\beta_i} u_i^*$$
$$+ r_{Hi}(t)[1 + c(t)w_i^{\gamma}] \left(\frac{\beta_i}{\alpha_i}\right)^{\alpha_i} \left(\frac{1}{r_{Hi}(t)}\right)^{\alpha_i} u_i^* \tag{4.16}$$

This expenditure function must equal the income of the household at location t, yielding the household bid rent function:

$$r_{Hi}(t) = \beta_i (\alpha_i)^{\frac{\alpha_i}{\beta_i}} \left(\frac{w_i - kt}{[1 + c(t)w_i^{\gamma}]u_i^*} \right)^{\frac{1}{\beta_i}}$$ (4.17)

Substituting Eq. (4.17) into Eqs. (4.14) and (4.15) results in the demand for goods and the bid max lot size as follows:

$$z_i(t) = \alpha_i(w_i - kt)$$ (4.18)

$$s_{Hi}(t) = \left(\frac{1}{\alpha_i(w_i - kt)} \right)^{\frac{\alpha_i}{\beta_i}} [1 + c(t)w_i^{\gamma}]^{\frac{1}{\beta_i}} (u_i^*)^{\frac{1}{\beta_i}}$$ (4.19)

4.2.4 City Boundary

The city boundary is determined by the intersection between the slope of the bid rent of the high-income household and the constant line for agricultural land rent. This is expressed by Eq. (4.20), implying that the fringe areas are populated by high-income households:

$$r_{H1}(-t_2) = rA$$ (4.20)

Thus, the following equation is obtained as follows:

$$\beta_1(\alpha_1)^{\frac{\alpha_1}{\beta_1}} \left(\frac{w_1 - kt}{[1 + c(t)w_1^{\gamma}]u_1^*} \right)^{\frac{1}{\beta_1}} = rA$$ (4.21)

Solving for t in Eq. (4.21), we determine the city boundaries in the left- and right-hand sides in the city as follows:

$$-t_2 = \frac{1}{k} \left\{ w_1 - \left(\frac{rA}{\beta_1(\alpha_1)^{\frac{\alpha_1}{\beta_1}}} \right)^{\beta_1} \right\} [1 + c(t)w_1^{\gamma}]u_1^*$$ (4.22)

$$t_2 = \frac{1}{k} \left\{ w_1 - \left(\frac{rA}{\beta_1(\alpha_1)^{\frac{\alpha_1}{\beta_1}}} \right)^{\beta_1} \right\} [1 + c(t)w_1^{\gamma}]u_1^*$$ (4.23)

4.2.5   Population

The population on normal land is determined as follows:

$$N_1 = \int_{-t_2}^{0} \frac{1}{s_{H1}} dt + \int_{0}^{t_3} \frac{1}{s_{H1}} dt + \int_{t_4}^{t_5} \frac{1}{s_{H1}} dt + \int_{t_6}^{t_7} \frac{1}{s_{H1}} dt + \int_{t_8}^{t_2} \frac{1}{s_{H1}} dt \quad (4.24)$$

Each term in Eq. (4.24) is calculated as follows:

$$
\begin{aligned}
\int_{-t_2}^{0} \frac{1}{s_{H1}} dt &= \int_{0}^{t_2} \frac{1}{s_{H1}} dt = \int_{0}^{t_2} (\alpha_1(w_1 - kt))^{\frac{\alpha_1}{\beta_1}} [1 + c_{02}w_1^{\gamma}]^{\frac{-1}{\beta_1}} (u_1^*)^{\frac{-1}{\beta_1}} dt \\
&= \frac{1}{k}\beta_1(\alpha_1)^{\frac{\alpha_1}{\beta_1}}(w_1)^{\frac{1}{\beta_1}} [1 + c_{02}w_1^{\gamma}]^{\frac{-1}{\beta_1}} (u_1^*)^{\frac{-1}{\beta_1}} - \frac{rA}{k} \\
&= f_H(0)[1 + c_{02}w_1^{\gamma}]^{\frac{-1}{\beta_1}} (u_1^*)^{\frac{-1}{\beta_1}} - \frac{rA}{k}
\end{aligned}
\quad (4.25)
$$

where

$$f_H(x) = \frac{1}{k}\beta_1(\alpha_1)^{\frac{\alpha_1}{\beta_1}}(w_1 - kx)^{\frac{1}{\beta_1}}$$

$$
\begin{aligned}
\int_{0}^{t_3} \frac{1}{s_{H1}} dt &= \int_{0}^{t_3} (\alpha_1(w_1 - kt))^{\frac{\alpha_1}{\beta_1}} [1 + c_{03}w_1^{\gamma}]^{\frac{-1}{\beta_1}} (u_1^*)^{\frac{-1}{\beta_1}} dt \\
&= f_H(0)[1 + c_{03}w_1^{\gamma}]^{\frac{-1}{\beta_1}} (u_1^*)^{\frac{-1}{\beta_1}} - f_H(t_3)[1 + c_{03}w_1^{\gamma}]^{\frac{-1}{\beta_1}} (u_1^*)^{\frac{-1}{\beta_1}}
\end{aligned}
\quad (4.26)
$$

$$
\begin{aligned}
\int_{t_4}^{t_5} \frac{1}{s_{H1}} dt &= \int_{t_4}^{t_5} (\alpha_1(w_1 - kt))^{\frac{\alpha_1}{\beta_1}} [1 + c_{45}w_1^{\gamma}]^{\frac{-1}{\beta_1}} (u_1^*)^{\frac{-1}{\beta_1}} dt \\
&= f_H(t_4)[1 + c_{45}w_1^{\gamma}]^{\frac{-1}{\beta_1}} (u_1^*)^{\frac{-1}{\beta_1}} - f_H(t_5)[1 + c_{45}w_1^{\gamma}]^{\frac{-1}{\beta_1}} (u_1^*)^{\frac{-1}{\beta_1}}
\end{aligned}
\quad (4.27)
$$

$$
\begin{aligned}
\int_{t_6}^{t_7} \frac{1}{s_{H1}} dt &= \int_{t_6}^{t_7} (\alpha_1(w_1 - kt))^{\frac{\alpha_1}{\beta_1}} [1 + c_{67}w_1^{\gamma}]^{\frac{-1}{\beta_1}} (u_1^*)^{\frac{-1}{\beta_1}} dt \\
&= f_H(t_6)[1 + c_{67}w_1^{\gamma}]^{\frac{-1}{\beta_1}} (u_1^*)^{\frac{-1}{\beta_1}} - f_H(t_7)[1 + c_{67}w_1^{\gamma}]^{\frac{-1}{\beta_1}} (u_1^*)^{\frac{-1}{\beta_1}}
\end{aligned}
\quad (4.28)
$$

$$\int_{t_8}^{t_2} \frac{1}{s_{H1}} dt = \int_{t_8}^{t_2} (\alpha_1(w_1 - kt))^{\frac{\alpha_1}{\beta_1}} [1 + c_{28} w_1^\gamma]^{\frac{-1}{\beta_1}} (u_1^*)^{\frac{-1}{\beta_1}} dt$$

$$= f_H(t_8) [1 + c_{28} w_1^\gamma]^{\frac{-1}{\beta_1}} (u_1^*)^{\frac{-1}{\beta_1}} - \frac{rA}{k} \tag{4.29}$$

Substituting Eqs. (4.25), (4.26), (4.27), (4.28), and (4.29) into Eq. (4.24) results in the number of high-income households in the city as follows:

$$N_1 = \left\{ f_H(0) [1 + c_{02} w_1^\gamma]^{\frac{-1}{\beta_1}} + f_H(0) [1 + c_{03} w_1^\gamma]^{\frac{-1}{\beta_1}} - f_H(t_3) [1 + c_{03} w_1^\gamma]^{\frac{-1}{\beta_1}} \right.$$
$$+ f_H(t_4) [1 + c_{45} w_1^\gamma]^{\frac{-1}{\beta_1}} - f_H(t_5) [1 + c_{45} w_1^\gamma]^{\frac{-1}{\beta_1}} + f_H(t_6) [1 + c_{67} w_1^\gamma]^{\frac{-1}{\beta_1}}$$
$$\left. - f_H(t_7) [1 + c_{67} w_1^\gamma]^{\frac{-1}{\beta_1}} + f_H(t_8) [1 + c_{28} w_1^\gamma]^{\frac{-1}{\beta_1}} \right\} (u_1^*)^{\frac{-1}{\beta_1}} - 2 \frac{rA}{k} \tag{4.30}$$

Finally, the equilibrium utility level in a high-income household is calculated as follows:

$$u_1^* = \left\{ f_H(0) [1 + c_{02} w_1^\gamma]^{\frac{-1}{\beta_1}} + f_H(0) [1 + c_{03} w_1^\gamma]^{\frac{-1}{\beta_1}} - f_H(t_3) [1 + c_{03} w_1^\gamma]^{\frac{-1}{\beta_1}} \right.$$
$$+ f_H(t_4) [1 + c_{45} w_1^\gamma]^{\frac{-1}{\beta_1}} - f_H(t_5) [1 + c_{45} w_1^\gamma]^{\frac{-1}{\beta_1}} + f_H(t_6) [1 + c_{67} w_1^\gamma]^{\frac{-1}{\beta_1}}$$
$$\left. - f_H(t_7) [1 + c_{67} w_1^\gamma]^{\frac{-1}{\beta_1}} + f_H(t_8) [1 + c_{28} w_1^\gamma]^{\frac{-1}{\beta_1}} \right\}^{\beta_1} \left(N_1 + 2\frac{rA}{k} \right)^{-\beta_1} \tag{4.31}$$

The population in the flood-prone areas is determined as follows:

$$N_2 = \int_{t_3}^{t_4} \frac{1}{s_{H2}} dt + \int_{t_5}^{t_6} \frac{1}{s_{H2}} dt + \int_{t_7}^{t_8} \frac{1}{s_{H2}} dt \tag{4.32}$$

where:

N_2: number of low-income households

Each term in Eq. (4.32) is calculated as follows:

$$\int_{t_3}^{t_4} \frac{1}{s_{H2}} dt = \int_{t_3}^{t_4} (\alpha_2(w_2 - kt))^{\frac{\alpha_2}{\beta_2}} [1 + c_{34} w_2^\gamma]^{\frac{-1}{\beta_2}} (u_2^*)^{\frac{-1}{\beta_2}} dt$$

$$= (g_H(t_3) - g_H(t_4)) [1 + c_{34} w_2^\gamma]^{\frac{-1}{\beta_2}} (u_2^*)^{\frac{-1}{\beta_2}} \tag{4.33}$$

where

$$g_H(x) = \frac{1}{k}\beta_2(\alpha_2)^{\frac{\alpha_2}{\beta_2}}(w_2 - kx)^{\frac{1}{\beta_2}}$$

$$\int_{t_5}^{t_6} \frac{1}{s_{H2}}dt = \int_{t_5}^{t_6}(\alpha_2(w_2 - kt))^{\frac{\alpha_2}{\beta_2}}\left[1 + c_{56}w_2^\gamma\right]^{\frac{-1}{\beta_2}}(u_2^*)^{\frac{-1}{\beta_2}}dt$$
$$= (g_H(t_5) - g_H(t_6))\left[1 + c_{56}w_2^\gamma\right]^{\frac{-1}{\beta_2}}(u_2^*)^{\frac{-1}{\beta_2}} \tag{4.34}$$

$$\int_{t_7}^{t_8} \frac{1}{s_{H2}}dt = \int_{t_7}^{t_8}(\alpha_2(w_2 - kt))^{\frac{\alpha_2}{\beta_2}}\left[1 + c_{78}w_2^\gamma\right]^{\frac{-1}{\beta_2}}(u_2^*)^{\frac{-1}{\beta_2}}dt$$
$$= (g_H(t_7) - g_H(t_8))\left[1 + c_{78}w_2^\gamma\right]^{\frac{-1}{\beta_2}}(u_2^*)^{\frac{-1}{\beta_2}} \tag{4.35}$$

Substituting Eqs. (4.33), (4.34), and (4.35) into Eq. (4.32) results in the number of low-income households in the flood-prone areas as follows:

$$N_2 = \left\{ (g_H(t_3) - g_H(t_4))\left[1 + c_{34}w_2^\gamma\right]^{\frac{-1}{\beta_2}} \right.$$
$$+ (g_H(t_5) - g_H(t_6))\left[1 + c_{56}w_2^\gamma\right]^{\frac{-1}{\beta_2}}$$
$$\left. + (g_H(t_7) - g_H(t_8))\left[1 + c_{78}w_2^\gamma\right]^{\frac{-1}{\beta_2}} \right\}(u_2^*)^{\frac{-1}{\beta_2}} \tag{4.36}$$

4.2.6   Market Equilibrium Conditions

This model has three markets: commodity market, labor market, and land market. Then, the equilibrium condition for the three markets, respectively, is described in Eqs. (4.37), (4.38), (4.39), (4.40), (4.41), (4.42), (4.43), (4.44), (4.45), (4.46), (4.47), (4.48), (4.49), (4.50), (4.51), (4.52), (4.53), (4.54), (4.55), (4.56), (4.57), (4.58), (4.59), (4.60), (4.61), (4.62), (4.63), (4.64), (4.65) and (4.66).

4.2.6.1   Commodity Market

Total output by the firms, which equals total consumption by households, is determined as follows:

$$X = \int_{-t_2}^{0} \frac{z_1}{s_{H1}} dt + \int_{0}^{t_3} \frac{z_1}{s_{H1}} dt + \int_{t_4}^{t_5} \frac{z_1}{s_{H1}} dt + \int_{t_6}^{t_7} \frac{z_1}{s_{H1}} dt + \int_{t_8}^{t_2} \frac{z_1}{s_{H1}} dt$$

$$+ \int_{t_3}^{t_4} \frac{z_2}{s_{H2}} dt + \int_{t_5}^{t_6} \frac{z_2}{s_{H2}} dt + \int_{t_7}^{t_8} \frac{z_2}{s_{H2}} dt + \int_{-t_2}^{0} \frac{kt}{s_{H1}} dt + \int_{0}^{t_3} \frac{kt}{s_{H1}} dt$$

$$+ \int_{t_4}^{t_5} \frac{kt}{s_{H1}} dt + \int_{t_6}^{t_7} \frac{kt}{s_{H1}} dt + \int_{t_8}^{t_2} \frac{kt}{s_{H1}} dt + \int_{t_3}^{t_4} \frac{kt}{s_{H2}} dt + \int_{t_5}^{t_6} \frac{kt}{s_{H2}} dt \qquad (4.37)$$

$$+ \int_{t_7}^{t_8} \frac{kt}{s_{H2}} dt + \int_{-t_2}^{0} \frac{r_{H1}}{s_{H1}} dt + \int_{0}^{t_3} \frac{r_{H1}}{s_{H1}} dt + \int_{t_4}^{t_5} \frac{r_{H1}}{s_{H1}} dt + \int_{t_6}^{t_7} \frac{r_{H1}}{s_{H1}} dt$$

$$+ \int_{t_8}^{t_2} \frac{r_{H1}}{s_{H1}} dt + \int_{t_3}^{t_4} \frac{r_{H2}}{s_{H2}} dt + \int_{t_5}^{t_6} \frac{r_{H2}}{s_{H2}} dt + \int_{t_7}^{t_8} \frac{r_{H2}}{s_{H2}} dt$$

Each term in Eq. (4.37) is calculated as follows:

$$\int_{-t_2}^{0} \frac{z_1}{s_{H1}} dt = \int_{0}^{t_2} \frac{z_1}{s_{H1}} dt = \int_{0}^{t_2} \alpha_1(w_1 - kt)(\alpha_1(w_1 - kt))^{\frac{\alpha_1}{\beta_1}} \left[1 + c_{02} w_1^{\gamma}\right]^{\frac{-1}{\beta_1}} (u_1^*)^{\frac{-1}{\beta_1}} dt$$

$$= -\frac{\beta_1 \alpha_1^{\frac{1}{\beta_1}}}{k(2\beta_1 + \alpha_1)} \left(\frac{rA}{\beta_1 \alpha_1^{\frac{1}{\beta_1}}}\right)^{2\beta_1 + \alpha_1} \left[1 + c_{02} w_1^{\gamma}\right] (u_1^*)$$

$$+ \frac{\beta_1}{k(2\beta_1 + \alpha_1)} \alpha_1^{\frac{1}{\beta_1}} w_1^{\frac{2\beta_1 + \alpha_1}{\beta_1}} \left[1 + c_{02} w_1^{\gamma}\right]^{\frac{-1}{\beta_1}} (u_1^*)^{\frac{-1}{\beta_1}}$$

$$(4.38)$$

$$\int_{0}^{t_3} \frac{z_1}{s_{H1}} dt = -\frac{\beta_1}{\alpha_1 k(2\beta_1 + \alpha_1)} (\alpha_1(w_1 - kt_3))^{\frac{2\beta_1 + \alpha_1}{\beta_1}} \left[1 + c_{03} w_1^{\gamma}\right]^{\frac{-1}{\beta_1}} (u_1^*)^{\frac{-1}{\beta_1}}$$

$$+ \frac{\beta_1}{k(2\beta_1 + \alpha_1)} \alpha_1^{\frac{1}{\beta_1}} w_1^{\frac{2\beta_1 + \alpha_1}{\beta_1}} \left[1 + c_{03} w_1^{\gamma}\right]^{\frac{-1}{\beta_1}} (u_1^*)^{\frac{-1}{\beta_1}} \qquad (4.39)$$

$$= \{h(t_3) - h(0)\} \left[1 + c_{03} w_1^{\gamma}\right]^{\frac{-1}{\beta_1}} (u_1^*)^{\frac{-1}{\beta_1}}$$

where

$$h_1(x) = -\frac{\beta_1}{\alpha_1 k(2\beta_1 + \alpha_1)} (\alpha_1(w_1 - kx))^{\frac{2\beta_1 + \alpha_1}{\beta_1}}$$

$$\int_{t_4}^{t_5} \frac{z_1}{s_{H1}} dt = \{h_1(t_5) - h_1(t_4)\}\left[1 + c_{45}w_1^{\gamma}\right]^{\frac{-1}{\beta_1}}\left(u_1^*\right)^{\frac{-1}{\beta_1}} \tag{4.40}$$

$$\int_{t_6}^{t_7} \frac{z_1}{s_{H1}} dt = \{h_1(t_7) - h_1(t_6)\}\left[1 + c_{67}w_1^{\gamma}\right]^{\frac{-1}{\beta_1}}\left(u_1^*\right)^{\frac{-1}{\beta_1}} \tag{4.41}$$

$$\int_{t_8}^{t_2} \frac{z_1}{s_{H1}} dt = -\frac{\beta_1 \alpha_1^{\frac{1}{\beta_1}}}{k(2\beta_1 + \alpha_1)}\left(\frac{rA}{\beta_1 \alpha_1^{\frac{\alpha_1}{\beta_1}}}\right)^{2\beta_1 + \alpha_1}\left[1 + c_{82}w_1^{\gamma}\right]\left(u_1^*\right)$$

$$+ h_1(t_8)\left[1 + c_{82}w_1^{\gamma}\right]^{\frac{-1}{\beta_1}}\left(u_1^*\right)^{\frac{-1}{\beta_1}} \tag{4.42}$$

$$\int_{t_3}^{t_4} \frac{z_2}{s_{H2}} dt = \{h_2(t_4) - h_2(t_3)\}\left[1 + c_{34}w_2^{\gamma}\right]^{\frac{-1}{\beta_2}}\left(u_2^*\right)^{\frac{-1}{\beta_2}} \tag{4.43}$$

$$\int_{t_5}^{t_6} \frac{z_2}{s_{H2}} dt = \{h_2(t_6) - h_2(t_5)\}\left[1 + c_{56}w_2^{\gamma}\right]^{\frac{-1}{\beta_2}}\left(u_2^*\right)^{\frac{-1}{\beta_2}} \tag{4.44}$$

$$\int_{t_7}^{t_8} \frac{z_2}{s_{H2}} dt = \{h_2(t_8) - h_2(t_7)\}\left[1 + c_{78}w_2^{\gamma}\right]^{\frac{-1}{\beta_2}}\left(u_2^*\right)^{\frac{-1}{\beta_2}} \tag{4.45}$$

where

$$h_2(x) = -\frac{\beta_2}{\alpha_2 k(2\beta_2 + \alpha_2)}\left(\alpha_2(w_2 - kx)\right)^{\frac{2\beta_2 + \alpha_2}{\beta_2}}$$

$$\int_{-t_2}^{0} \frac{kt}{s_{H1}} dt = \int_{0}^{t_2} \frac{kt}{s_{H1}} dt = \int_{0}^{t_2} kt(\alpha_1(w_1 - kt))^{\frac{-\alpha_1}{\beta_1}}\left[1 + c_{02}w_1^{\gamma}\right]^{\frac{1}{\beta_1}}\left(u_1^*\right)^{\frac{1}{\beta_1}} dt$$

$$= -\frac{rA}{k} + \beta_1 \alpha_1^{\frac{-\alpha_1}{\beta_1}} w_1^{\frac{1}{\beta_1}}\left[1 + c_{02}w_1^{\gamma}\right]^{\frac{1}{\beta_1}}\left(u_1^*\right)^{\frac{1}{\beta_1}}$$

$$= -\frac{rA}{k} - m_1(0)\left[1 + c_{02}w_1^{\gamma}\right]^{\frac{1}{\beta_1}}\left(u_1^*\right)^{\frac{1}{\beta_1}} \tag{4.46}$$

where

$$m_1(x) = -\beta_1 \alpha_1^{\frac{-\alpha_1}{\beta_1}}(w_1 - kx)^{\frac{1}{\beta_1}}$$

$$\int_{0}^{t_3} \frac{kt}{s_{H1}} dt = \int_{0}^{t_3} kt(\alpha_1(w_1 - kt))^{\frac{-\alpha_1}{\beta_1}}\left[1 + c_{03}w_1^{\gamma}\right]^{\frac{1}{\beta_1}}\left(u_1^*\right)^{\frac{1}{\beta_1}} dt$$

$$= \{m_1(t_3) - m_1(0)\}\left[1 + c_{03}w_1^{\gamma}\right]^{\frac{1}{\beta_1}}\left(u_1^*\right)^{\frac{1}{\beta_1}} \tag{4.47}$$

$$\int_{t_4}^{t_5} \frac{kt}{s_{H1}} dt = \{m_1(t_5) - m_1(t_4)\}\left[1 + c_{45}w_1^{\gamma}\right]^{\frac{1}{\beta_1}}\left(u_1^*\right)^{\frac{1}{\beta_1}} \tag{4.48}$$

$$\int_{t_6}^{t_7} \frac{kt}{s_{H1}} dt = \{m_1(t_7) - m_1(t_6)\}\left[1 + c_{67}w_1^{\gamma}\right]^{\frac{1}{\beta_1}}\left(u_1^*\right)^{\frac{1}{\beta_1}} \tag{4.49}$$

$$\int_{t_8}^{t_2} \frac{kt}{s_{H1}} dt = -\frac{rA}{k} - m_1(t_8)\left[1 + c_{82}w_1^{\gamma}\right]^{\frac{1}{\beta_1}}\left(u_1^*\right)^{\frac{1}{\beta_1}} \tag{4.50}$$

$$\int_{t_3}^{t_4} \frac{kt}{s_{H2}} dt = \int_{t_3}^{t_4} kt(\alpha_2(w_2 - kt))^{\frac{-\alpha_2}{\beta_2}}\left[1 + c_{34}w_2^{\gamma}\right]^{\frac{1}{\beta_2}}\left(u_2^*\right)^{\frac{1}{\beta_2}} dt$$
$$= \{m_2(t_4) - m_2(t_3)\}\left[1 + c_{34}w_2^{\gamma}\right]^{\frac{1}{\beta_2}}\left(u_2^*\right)^{\frac{1}{\beta_2}} \tag{4.51}$$

where

$$m_2(x) = -\beta_2 \alpha_2^{\frac{-\alpha_2}{\beta_2}}(w_2 - kx)^{\frac{1}{\beta_2}}$$

$$\int_{t_5}^{t_6} \frac{kt}{s_{H2}} dt = \{m_2(t_5) - m_2(t_6)\}\left[1 + c_{56}w_2^{\gamma}\right]^{\frac{1}{\beta_2}}\left(u_2^*\right)^{\frac{1}{\beta_2}} \tag{4.52}$$

$$\int_{t_7}^{t_8} \frac{kt}{s_{H2}} dt = \{m_2(t_7) - m_2(t_8)\}\left[1 + c_{78}w_2^{\gamma}\right]^{\frac{1}{\beta_2}}\left(u_2^*\right)^{\frac{1}{\beta_2}} \tag{4.53}$$

$$\int_{-t_2}^{0} \frac{r_{H1}}{s_{H1}} dt = \int_{0}^{t_2} \frac{r_{H1}}{s_{H1}} dt = -\frac{\beta_1}{k(2\beta_1 + \alpha_1)}\beta_1 \alpha_1^{\frac{1}{\beta_1}}\left(\frac{\frac{rA}{\alpha_1}}{\beta_1 \alpha_1^{\frac{1}{\beta_1}}}\right)^{2\beta_1 + \alpha_1}\left[1 + c_{02}w_1^{\gamma}\right]^{\frac{-1}{\beta_1}}\left(u_1^*\right)^{\frac{-1}{\beta_1}}$$
$$+ \frac{\beta_1}{k(2\beta_1 + \alpha_1)}\beta_1 \alpha_1^{\frac{1}{\beta_1}}(w_1)^{\frac{2\beta_1 + \alpha_1}{\beta_1}}\left[1 + c_{02}w_1^{\gamma}\right]^{\frac{-1}{\beta_1}}\left(u_1^*\right)^{\frac{-1}{\beta_1}}$$
$$= \left\{-\frac{\beta_1}{k(2\beta_1 + \alpha_1)}\beta_1 \alpha_1^{\frac{1}{\beta_1}}\left(\frac{\frac{rA}{\alpha_1}}{\beta_1 \alpha_1^{\frac{1}{\beta_1}}}\right)^{2\beta_1 + \alpha_1} - l_1(0)\right\} \times \left[1 + c_{02}w_1^{\gamma}\right]^{\frac{-1}{\beta_1}}\left(u_1^*\right)^{\frac{-1}{\beta_1}} \tag{4.54}$$

where

$$l_1(x) = -\frac{\beta_1}{k(2\beta_1 + \alpha_1)}\beta_1 \alpha_1^{\frac{1}{\beta_1}}(w_1 - kx)^{\frac{2\beta_1 + \alpha_1}{\beta_1}}$$

$$\int_{0}^{t_3} \frac{r_{H1}}{s_{H1}} dt = \{l_1(t_3) - l_1(0)\}\left[1 + c_{03}w_1^{\gamma}\right]^{\frac{-1}{\beta_1}}\left(u_1^*\right)^{\frac{-1}{\beta_1}} \tag{4.55}$$

$$\int_{t_4}^{t_5} \frac{r_{H1}}{s_{H1}} dt = \{l_1(t_5) - l_1(t_4)\} \left[1 + c_{45} w_1^{\gamma}\right]^{\frac{-1}{\beta_1}} \left(u_1^*\right)^{\frac{-1}{\beta_1}} \tag{4.56}$$

$$\int_{t_6}^{t_7} \frac{r_{H1}}{s_{H1}} dt = \{l_1(t_7) - l_1(t_6)\} \left[1 + c_{67} w_1^{\gamma}\right]^{\frac{-1}{\beta_1}} \left(u_1^*\right)^{\frac{-1}{\beta_1}} \tag{4.57}$$

$$\int_{t_8}^{t_2} \frac{r_{H1}}{s_{H1}} dt = \left\{ -\frac{\beta_1}{k(2\beta_1 + \alpha_1)} \beta_1 \alpha_1^{\frac{1}{\beta_1}} \left(\frac{rA}{\beta_1 \alpha_1^{\frac{\alpha_1}{\beta_1}}}\right)^{2\beta_1 + \alpha_1} - l_1(t_8) \right\} \times \left[1 + c_{28} w_1^{\gamma}\right]^{\frac{-1}{\beta_1}} \left(u_1^*\right)^{\frac{-1}{\beta_1}}$$

$$\tag{4.58}$$

$$\int_{t_3}^{t_4} \frac{r_{H2}}{s_{H2}} dt = \{l_2(t_4) - l_2(t_3)\} \left[1 + c_{34} w_2^{\gamma}\right]^{\frac{-1}{\beta_2}} \left(u_2^*\right)^{\frac{-1}{\beta_2}} \tag{4.59}$$

where

$$l_2(x) = -\frac{\beta_2}{k(2\beta_2 + \alpha_2)} \beta_2 \alpha_2^{\frac{\alpha_2}{\beta_2}} (w_2 - kx)^{\frac{2\beta_2 + \alpha_2}{\beta_2}}$$

$$\int_{t_5}^{t_6} \frac{r_{H2}}{s_{H2}} dt = \{l_2(t_5) - l_2(t_6)\} \left[1 + c_{56} w_2^{\gamma}\right]^{\frac{-1}{\beta_2}} \left(u_2^*\right)^{\frac{-1}{\beta_2}} \tag{4.60}$$

$$\int_{t_7}^{t_8} \frac{r_{H2}}{s_{H2}} dt = \{l_2(t_7) - l_2(t_8)\} \left[1 + c_{78} w_2^{\gamma}\right]^{\frac{-1}{\beta_2}} \left(u_2^*\right)^{\frac{-1}{\beta_2}} \tag{4.61}$$

Substituting Eqs. (4.38), (4.39), (4.40), (4.41), (4.42), (4.43), (4.44), (4.45), (4.46), (4.47), (4.48), (4.49), (4.50), (4.51), (4.52), (4.53), (4.54), (4.56), (4.57), (4.58), (4.59), (4.60), and (4.61) into Eq. (4.37) results in the total commodities being calculated as follows:

$$\begin{aligned}
X = \quad & (4.38) + (4.39) + (4.40) + (4.41) \\
& + (4.42) + (4.43) + (4.44) + (4.45) \\
& + (4.46) + (4.47) + (4.48) + (4.49) \\
& + (4.50) + (4.51) + (4.52) + (4.53) \\
& + (4.54) + (4.55) + (4.56) + (4.57) \\
& + (4.58) + (4.59) + (4.60) + (4.61).
\end{aligned}$$

4.2.6.2 Labor Market

The labor supply of each type of household equals the number of each type of household. Then, the equilibrium condition in the labor market is reached when the labor supply from each type of household equals labor demand. Then, the equalities are written as follows:

$$ls_1 = ld_1 = N_1 \tag{4.62}$$

$$ls_2 = ld_2 = N_2 \tag{4.63}$$

4.2.6.3 Land Market

Denoting agricultural land by rA, which is an exogenous variable, the market rent function over the city in equilibrium, $r(t)$, is denoted as follows:

$$r(t) \equiv \max\{r_{H1}(t), r_{H2}(t), rA\} \text{ (on normal land)} \tag{4.64}$$
$$r(t) \equiv \max\{r_{H1}(t), r_{H2}(t)\} \quad \text{(in flood} - \text{prone areas)} \tag{4.65}$$

Given the periodical floods, flood-prone areas cannot be used for agriculture. Flood-prone areas are assumed to be located in the residential area. Hence, when we assume that the city center—in which the business area is located—is a point and the residential area surrounds the city center, the land equilibrium condition is expressed as follows:

$$r(t) = r_{H1}(t) \geq r_{H2}(t) \quad \text{for } t \in \quad \text{residential area on normal land} \tag{4.66}$$
$$r(t) = r_{H2}(t) \geq r_{H1}(t) \quad \text{for } t \in \quad \text{in flood-prone areas} \tag{4.67}$$
$$r(t) = r_{H1}(t) = rA \quad \text{for } t \in \text{ city boundary} \tag{4.68}$$

4.3 Numerical Simulations

The following section presents numerical simulations using statistical data and field survey data of Palangkaraya City. However, the available data might be less consistent given poor data management. Therefore, some difficult estimations were merely approached through approximations.

4.3.1 Estimating Parameters

Parameter α in the utility function of both households is calculated as follows:

$$\alpha_1 = \frac{px_1}{w_1} \quad \text{and} \quad \alpha_2 = \frac{px_2}{w_2}$$

where:

α_1, α_2: elasticity parameters
p: price of consumption goods
x_1, x_2: consumption goods by high-income and low-income households
w_1, w_2: wage of high-income and low-income households

and because

$$\alpha + \beta = 1$$

then parameter β can be easily determined. Furthermore, parameter γ in the asset function is a bit difficult to estimate given a lack of appropriate statistical data provided by the local government. However, by using field survey data, parameter γ for both types of households can be roughly estimated using the following equations:

$$\ln A_1 = \gamma_1 + \ln w_1$$
$$\gamma_1 = \ln A_1 - \ln w_1$$

and

$$\ln A_2 = \gamma_2 + \ln w_2$$
$$\gamma_2 = \ln A_2 - \ln w_2$$

Herewith, Table 4.1 presents the parameters α, β, and γ.

Other parameters, such as θ, σ, ζ, are very difficult to estimate given a lack of data. However, by employing a calibration technique and conducting a sensitivity analysis numerous times, these parameters can be roughly approached as presented in Table 4.2.

Table 4.1 Elasticity parameters in the utility function

Elasticity parameters		
θ	σ	ζ
1.5	0.1	0.3

Table 4.2 Elasticity parameters in the production function

	Elasticity parameters		
	α	β	γ
High-income household	0.62	0.38	1.49
Low-income household	0.73	0.27	1.13

4.3.2 *Analysis Results*

The results of the numerical simulation are summarized and discussed as follows.

4.3.2.1 Bid Rent

The numerical simulation results using necessary data on Palangkaraya City in Fig. 4.2 showed that, in the flood-prone areas, the bid rent of the representative high-income households becomes lower than that of the representative low-income households, suggesting that these representative low-income households reside in flood-prone areas. This result can be highlighted as a new finding, thus appropriately providing a systematic explanation of the existence of illegal settlements in flood-prone areas.

The implication of the model is that in flood-prone areas in which the expected damage rate on a household's asset takes the value $0 < c < 1$, the high-income household faces a significant loss on its assets. Hence, while enjoying a fixed utility level, the household's ability to pay land rent declines significantly to even lower than the bid rent of low-income households. Therefore, as a result, the low-income households reside in the flood-prone areas. Summarizing this interpretation, we obtain *Proposition 1*.

Proposition 1
In flood-prone areas in which the expected damage rate on household assets takes the bid rent value $c > 0$, the representative high-income households under the appropriate utility level becomes lower than that of the low-income households.

Furthermore, by applying the bid rent approach to the left side and right side of the city, a theoretical residential land use pattern in the city was depicted that shows

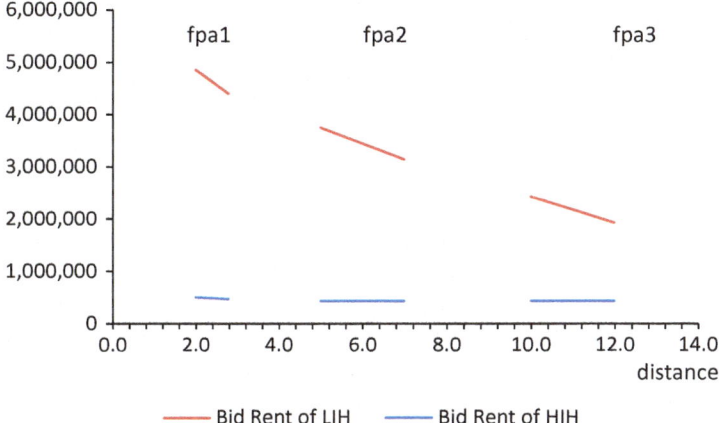

Fig. 4.2 Hierarchical structure of the model

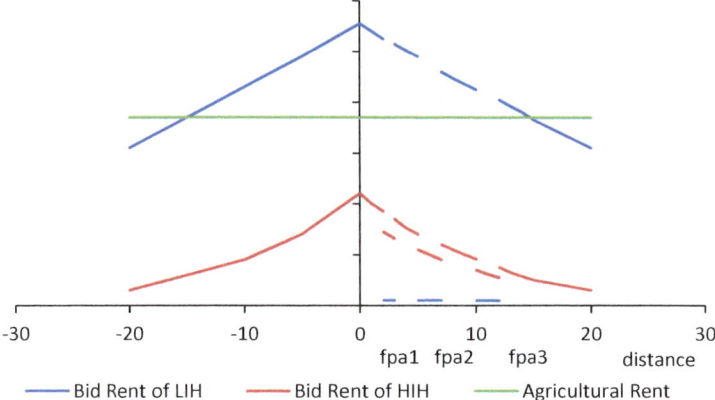

Fig. 4.3 Hierarchical structure of industries

that the high-income households populate normal land, whereas the low-income households mushroomed in the tiny flood-prone areas, as is shown in Fig. 4.3.

The next implication of the model is as follows. Because $w_1 > w_2$ and the expected damage rate on a household's assets must take the value $c = 0$ in normal land areas in which no floods occur, the bid rent of the representative high-income households becomes higher than that of the representative low-income households. Hence, normal land is used by the high-income households.

Conversely, in flood-prone areas in which floods frequently occur, the bid rent of the representative low-income households under an appropriate utility level becomes higher than that of the representative high-income households, leaving the flood-prone areas to be used by the low-income households. Summarizing this interpretation, we obtain *Proposition 2*.

Proposition 2

In a city in which flood-prone areas exist, the high-income households reside on the normal land, whereas the low-income households populate the flood-prone areas that depict a residential land use pattern.

4.3.2.2 Bid Max Lot Size

The bid max lot size determines the optimal lot size afforded by the representative households. The model implies that the optimal lot size is obtained when the bid rent given by the budget line is tangent to a household's utility at a fixed level. In the flood-prone areas, because the wage of the representative high-income household is higher than the wage of the representative low-income household, the optimal lot size of the high-income household is larger than that of the low-income household. Figure 4.4 shows that the representative low-income households are afforded smaller lot sizes relative to those of the high-income households in flood-prone areas.

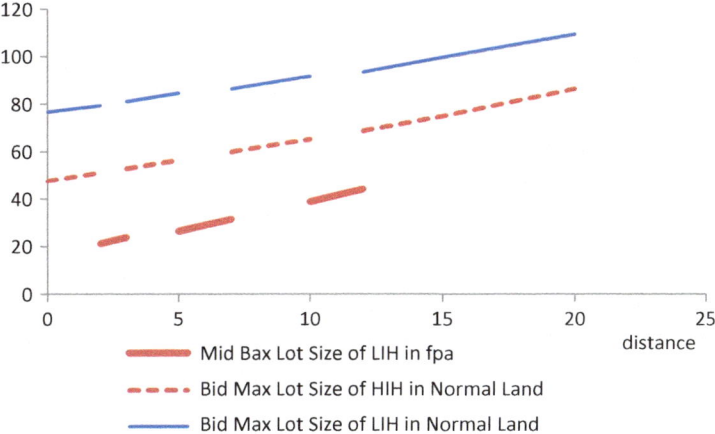

Fig. 4.4 Hierarchical structure of households

Furthermore, the optimal lot size in the flood-prone areas was compared and shown to be smaller than the optimal lot size for the normal land. Summarizing this interpretation, we obtain *Proposition 3*.

Proposition 3
The optimal lot size in the flood-prone areas is smaller than that for the normal land.

However, given that the bid rent of low-income households prevailed in the flood-prone areas, the optimal lot size in these areas is represented by the optimal lot size of the low-income households. Summarizing this interpretation, we obtain *Proposition 4*.

Proposition 4
Because the bid rent of the low-income households prevails in the flood-prone areas, the optimal lot size in the flood-prone areas is represented by the optimal lot size of the low-income households.

In addition, because density is a reciprocal of the bid max lot size, Fig. 4.5 shows that densities in fixed flood-prone areas are highest relative to other densities for normal land. Not only is this conclusion natural, but it also reflects the high density in most of the occupied flood-prone areas, as observed in many urban areas. Summarizing this interpretation, we obtain *Proposition 5*.

Proposition 5
The density in flood-prone areas is higher than that for normal land areas, implying that flood-prone areas are more populous than normal land areas.

Furthermore, the numerical simulation results show that densities in the flood-prone areas decrease as utility levels increase. In this case, the utility level is outside the city in surrounding rural areas and equals the utility level in the flood-prone areas, which is called the supreme utility level. This result indicates that an increase in the supreme utility level in surrounding rural areas by supreme utility

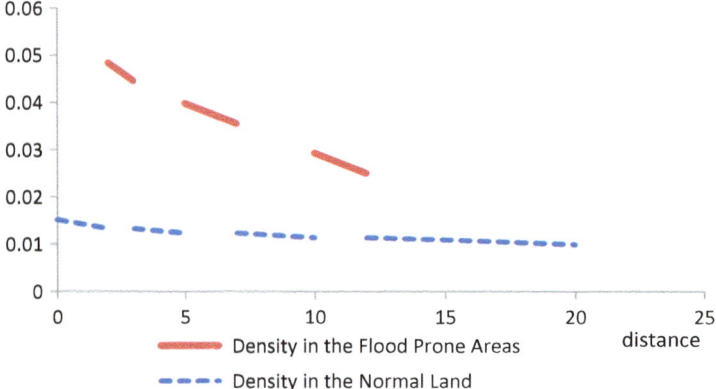

Fig. 4.5 Density in the city

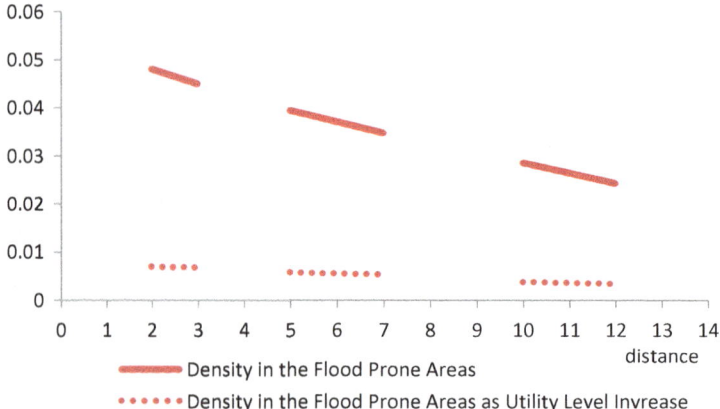

Fig. 4.6 Shift of density in flood-prone areas as utility level increases

development projects could possibly deflate the flood-prone areas such that they are more open space, thus preserving their ecological functions. The supreme utility development policy may positively reduce densities in the occupied flood-prone areas. The result of the numerical simulation is shown in Fig. 4.6.

4.3.2.3 Policy Simulations

In the previous simulation, changes in the utility level were shown to positively alter the bid max lot size. In that case, the utility level must be a supreme utility level outside the city in surrounding rural areas; otherwise, the increase in the utility level must shift household budget lines. Therefore, the supreme utility development policy implements supreme utility development projects in the surrounding rural areas and is expected to reduce the densities in the flood-prone areas. This section evaluates four cases for three flood-prone areas.

Base Case No supreme utility development policy intervention, business as usual

Case 1 Introduction of supreme utility development policy, which is implemented through utility development projects in surrounding rural areas. The policy's effectiveness level is 50% and could be assumed to increase by half or 50% of the previous utility level in the surrounding rural areas—equal to the utility level in flood-prone areas.

Case 2 Supreme utility development policy takes an effectiveness level of 75%, which could be assumed to increase the utility level in the surrounding rural areas by 75% of the previous utility level.

Case 3 Supreme utility development policy takes a full effectiveness level at 100%, which could be assumed to increase the utility level in the surrounding rural areas by doubling the rate or at 100% from the previous utility level.

Moreover, the increases in the previous utility level (in the base case) at 50%, 75%, and 100% reflect by assumption the effectiveness level of the supreme utility development policies. If the effectiveness level is 50%, then the utility level in the surrounding rural areas by assumption increases by 50%. If the effectiveness level is 75%, then the utility level by assumption also increases by 75%. Moreover, if the policy assumes a full effectiveness level—successfully doubling the previous utility level—then the utility level is assumed to increase by 100%. These assumptions can be intuitively justified as based on the common opinion that a successful and effective policy normally changes the utility level at a full rate. In this case, a 100% increase in the level can be regarded as a full rate.

Furthermore, two attributes of the changes in density are observed in this simulation. One attribute is the average percentage change of the densities for case 1, case 2, and case 3 relative to the base case, which is aimed at measuring the significance of the density reductions stimulated by the policy's effectiveness level. Another attribute is the slope steepness of the density curves for case 1, case 2, and case 3, which is a further step in the observation and aims to investigate the case that implies a better outcome.

1. Base case

Let us first examine the three flood-prone areas. Because the bid rent of low-income households prevails in flood-prone areas, the optimal lot size in these areas is represented by the lot size of low-income households. Here, flood-prone area 1 (fpa1) is the Danau seha neighborhood located 2–3 km from the CBD, flood-prone area 2 (fpa 2) is the Flamboyan neighborhood located 5–7 km from the CBD, and flood-prone area 3 (fpa 3) is the Mendawai neighborhood located 10–12 km from the CBD. In addition, the location and size of flood-prone areas are fixed. Figure 4.7 shows the optimal lot size in the three flood-prone areas.

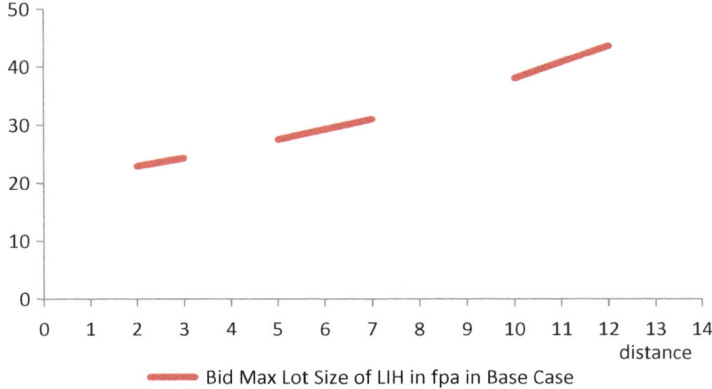

Fig. 4.7 Lot size in flood-prone areas in the base case

As shown in Fig. 4.7, the optimal lot size increases as the distance increases. The smallest optimal lot size is in fpa 1 with an average size of 23.59 m^2 per household, whereas the largest is in fpa 3 with an average size of 40.59 m^2 per household. Given the range of 23.59 m^2–40.59 m^2 per household, the three flood-prone areas are classified as slum areas, in which living conditions are deteriorating because minimum living space exists.

(1) Case 1

Introduction of the supreme utility development policy is aimed at reducing the density in flood-prone areas. For instance, a supreme utility development policy, such as national health insurance, basic national education support, and others, must be implemented in the surrounding rural areas and must equal the utility level in flood-prone areas. In case 1, the effectiveness level of the supreme utility development policy is 50%, implying that the policy is in an approximate half effective state.

(2) Case 2

The utility level in the surrounding rural areas increased by 75% from the base value because the supreme utility development induced 75% of the utility level from the base value.

(3) Case 3

The utility level in the surrounding rural areas increased 100% from the base value because the supreme utility development induced 100% of the utility level from the base value. Alternatively, we may state that, in case 3, the policy requires full effectiveness to increase the utility level in the surrounding rural areas by 100% from the base case.

Then, the results of case 1, case 2, and case 3 are compared with that of the base case and are arrayed in Figs. 4.8 and 4.9.

Figures 4.8 show that the optimal lot size in flood-prone areas increased by ratios of 3.49, 6.95, and 12.03 as the previous utility levels in the surrounding rural areas

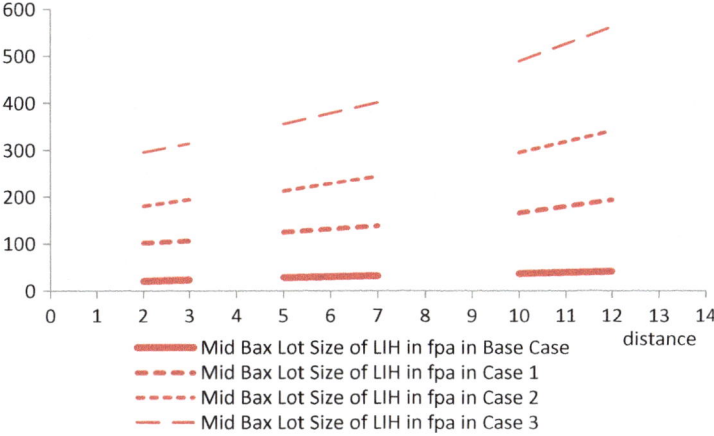

Fig. 4.8 Change in lot size in flood-prone areas

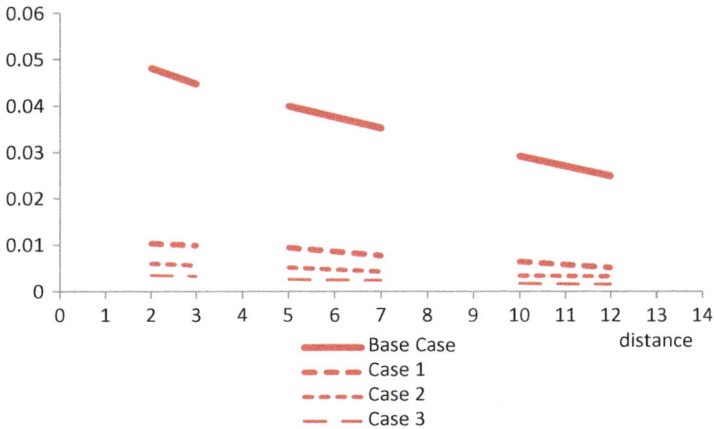

Fig. 4.9 Change in density in flood-prone areas for case 1, case 2, and case 3

increased by 50%, 75%, and 100%. In addition, the smallest previous lot size is 23.59 m² as a result of the utility level increases of 50%, 75%, and 100%. Hence, the optimal size became 105.91, 187.44, and 307.36, respectively.

Percentage changes in the density in flood-prone areas for case 1, case 2, and case 3 relative to the base case are calculated and shown in Table 4.3.

Figure 4.9 shows that the density in flood-prone areas decreased by 76%, 86%, and 92% as the previous utility increased by 50%, 75%, and 100%. Table 4.3 shows that the 50% effect of the supreme utility development relative to the base case significantly reduced the density in flood-prone areas by 76% from the highest density of 0.03–0.009, on average.

Table 4.3 Percentage change in density in flood-prone areas in case 1, case 2, and case 3 relative to the base case

	Percentage change of density reduction in the flood-prone areas as compared with the base case
Case 1	76%
Case 2	86%
Case 3	92%

Table 4.4 Slope steepness of density curves in case 1, case 2, and case 3

	Slope steepness of density curves in case 1, case 2, and case 3
Case 1 (50%)	0.0006
Case 2 (75%)	0.0003
Case 3 (100%)	0.000019

Furthermore, the slope steepness of the density curves in the flood-prone areas in case 1, case 2, and case 3 are compared and shown in Table 4.4.

The simulation results show that the slopes of the density curves in case 1, case 2, and case 3 take the values of 0.0006, 0.0003, and 0.000019, respectively. By comparing the results, one can conclude that the slope of the density curve in case 1 is steeper than that in case 2 and case 3. This conclusion indicates that the 50% effectiveness level of the supreme utility development policy in the surrounding rural areas results in a more persistent decline in density by distance to flood-prone areas than the 75% or even 100% effectiveness levels.

4.4   Concluding Remarks

This study has applied a new urban economics approach to analyzing illegal settlements in flood-prone areas. This study formulated a new urban economics model, namely, the general equilibrium model. Different from other urban economics models, the model in this study introduced an EFDR on household assets—a new method to estimate flood damage to household assets. Hence, by applying the method, one can predict the EFDRs for household assets in a city and, thus, can constitute the quality of such land in a city. This attempt is highlighted because it has not appeared in traditional urban economics models.

The model yields variants of the bid rent function and the bid max lot size function. These functions are considerably different than in Fujita's model when considering land heterogeneity. Hence, the model can be applied to analyze a land use pattern in a city in which land heterogeneity exists, as identified in Palangkaraya City in the Central Kalimantan Province, Indonesia.

The model takes into account an agglomeration economy and production sectors. In addition, the agglomeration economy significantly contributes to developing the city and urban areas, thus, allowing for the existence of a CBD. Moreover, all of the production sectors in which both types of households endow working time are assumed to be in the CBD. Therefore, in that sense, the model then could allow for complex interactions by the economic agents in the city. To that point, the model can be considered far more realistic than the partial equilibrium model.

The numerical simulation based on Palangkaraya City's data shows that on normal land, the bid rent of the representative high-income households is higher than that of low-income households, thus reproducing such land use patterns in which high-income households populate normal land areas. Conversely, in the flood-prone areas, the bid rent of the representative low-income households could become higher than that of the representative high-income households. As a result, low-income households overpopulate the flood-prone areas. The reverse bid rent in the flood-prone areas is highlighted as a new finding because it has never appeared in the literature on urban economics.

Furthermore, by arraying these results, a land use pattern in the city was depicted. High-income households reside on normal land, and low-income households occupied flood-prone areas.

Moreover, the numerical simulation on the bid max lot size, which determines the optimal lot size afforded by the representative households in the city, showed that the bid max lot size in the flood-prone areas is smaller than that in normal land areas, hence reciprocally pointing out that flood-prone areas are denser than normal land areas. The numerical simulation also showed that in the flood-prone areas, the optimal lot size of the representative high-income households is larger than that of the low-income households. However, because the bid rent of low-income households prevailed in flood-prone areas, the optimal lot size in these areas is represented by low-income households.

An area's density reflects the population living in a fixed area. Therefore, the higher density in fixed flood-prone areas implies that these areas are more populous than normal land areas.

Next, a simulation of the policy showed that a 50% increase in the previous utility level indicated an assumed 50% effectiveness of the supreme utility development policies in the surrounding rural areas. This increase significantly reduced the density in flood-prone areas, as indicated by a 76% change. Hence, the optimal lot size increases from 23.59 to 105.91 m^2.

Furthermore, a comparison of the steepness of the slope in the density curves in case 1, case 2, and case 3 showed that a 50% increase in the effectiveness of supreme utility development policies sets a more persistent decline in density on the basis of distance in flood-prone areas than do 75% and 100% increases in the policy's effectiveness at the household's utility level.

Chapter 5
Conclusion and Policy Recommendations

5.1 Conclusion

This study developed urban economics models, namely, the partial equilibrium model and the general equilibrium model, to analyze illegal settlements in Palangkaraya city in the Central Kalimantan Province, Indonesia. The partial equilibrium model is aimed at developing a preliminary theoretical analysis. The models are developed by employing the bid rent approach. Because the city is in a tropical region surrounded by river basins and has suffered massive deforestation of its surrounding forest, frequent floods and their corresponding damage to household assets in the city are inevitable.

The models introduced the EFDR on household assets. Because floods occur stochastically and given the unreliability of the data records on historical flood occurrences, water inundation is estimated by employing the annual expected depth of flood water, as introduced by Miyata and Abe (1991). In the models, this method was modified slightly by incorporating a damage level for household assets that corresponds to water volume. Hence, by applying the modified method, such EFDR to household assets can be estimated.

Furthermore, the EFDR value can be employed to constitute land quality in the city. If the EFDR value is 0, then the land is safe from water inundation. If the EFDR value is greater than 0, then the land faces water inundation. This method is regarded as a new attempt to analyze illegal settlements in flood-prone areas from an urban economics point of view, hence extending the previous studies on urban economics theory.

In addition, land quality is considered in the utility function. Each household is assumed to feel unsecured if it is in a flood-prone area because of the expectation of frequent floods. Therefore, the utility function is assumed to be discounted in a flood-prone area. Moreover, households maximize their ability to pay for land through an appropriate choice of goods and land—in this case, including its quality.

© Springer Nature Singapore Pte Ltd. 2018
Y. Miyata et al., *Environmental and Natural Disaster Resilience of Indonesia*,
New Frontiers in Regional Science: Asian Perspectives 23,
https://doi.org/10.1007/978-981-10-8210-8_5

The bid rent approach employed in this study mimics the approach by Fujita. However, in contrast to Fujita's approach, the models in this study consider land quality constituted by the EFDR. Hence, the models could yield variants of the bid rent and the bid max lot size that differ from the previous literature.

Furthermore, the partial equilibrium model slightly lacks reality because the supply side is neglected; thus, income is given exogenously. Instead, the general equilibrium model accounted for an agglomeration economy and production sectors. Henceforth, this model could allow for complex interactions by economic agents in the city. Therefore, in that sense, the general equilibrium model is far closer to reality than the partial equilibrium model. Thus, the general equilibrium model established a significant distinction from the partial equilibrium model. Now, the firms are accounted for and are in the CBD; hence, both types of households could endow available working time to obtain income. In the household locational equilibrium, the household utility level takes the same value irrespective of the household's residential place. The representative households maximize their ability to pay for land by appropriately choosing goods and land; therefore, the bid rent and the bid max lot size are achieved.

Because the income of the representative high-income households is relatively higher than the income of the representative low-income households, the general equilibrium model suggests that for normal land areas with no risk of flood, a high-income household offers a higher bid rent than a low-income household under appropriate elasticity parameters. As a result, the high-income households reside in normal land areas. Conversely, in the flood-prone areas, the bid rent of high-income household becomes lower than that of low-income households. As a result, the flood-prone areas are populated by low-income households. Then, by arraying the results altogether, a land use pattern in the city is depicted. The high-income households occupied normal land areas for residential use; conversely, low-income households reside in flood-prone areas.

Furthermore, the bid max lot size that determines the optimal lot size afforded by both types of households is derived when the bid rent slope given by the budget line is tangent to the households' fixed utility level. The numerical simulation showed that the optimal lot size of the representative households in flood-prone areas in which the EFDR takes a value higher than 0 is smaller than that in normal land areas. This result implies that density in fixed flood-prone areas is higher than that in normal land areas. The conclusion can be made that flood-prone areas are more populous than normal land areas. This conclusion is convincing as observed in the real world in which occupied flood-prone areas are often identified as areas with high density and low quality of life. High density may lead to deterioration of the environment and quality of life, as observed in many slum areas in developing countries. In addition, as the numerical simulation also shows, although the optimal lot size of the representative high-income households in flood-prone areas is larger than that of the representative low-income households, the low-income households' optimum lot size represents the density in the area. Because the bid rent of the low-income households prevails in flood-prone areas, the optimal lot size in flood-prone areas is determined by the low-income households.

Moreover, policy simulations showed that increases in households' utility levels through the introduction of supreme utility development policies reduce density in flood-prone areas, resulting in flood-prone areas having more open space.

As the final chapter, this chapter aims to summarize the major results of this dissertation.

In Chap. 3, the partial equilibrium model was developed by taking into account the EFDR and the asset function, thus yielding the bid rent function and the bid max lot size function that are highlighted as being different from Fujita's models.

By employing the function, a numerical simulation demonstrated that the EFDR significantly affected the bid rent of high-income households, which becomes lower than that of low-income households in flood-prone areas. Therefore, flood-prone areas are populated by low-income households. This conclusion is highlighted as a new finding.

Furthermore, a residential land use pattern in the city is then determined by the bid rents of both high-income and low-income households. In normal land areas in which no flood occurrences damage household assets, the bid rent of the representative high-income households is higher than that of the representative low-income households. Hence, normal land areas are occupied for residential use by high-income households. Conversely, in flood-prone areas, the EFDR takes a value >0, meaning that flood occurrences could damage household assets and the bid rent of the representative high-income households becomes lower than that of the representative low-income households. Hence, flood-prone areas are occupied for residential use by low-income households. In addition, household income determines household assets. Hence, in that sense, one can intuitively conclude that the representative high-income households own more assets than the representative low-income households. However, for the sake of simplification, the partial equilibrium model did not take into account the firm; hence, in this case, the income of representative households is exogenously given. Realizing that the model is slightly lacking in reality, in that sense, the necessity to construct a general equilibrium model came into being.

Therefore, in Chap. 4, the partial equilibrium model was extended to a general equilibrium model. The study area is assumed to be a monocentric city. In this city, firms are assumed to be in the CBD and are homogenous producing single commodity types. Then, the representative of both types of households endows working time to obtain wages as household income. The high-income household's level of education allows it to earn more wages than low-income households. Hence, because the asset function is defined as an increasing function of wages, then one can intuitively conclude that high-income households own more assets than low-income households. Then, because income is currently internalized, the representative households can maximize the bid rent of appropriately choosing goods and land. In flood-prone areas, land is inundated by water from flood occurrences; hence, land quality is influenced by the EFDR. In flood-prone areas, the representative households maximize their bid rent by appropriately choosing goods and land consumption while facing the same flood damage rate to household assets. As a result, the bid rent of high-income households becomes lower than that of low-income households. Therefore, flood-prone areas are occupied by low-income households. This conclusion is highlighted as a new finding that differs from traditional urban economics.

Furthermore, the results of the numerical simulation on bid max lot size, which determine optimal lot size, showed that optimal lot size in the city in normal land areas is higher than in flood-prone areas. This result implied reciprocally that density in flood-prone areas is higher than in normal land areas. Convincingly, flood-prone areas are more populous, which may lead to greater deterioration of living conditions than for normal land areas.

Other results showed that in flood-prone areas, the optimal lot size of high-income households is larger than that of low-income households. However, given that the bid rent of low-income households prevailed in flood-prone areas, the optimal lot size in the area is represented by the optimal lot size of low-income households. Because optimal lot size reciprocally constitutes density, one can conclude from the result that density in flood-prone areas is higher than that in normal land areas, implying that flood-prone areas are more populous than normal land areas. This conclusion confirmed that occupied flood-prone areas that are crowded with squatters cause deterioration in living quality, as is observed in flood-prone areas in many urbanized cities of developing countries.

Furthermore, policy simulations of three cases showed that a 50% increase in the previous utility level indicated an assumed 50% effectiveness of the supreme utility development policies in the surrounding rural areas, which significantly reduced the density in flood-prone areas, as indicated by the 76% change. This result is quite significant because the previous optimal lot size, which is lower than the standard human living space, was changed to the standard. Moreover, a 50% increase in the previous utility level to represent 50% effectiveness of the supreme utility development policies in surrounding rural areas sets a more persistent decline in density based on distance in flood-prone areas than from 75% and 100% increases. Therefore, a 50% increase in the effectiveness of the supreme utility development policies is necessary.

Finally, as an overall conclusion, the two models have provided an analysis of illegal settlements in flood-prone areas from the urban economics point of view. The models scientifically explain the existence of illegal settlements and assess policy that leads to depletion of occupied flood-prone areas and, thus, maintaining these areas as open spaces. Initiated by a partial equilibrium model and extended to a general equilibrium model that incorporates the EFDR on household assets, thus constituting land quality, the reverse result of the bid rent of high-income households and low-income households is derived. The reverse result—the bid rent of low-income households could become higher than that of high-income households—explains the occupation of flood-prone areas in Palangkaraya city primarily by low-income households. Because the models differ from traditional urban economics models, this study can be highlighted as an attempt to conduct new city analysis.

5.2 Policy Recommendations

This study provided a systematic explanation of the existence of illegal settlements in flood-prone areas in Palangkaraya city, thus leading to policies that can be adopted by the Palangkaraya municipality to reduce flood-prone areas. As simulated in three cases of supreme utility development policies, such as national health insurance, national basic education support, and a social safety net, addressing rural inhabitants could increase the optimal lot size, hence decreasing the densities in flood-prone areas.

However, measuring the precise effect of supreme utility development policies on an increment in the utility level in the surrounding rural areas was realized as being the most difficult or almost impossible. Therefore, to avoid such a difficulty, we simply assumed—on the basis of common opinion—that the 100% effectiveness level of the policy affects the utility level at a full rate. In this case, 100% can be regarded as the full rate and represents the full effectiveness level of the policy and the full rate of the utility level increment. Hence, assuming that the policies are fully effective and would increase the utility level at a full rate was quite logical.

Furthermore, the policy simulations showed that supreme utility development policies in the surrounding rural areas can significantly affect the increments of the optimal lot size. Hence, the density in flood-prone areas reciprocally decreases. This study numerically demonstrated that if the effectiveness level of the supreme utility development policies is 50%—assuming that the policies take half effectiveness and the increase in the utility level is 50% of the previous value (base case)—then the density in the flood-prone areas is reduced by 76%. This rate is quite significant because the optimal lot size changed from 23.59 m^2 per household to 105.91 m^2 per household. The 23.59 m^2 per household value is regarded as lower than the standard living space (9 m^2 per person is the minimum living space according to HABITAT-UN), whereas 105.91 m^2 per household is obviously higher than the minimum standard.

Moreover, the most important point from the results is that flood-prone areas could be recovered as open space. Hence, ecological functions are preserved through an increase in the utility level in surrounding rural areas as a result of the implementation of supreme utility development projects in these areas.

This conclusion leads to possible efforts to recover occupied flood-prone areas as open space, thus preserving the ecological functions. An improvement in the utility level in surrounding rural areas through supreme utility development projects could be considered an option. Furthermore, such an effort aimed at preserving and conserving the ecological functions of flood-prone areas, along with an urbanization process, can be highlighted as an endeavor that promotes sustainable development in Palangkaraya city as the capital of the Central Kalimantan Province, where green government policies are implemented.

Moreover, these efforts are in line with green government policies that aim to reduce carbon emissions from the mistreatment of wetland areas as desired for the Central Kalimantan Province. The region preserves tropical rainforests and wetland areas, hence also stores significant carbon deposits in its grounds. This characteristic gives Palangkaraya city a significant role, among the others, in the mitigation of global warming.

Furthermore, because the Palangkaraya city authority has made several efforts to mitigate the deterioration in its flood-prone areas—thus, in general, preserving the existence of wetland areas in the Central Kalimantan Province—a model that can measure policy interventions and ease their implementations at the ground level is highly regarded. In the past, most of the policies implemented by the authority failed to reduce the targeted flood-prone areas. Most of this failure was blamed on the inability of the policy-makers to understand the occupation of flood-prone areas within the city context. Occupation for residential use was merely regarded simply because the poor migrated to city areas with no formal affordable housing. Hence, they resided informally in flood-prone areas—a vulnerable and vacant land, that is, no such comprehensive models exist to assist in formulating policies. Therefore, not surprisingly, past policies to deflate flood-prone areas were blindly designed, and the results were poor and far from what was expected.

The policy recommendation derived from this study is not merely aimed as a panacea in addressing misuses of flood-prone areas in Palangkaraya city. Their effect in deflating occupied flood-prone areas was only observed in the numerical simulations, and observing such an effect in the real world is necessary. However, the most important point is that the models can be employed to simulate and predict the results of supreme utility development policies implemented by the Palangkaraya city authority in the surrounding rural areas that aim to increase utility levels and, in turn, reduce density in flood-prone areas. Henceforth, these models can provide excellent guidance to the Palangkaraya city authority and the Central Kalimantan provincial government in formulating utility development projects and action programs, particularly at the ground level.

Finally, although beyond the scope of the study, the Central Kalimantan Province, and, in particular, Palangkaraya city, is facing paradoxical challenges in preserving and conserving its ecology in accordance with a global movement to mitigate climate change. As a region with significant carbon stock and reserved rainforests and wetlands, the Central Kalimantan Province has attracted a United Nation's initiative on climate change mitigation through the REED program. The program aims to reduce carbon emissions by preserving and conserving forests and wetlands. Moreover, the fact is that the rapid development of cities and urban areas is severely depleting the existence of forests and wetlands. Therefore, a paradox exists. On the one hand, city authorities seek to create vibrant urban areas and attractive cities and to increase economic growth. On the other hand, such authorities demand more land and more natural resources to exploit. In that case, wetland and forest areas would be wiped out eventually. Therefore, to address that paradox and the related complex challenges, sustainable development and eco-friendly exploitation need to be considered by the provincial government, the city authorities, and the urban managers. In that sense, the outcomes of this study can be taken into account when initiating eco-friendly policy assessments that lead to the future preservation and conservation of forests and wetlands throughout the Central Kalimantan Province.

Reference

Miyata, Y., & Abe, H. (1991). Evaluating the impacts of the flood control project using the land price function. *Journal of the City Planning Institute of Japan, 26*, 109–114. (in Japanese).

Part II
Studies on Economic and Environmental Efficiency of Makassar City in Indonesia: AHP and CGE Modeling Approaches

Chapter 6
Economic and Environmental Issues in Makassar City

6.1 Economy and Environmental Interactions

Every economic action can have some effect on the environment, and every environmental change can have an impact on the economy: every economic change is usually associated with a change in the welfare of society (Meadows 1972; Hanley et al. 1997; Wainwright and Barnes 2009). Human activity in the environment impacts human welfare. There is an interaction between the economy and the environment. This interaction is dynamic because the economy and the environment continually change one another.

In describing interactions between economics and the environment, economy refers to economic agents, institutions (government, firms, and household), and connections between agents and institutions, such as markets. With respect to the environment, life exists on the Earth's surface, the atmosphere, and the geosphere; flora and fauna include life forms, energy, and material resources (Nisbet 1991; Hanley et al. 1997). Humans affect the environment through economic activities such as market production and consumption. The environment supplies resources, either as a partial recycling factory or as a waste receptacle. The production sector extracts resources from the environment and transforms them into outputs for the consumption sector. These sectors produce waste from their activities, and they return waste to the environment.

The economy and the environment connect in several ways (Hanley et al. 1997). The environment supplies material and energy resource inputs, waste assimilative capacity, amenities, and educational and spiritual values; and global life of the planet supports to the economic process. Figure 6.1 describes the interaction between economics and the environment. Economic exchanges of goods, services, and factors of production occur between the production and consumption sectors in the market. There is a partial recycling process within the production and consumption

© Springer Nature Singapore Pte Ltd. 2018
Y. Miyata et al., *Environmental and Natural Disaster Resilience of Indonesia*,
New Frontiers in Regional Science: Asian Perspectives 23,
https://doi.org/10.1007/978-981-10-8210-8_6

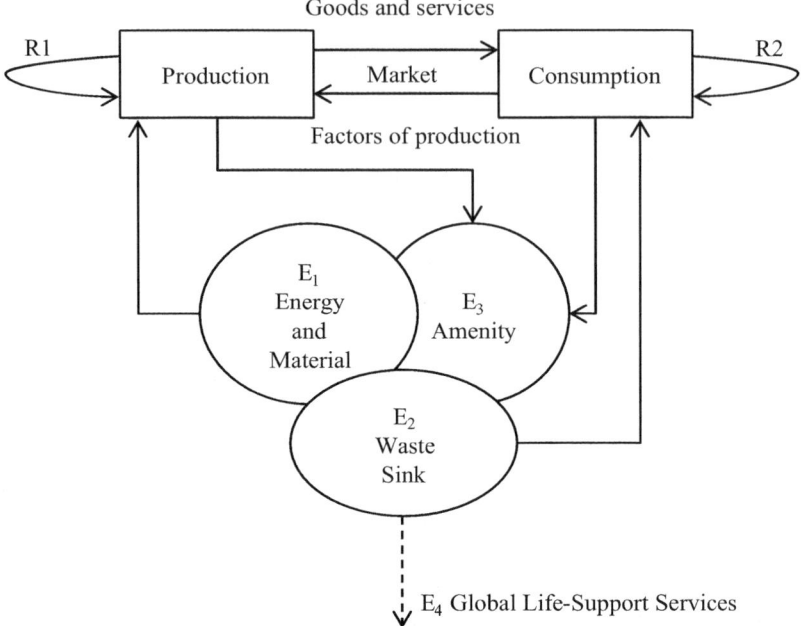

Fig. 6.1 Economy-environment interactions (Hanley 1997)

sectors, as shown by R1 and R2. E1, E2, and E3 denote the environment, and E4 denotes the all-encompassing boundary. The production sector extracts energy and material resources from the environment and transforms them into outputs as consumer goods and services and waste products (e.g., carbon dioxide (CO_2)).

Wastes derived from the production and consumption sectors are returned to the environment either directly or indirectly. These wastes are biologically or chemically processed by the environment. However, the environment has limited space for waste. Environmental capacity for waste depends on its volume. Figure 6.1 shows that using the environment for any purpose can reduce its ability to supply other services. The three circles E1, E2, and E3 overlap, which indicates conflicts in resource use.

The many conflicting demands on the environment cause scarce resource; simultaneously, absolute scarcities of environmental services are increasing (Daly 1991). The primary cause of absolute scarcity is economic growth, which can increase demand for materials and energy, waste output, and environmental quality. However, if environmental resources are fixed, then absolute scarcity will increase with world economic growth (Haley 1991). Economics plays a role in allocating resources to conflicting demands.

6.2   Economic Development and Sustainable Environment in Indonesia

Economic growth has led to increased action on the environment. Economic growth is economic development that has already occurred. Economic development is usually a long-term process that promotes growth, encourages competitiveness, increases employment opportunities and wages, enhances higher education, reduces poverty, and diminishes inequalities (Munier 2004). Based on this definition, economic development offers an improved standard of life. According to the World Commission on Environment and Development, sustainable development is development that allows the current population to meet its needs without compromising the ability of future generations to meet their needs. Sustainable development indicates that resources must be used wisely.

Economic development and a sustainable environment are inextricably linked. Development increases the demand for energy resources, whereas the availability of those resources stimulates even more development by allowing trade and economic specialization. Industrialization in economic development has created a considerable need for energy in the production and consumption sectors. The availability of natural resources is one method of measuring region's prosperity. The amount and quality of natural resources are the result of economic development, which further encourages sustainable development.

6.2.1   Sustainable Development and the Indonesia Environment

Indonesia has experienced many advances in economic development. Indonesia's economy began as one that was traditional and agriculture-based currently; however, manufacturing and services predominate. Economic progress has improved societal welfare, reflected in the increase in per capita income and improvement of social and economic indicators such as the Human Development Index (HDI). Between 1980 and 2010, Indonesia's HDI increased from 0.39 to 0.60.

Indonesia also plays a growing role in the global economy. Currently, Indonesia ranks as the 17th largest economy in the world. Prior to the global economic crisis, various international agencies noted Indonesia's success.

Indonesia is rapidly developing and requires considerable energy to support that development. Energy demand and development will increase simultaneously, with economic and population growth, particularly in the industry sector. Indonesia's domestic needs are still primarily met by its energy resource, which also produce commodities and foreign exchange revenues. The considerable and continuous use of energy resources has caused the depletion of Indonesia's energy reserves. Therefore, we need wiser environmental management to preserve those resources.

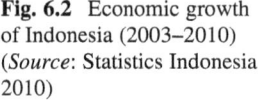

Fig. 6.2 Economic growth of Indonesia (2003–2010) (*Source*: Statistics Indonesia 2010)

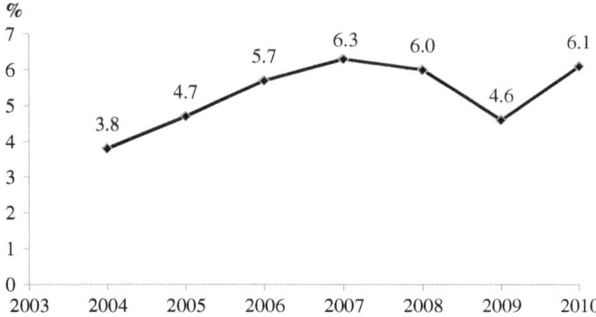

Undang-Undang Dasar 1945 (UUD 1945) is Indonesia's constitution and the primary source of its development policy. In 2002, the Indonesian government incorporated the principle of a sustainable environment in the fourth amendment to that constitution. Indonesia's national economy is based on economic democracy and the principles of togetherness, efficiency, sustainability, the environment, independence, and maintaining a balance of economic growth and national unity. With the adoption of the principles of sustainable development and sustainable environment, Indonesia's constitution became "green." It guarantees the rights of every community to health and a clean environment.

The government has implemented several macroeconomic policies for achieving economic growth with sustainable development and environment. For example, the state maintains the availability of energy resources has increased the use of renewable energy and has improved the quality and quantity of the supporting infrastructure. Efficiency in production and consumption improves the quality and management of the carbon emission programs and the environment.

The growth of the national economy parallels the growth of the industry sector. Figure 6.2 shows that the economic growth of Indonesia has increased almost every year. Most industrial activities utilize fossil fuels that are used for electricity and heat production. Fossil fuels also supply industrial processes such as those of the fertilizer industry (natural gas), the steel industry (coal), and the chemical industry (kerosene and gasoline). Based on the *Handbook of Energy and Economic Statistics of Indonesia* (Ministry of Energy and Mineral Resources), the industry sector's share of total commercial energy consumption in Indonesia is approximately 53% (including supply for industrial processes) or approximately 47%, if natural gas to supply the fertilizer production process is not included.

Table 6.1 compares Indonesia's primary energy supply and final energy consumption over the past 11 years. Growth increased every year by 3.7% for energy supply and by 3.4% for final energy consumption. On average, Indonesia's annual economic growth during the period was 5% per year (Ministry of Finance of Indonesia 2010).

With its plantations and mineral resources, Indonesia intends to become the center of world food security and an agricultural products processing center. Without ignoring the principles of sustainable development, Indonesia also expects to

Table 6.1 Energy supply and consumption in Indonesia

Year	Primary energy supply BOE	Final energy consumption
2000	995,741,609	777,925
2001	1,041,252,219	802,325
2002	1,070,035,892	799,926
2003	1,131,058,046	839,748
2004	1,144,483,636	875,261
2005	1,166,487,651	864,601
2006	1,175,503,577	880,153
2007	1,230,902,805	916,720
2008	1,262,003,306	906,846
2009	1,294,631,364	978,380
2010	1,429,328,278	1,067,529
2011	1,516,241,607	1,114,767

Source: *Handbook of Energy and Economic Statistics of Indonesia* Ministry of Energy and Mineral Resources (2010)

become a global logistics center based on the potential mobility and geographic advantages of its resources.

The energy demand of various industry sub-sectors is expected to increase and to follow their production capacity growth. On average, energy utilization in the Indonesian industry sector is not as efficient as in other countries because in industry sub-sectors, older technologies are still applied (Ministry of Energy and Mineral Resources of Indonesia 2007).

6.3   Environmental Problems in Indonesia

Instead of increasing the standard of life, economic development usually imposes a heavy environmental burden. Economic development produces pollution, depletes nonrenewable resources, increases waste, and uses water. The growth and acceleration of economic development requires more resources for the production process will ultimately reduce the availability of existing resources and will increase the burden on the environment. Pollution or so-called an emission is a substance or energy introduced into the environment that has undesired effects or adversely affects the usefulness of a resource. Pollution can disrupt the sustainability of an ecosystem and will reduce the quality of human life.

Climate change is the single largest environmental and humanitarian crisis of our time. We must act now to adopt cleaner energy sources because climate change is changing economies, health, and communities in diverse ways. Scientists warn that if we do not aggressively curb climate change now, the results will likely be disastrous. In recent years, climate change caused by CO_2 emissions has become increasingly important for discussion. There is uncertainty as to the extent of global warming caused by, e.g., a doubling of current CO_2 levels, and even more uncertainty regarding the physical effects that this warming will have. Environmentalists often argue that society should take action before that uncertainty is resolved. The costs of not acting immediately may be greater than the costs of preventative or anticipatory action particularly when failing to act immediately will lead to irreversible, undesirable environmental consequences (Taylor 1991).

In 2005, baseline CO_2 emissions in Indonesia were estimated at 2.1 Gt CO_2; these amounts make Indonesia the third largest CO_2 emitter in the world. CO_2 emissions in Indonesia are expected to grow by 1.9% per year and will reach 2.5 Gt CO_2 in 2020. In 2005, the following five sectors generated the majority of Indonesia's emissions: forestry, agriculture, power, transportation, and buildings and cement. Indonesia's climate change strategy proposes cutting emissions in the following three ways: developing geothermal powers, driving energy efficiency, and reducing deforestation (Ministry of Finance of Indonesia 2009). The CO_2 emissions generated from the energy sector were 244.31 million tons in 2000, and on average, those emissions increase by 4.82% per year. Meanwhile, from 2000 to 2010, Indonesia's energy resource reserves declined 4.61% per year, on average (Ministry of Energy and Mineral Resources of Indonesia 2007, 2008, 2010).

The Ministry of Finance of the Republic of Indonesia has identified economic and fiscal policy strategies to mitigate climate change. It recommends reducing carbon dioxide emissions using the policies that are the most cost-effective and efficient in both the short and long terms. The strategies identified by the Ministry for the energy sector are as follows: (1) the implementation of a carbon tax on fossil-fuel combustion and (2) energy efficiency through the deployment of low-emissions technology.

In 2011, to mitigate climate change, the government issued Presidential Regulation No. 61/2011 on the National Action Plan to reduce greenhouse gas emissions and Presidential Regulation No. 71/2011 on the National Inventory of Greenhouse Gas. Those mitigation efforts include not only quantitative targets to reduce emissions by sector and sub-sector but also the necessary time to achieve them. Moreover, on September 25, 2009, at the G-20 summit in Pittsburg (United States), Indonesia's President committed to a 26% reduction in CO_2 emissions by 2020. The Indonesian government's national mitigation targets for greenhouse gas (GHG) are described in detail in Table 6.2.

6.4 Economic and Environmental Conditions in Makassar City

The acceleration and expansion of Indonesian economic development has included the development of centers of economic growth through industry clusters and special economic zones (SEZ). Essential to this approach is the integration of sectoral and regional methods. Each region develops a product that becomes superior. The development of economic growth centers maximizes the benefits of agglomeration

Table 6.2 National target greenhouse gas (GHG) mitigation

Sectors and sub-sectors	Emissions 2020 Gt CO$_2$	Emissions target self (26%) 2020 Gt CO$_2$	Emissions target from international (15%) 2020 Gt CO$_2$	Total emissions target (41%) 2020 Gt CO$_2$	(%)
1. Energy	**1.07**	**0.039**	**0.022**	**0.061**	**5.13**
Energy supply and transmission	1	0.03	0.01	0.04	
Industry	0.06				
Transportation	0.01				
2. Forestry	**1.57**	**0.672**	**0.367**	**1.039**	**87.38**
Peat land conservation	1.44	0.28	0.057	0.337	
Carbon sinks, forest sustainability	0.13	0.392	0.31	0.702	
Preventing and reducing deforestation fires					
3. Agricultural	**0.06**	**0.008**	**0.003**	**0.011**	**0.93**
Reducing weed burning	0.06	0.008	0.003	0.011	
Reducing the use of chemical fertilizers					
4. Waste	**0.25**	**0.048**	**0.03**	**0.078**	**6.56**
5. Other					
1Coastal, small island, oceans, fisheries					
Total	**2.95**	**0.767**	**0.422**	**1.189**	

Source: National Development Planning Agency (2010)

and explores potential areas of excellence to ameliorate the spatial inequality of Indonesia's economic development.

One center of economic growth in Indonesia is Makassar City. The city is the gateway to and main development area of eastern Indonesia.

6.4.1 Economic Growth in Makassar City

Makassar is one of Indonesia's largest metropolises and the provincial capital of the South Sulawesi. The city is an industrial center and an international harbor for eastern Indonesia area. Accordingly, in recent years it has experienced rapid development growth.

In 2006, Makassar's total population of Makassar was 1,223,540, its population density was 7.1/km^2, its total area was 17,807.01 hectares, and its population growth

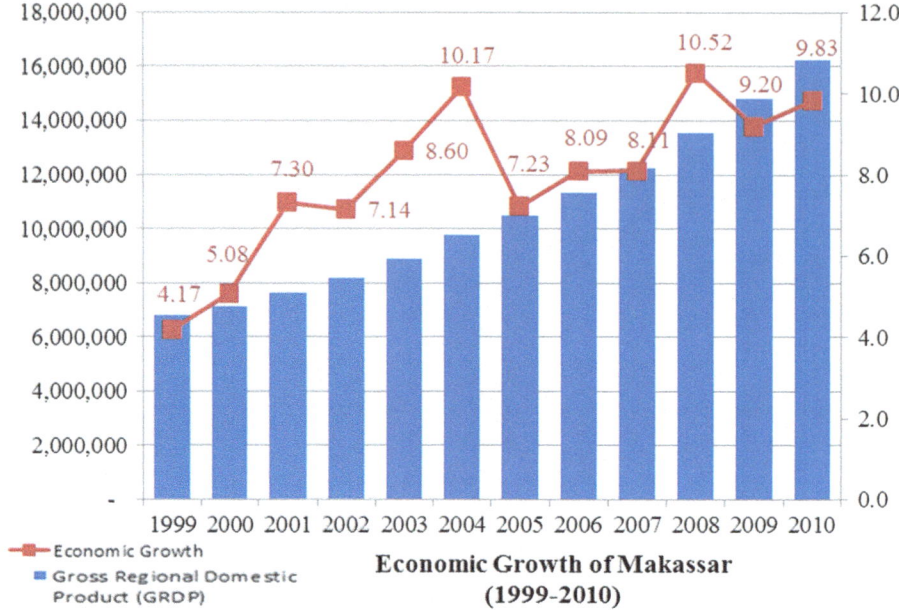

Fig. 6.3 The economic growth of Makassar City from 1999 to 2010 (*Source*: Makassar City Statistical Bureau 2010)

had reached 1.79% per year. In addition, the average annual population growth of people with low incomes is 5.7% per year. Urbanization has led to population growth, and poverty is increasing in this city. Municipalities carefully consider the problem of poverty. Since 2005, the government has operated free rice and fuel subsidy programs for the poor.

Figure 6.3 shows that from 1999 to 2010, Makassar's economic growth has increased every year by an average of 8.8%, indicating high rate of urbanization.

Makassar City is classified as a consumerist society characterized by higher levels of consumption than investment. This behavior has changed the city's urban structure and economic growth.

6.4.2 Environmental Conditions in Makassar City

Table 6.3 explains that the analysis of environmental data showed that Makassar City either met environmental standards or provided (on average) good environmental conditions. The city government has created a program to make the city a clean, comfortable, safe, and healthy place to live and work. In 2011, Makassar City received ASEAN's Clean Air for Big Cities Certificate of Recognition at ASEAN's Environmentally Sustainable Cities (ESC) Award program. This award is given to

Table 6.3 Assessment of environmental sustainability in Makassar City, 2010

Component of environment		Unit	Scala of indicators					Description	Method of analysis	Equipment
			1 Very bad	2 Bad	3 Average	4 Good	5 Very good			
I	**Climate**									
1	Temperature	°C	<35	31–30	28–30	21–27 **27.5**	16–20			
2	Rainfall	mm	<50	51–100	101–200	201–250	>250 **306.6**	Good	–	–
3	Humidity	%	>100	85–100	80–85 **82.7**	75–79	56–74	Very good	–	–
4	Wind velocity	km/hour	>41	31–40	21–30	11–20	<10 **4.0**	Average	–	–
II	**Physiography**							Very good	–	
1	Topography	%	>50	30–40	15–30	5–15	0–5 **2**	Very good	–	–
III	**Quality of water**									
1	Residue dissolved	mg/l	>1000	700–1000	400–699	200–399 **244.0**	<200	Good	Gravimetric	Timbangan analitik dan Kertas saring 0.45 µm
2	BOD	mg/l	>6	6-May	3–4	2–3 **2.64**	<2	Good	Titrimetri Potensiometri	Buret DO meter
3	COD	mg/l	>10 **10.91**	8–10	5–7	2–4	<2	Very bad	Titrimetri	Buret

(continued)

Table 6.3 (continued)

Component of environment		Unit	Scala of indicators					Description	Method of analysis	Equipment
			1 Very bad	2 Bad	3 Average	4 Good	5 Very good			
4	Dissolved oxygen	mg/l	>3	2.5–3	2–2.4	1.5–2.4	<1.4		Titrimetri	Buret
			5.94					Very bad	Potensiometri	DO meter
5	pH		>10.5	9.5–10.5	8.5–9.5	7.5–8.5	6.5–7.5		Potensiometri	pH meter
							6.2	Very good		
6	Detergent	mg/l	>0.2	0.17–0.2	0.014–0.16	0.01–0.013	<0.01		Spektrofotometri	Spektrofotometer
			0.435					Very bad		
IV	**Quality of air**									
1	SO_2	$\mu g/Nm^3$	>0.3	0.21–0.3	0.11–0.2	0.05–0.1	<0.05			
						0.073		Good	Pararosanilin	Spektrofotometer
2	CO	$\mu g/Nm^3$	>20	15–20	11–14	5–10	<5			
							2.179	Very good	NDIR	NDIR analyzer
3	NO_2	$\mu g/Nm^3$	>0.21	0.15–0.2	0.1–0.14	0.05–0.09	<0.05			
							0.005	Very good	Saltzman	Spektrofotometer
4	TSP (dust)	$\mu g/Nm^3$	>250	200–250	121–199	51–120	<50			
				108.18				Bad	Gravimetric	Hi – Vol
5	Lead (pb)	$\mu g/Nm^3$	>2	1.5–1.9	1–1.4	0.5–0.9	0–0.4			
					1.195			Average	Gravimetric	Hi – Vol

No.	Parameter	Unit						Status	Chemiluminescent	Spektrofotometer
6	O$_3$ (oxidants)	μg/Nm^3	>250	200–250	121–199	51–120	<50 **45.65**	Very good	–	–
7	PM$_{10}$ (particle <10 μm)	μg/Nm^3	>2	1.5–1.9	1–1.4	0.5–0.9	0–0.4 **0.006**	Very good	Gravimetric	Hi – Vol
8	Noise level	dBA	>70 **75.63**	61–70	51–60	46–50	41–45	Very bad	–	–
V	**Social and population**									
1	Population density	Population/km^2	>20.000	15.000–20.000	10.000–14.999	5.000–9.999 **7620**	<5.000	Good	–	
2	Level of education	%	<20	20–40	41–55	56–75	>75 **90.96**	Very good	–	–
VI	**Economical**									
1	Unemployment	%	>75	56–75	41–55	20–40	<20 **7.43**	Very good	–	–
2	GRDP people per capita	Million	<2	2.1–5	5.1–10	10.1–20	>20 **27.630.409**	Very good	–	–
VII	**Community health**									
1	Type of building	%	<15	15–25	26–50	51–75 **56.47**	76–100	Good	–	–
2	Water supply	%	<25	25–50	51–70 **56.34**	71–90	>90	Average	–	–
3	Sanitation	%	<25	25–50	51–70	71–90	>90 **95.74**	Very good	–	–

(continued)

Table 6.3 (continued)

Component of environment		Unit	Scala of indicators					Description	Method of analysis	Equipment
			1	2	3	4	5			
			Very bad	Bad	Average	Good	Very good			
4	Level of community nutrition	%	<20	21–40	41–60	61–85 **82.39**	>85	Good	–	–
5	Level of health service	%	<20	21–40	41–60	61–85 **83.33**	>85	Good	–	–
Total			**4**	**1**	**3**	**8**	**12**			
Value of indicators = ΣI × Scala			**4**	**2**	**9**	**32**	**60**			
Score of indicators = 28 × Scala			**28**	**56**	**84**	**112**	**140**			
Total of value			**107**					**Good**		

Source: Authors' calculation; The Central Board of Statistics of Makassar City (2011), Ministry of Environment of Indonesia (2011), Sari (2003)

ASEAN cities that have remained clean, green, and livable notwithstanding their growth as centers of economic and industrial activity.

Nevertheless, it is possible that with increasing development activity, elements of environmental pollutants will increase every year. Considering an increase of economic growth and population, an increase in environment degradation is also possible.

Industrial activities and traffic congestion are sources of CO_2 emissions in Makassar (BLHD Makassar 2012) because the industrial and transportation sectors are the city's largest energy users. Highway transportation consumes 80% of the energy primary in all transportation sectors.

6.5 Economic Efficiency for Environmental Protection

A variety of criteria have been used to measure the performance of an economic system and to evaluate economic policy: one such criterion is efficiency. Generally, efficiency in the economy refers to "how well" or "how effectively" a maximum output is produced from a combined set of inputs. Efficiency is the percentage of attainable production that is actually achieved and that can be distinguished from productivity, which considers the amount of output produced from a particular amount of input (Graham 2004).

The allocative efficiency of resources can achieve success by satisfying some of the following assumptions:

- The market is in a perfectly competitive condition.
- The household or industries cannot control price but instead are price-takers.
- Households have perfect information regarding the quality of all available products and prices, and the industry has perfect knowledge of technology and input prices.
- Decision-makers always consider all of the costs and benefits of their decisions, and thus, there are no external costs.

These conditions present perfect competition in the economy. Perfect competition provides the following results:

- Resources among industries are allocated efficiently.
- Final products among households are distributed efficiently.
- The economic system will produce goods and services for household utility.

Economic development will require more resources to produce goods and will produce an undesirable output, such as emissions.

Economic development and environmental quality have a correlation that is depicted in Fig. 6.4. Figure 6.4 shows the hypothesis of an inverted U-shaped relationship between economic output per capita and several measures of environmental quality. Figure 6.4 shows that economic development initially may increase

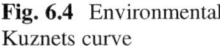 **Fig. 6.4** Environmental Kuznets curve

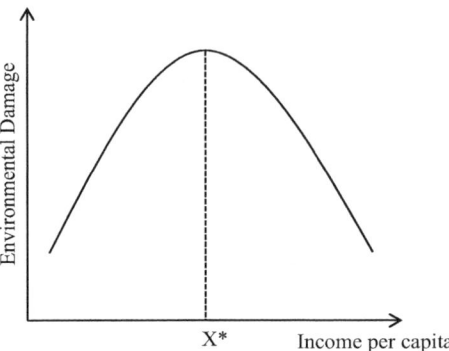

but then may actually decrease or reach zero because the physical system is so badly damaged that there are simply no more costs as environmental damage increases.

In some cases of environmental management, there is uncertainty about the environmental effects of activity and the impact on humans of subsequent environmental changes. The extent of this uncertainty is considerable.

Economic efficiency for environmental protection applies efficient policies to achieve economic and environmental objectives. Efficiency is desirable when considering environmental concerns with the lowest possible costs. Similarly, economic targets should be pursued with minimum environmental impact.

However, the efficiency of the economy versus that of the environment can differ significantly, depending on the characteristics and source of the pollution. An emission charge requires continuous data on the quantities of emissions from controlled sources. Regulators must also have the administrative capacity to use the data to establish and collect appropriate penalties.

In recent years, economists' focus has returned to an important issue: the efficiency of scarce resource allocation. Most developing economies can no longer expect large aid inflows and commercial financing from developed economies. This study examine two objectives: increasing development and reducing CO_2 emissions through the efficiency of resource allocation.

This study addresses economics and the environment using a methodology to analyze the efficiency of resource allocation. Resource allocation can be viewed as a trade-off that can be resolved by the price mechanism.

6.6   Conclusion

CO_2 emissions and the decline of natural resources caused by human economic activity to improve the standard of life, two causes of GHG, can alter both the natural balance and the climate change process. Environmental degradation must be prevented, and the damage caused by economic development must be reduced. Economic development can be sustainable or compatible with the viability of natural systems. Economic and environmental development required an analytical instrument to evaluate the most appropriate economic and environmental strategies. This study attempts to achieve the best possible result for the environment while assuming the smallest possible loss of economic development.

This study examines both the provision of public goods such as road construction and urban economics. It applies an analytic hierarchy process (AHP) to design efficiency with respect to the selection of the best road construction in a conservation area. We assume that the government is concerned with only two objectives: (1) increasing development through road improvement and (2) maintaining environmental balance, including the reduction of CO_2 emissions. Economists have proposed a public participation method AHP concept by substituting the criterion entity for the person entity (economics). Accordingly, efficiency is a feasible solution for the environment where the value of one criterion can only be achieved by degrading the value of at least one other criterion.

We extend the research approach by using a computable general equilibrium model by that adds environmental objectives to of economic objectives. After calibrating the model to the Makassar City economy and choosing the reduction of CO_2 emissions as the environmental objective, we can establish efficient economic development. Accordingly, we can estimate how much economic growth must be sacrificed to achieve each environmental goal. It is also possible to determine in which direction the mixed policy should be reformulated to obtain combinations of efficient economic activity and minimal environmental impact.

References

Badan Perencanaan Pembangunan Nasional (*National Development Planning Agency*). (2010). *Indonesia climate change sectoral roadmap*. Jakarta: Author. Retrieved from: http://bappenas.go.id/files/8913/5022/6069/climate-change-roadmap-waste-sector__20110218181950__0.pdf (2014.6.1).

Center of Data and Information on Energy and Mineral Resources. (2010). *Handbook of energy and economic statistics of Indonesia*. Ministry of Energy and Mineral Resources. Retrieved from: http://prokum.esdm.go.id/Publikasi/Handbook%20of%20Energy%20&%20Economic%20Statistics%20of%20Indonesia%20/Handbook%202010.pdf (2014.6.1).

Daly, H. E. (1991). Elements of environmental macroeconomics. *Ecological Economics: The Science and Management of Sustainability*, 32–46.

Graham, M. (2004). *Environmental efficiency: Meaning and measurement and application to Australian Dairy Farms*. Paper presented at the AARES 2004: Contributed papers.

Haley, U. C. (1991). Corporate contributions as managerial masques: Reframing corporate contributions as strategies to influence society. *Journal of Management Studies, 28*(5), 485–510.

Hanley, N., Shogren, J. F., & White, B. (1997). The Economics of sustainable development. In *Environmental economics in theory and practice* (pp. 425–449). Basingstoke: Macmillan Education.

Meadows, D. L. (1972). Toward a science of social forecasting. *Proceedings of the National Academy of Sciences, 69*(12), 3828–3831.

Ministry of Environment; Ecoregion Management Centre Sulawesi, Maluku and Papua. (2011). *Annual report of environmental status Sulawesi Ecoregion*. Indonesia: Author.

Munier, N. (2004). *Multicriteria environmental assessment: A practical guide*. Dordrecht: Springer.
Nisbet, E. G. (1991). *Leaving Eden: To protect and manage the Earth*. Cambridge: Cambridge University Press.
Sari. (2003). *Environmental sustainability level of Bandung City 2003*. Bandung: Institute of Technology Bandung.
Taylor, L. (1991). Economic openness: Problems to the century's end. *Economic Liberalization: No Panacea, 1989*, 99–147.
Wainwright, J., & Barnes, T. J. (2009). Nature, economy, and the space—Place distinction. *Environment and Planning D: Society and Space, 27*(6), 966–986.

Chapter 7
An Analytic Hierarchy Process (AHP) Approach to Economic and Environmental Policy

7.1 Introduction

Environmentalists and economists agree that indifference to the environment has caused environmental degradation and the depletion of natural resources. The underlying reason for the underestimation of assets is that not all environmental goods and services are included in the economic analysis of programs and policies. Many of the advantages provided by natural resources are public goods with no market price. When natural resources are supplied to one person, they are also available to others.

Roads are public goods; therefore, the government should provide roads because no single person wants to pay for good that had benefits for everybody. Several issues to consider are which development programs should be applied and how much money should be provided by the government for road development; it is an issue. We cannot apply a price system to determine the efficiency of economic resources provided for it. Wicksell's theory (1977) found that the political process is important for managing resource allocation in the economy. Wicksell argued that in a perfectly competitive market, using the voting system in decision-making would achieve the same results as using the price mechanism. However, the public cannot explain references to the public good. In a democratic society, voting should reflect both preferences and a willingness to pay for public services. Voting distribution and preferences determine voting results.

Road construction is a specific sector in which the use of professionals is one method of public participation that enables decision-making. The relevant professionals are the community of experts in road planning and development. The complexity of professional knowledge and understanding of planning and development can be simplified through an analytic hierarchy process (AHP) approach. This method is a mathematical concept to structure a problem with a matrix. All factors are arranged and selected and then descend a hierarchy structure to criteria and

© Springer Nature Singapore Pte Ltd. 2018   119
Y. Miyata et al., *Environmental and Natural Disaster Resilience of Indonesia*,
New Frontiers in Regional Science: Asian Perspectives 23,
https://doi.org/10.1007/978-981-10-8210-8_7

alternatives on successive levels. Determination of the criteria for road construction selection is not the main parameter for road construction but should be considered in decision-making.

Although the construction sector is one of the major contributors to Indonesia's economic development, the construction process and operation consume considerable energy and create CO_2 emissions. We must estimate the amount of CO_2 emissions that are produced by construction activities to prevent or ameliorate their environmental impact. Public preferences for the best type of construction must support the government's CO2 emission reduction.

The government of Indonesia has scarce financial resources, which, therefore, must be allocated efficiently. Selection can be conducted by evaluating the efficiency of economic resources. This evaluation will consider the most efficient allocation of resources and allow us to accomplish more with fewer resources. Road investment benefits the community. The method of evaluating an economic resource provides an integrated framework to evaluate investment from a public viewpoint. The evaluation method is based on analyses of the benefit–cost (B/C), net present value (NPV), and internal rate of return (IRR). The method will prove that public reference is the best choice for implementation.

7.2   Urban and Regional Economy

Movement of people and goods is the lifeblood that creates well-being and prosperity and makes the development of road networks a government priority. Population densities tend to follow patterns, and thus, new roads improve sustainable economic growth (Donald R. Glover 1975; Miyata et al.2005). There are two reasons of building or widening roads. The first reason increases road capacity by adding lanes or building new construction alongside pre-existing construction. The second reason involves building new roads in areas of development. Roads have both horizontal and vertical curvature and should be designed to fit the terrain to achieve the desired aesthetic qualities and harmonize with the surrounding environment (Mackay City Council 2008).

Recently, environmental issues have gained public attention, and people have become more aware that the consumption of goods and services has an impact on natural resources. The public and private sectors have started to consider reducing adverse effects and evolving methods to prevent such impacts. Selection of the highest-quality construction and material is one tool to evaluate sustainability and adverse environmental and societal impacts. Economic criteria, aesthetic value, environmental factors, and design factors must be considered before choosing material and a method of construction (Horvath and Hendrickson 1997).

Road construction has both benefits and consequences. The purpose of road construction is to maximize safety, serve the community, shorten distances and travel times, and increase economic output and quality of life. Vehicle speed greatly affects the benefits achieved. Geometric conditions also limit street services (Zheng 1997). The planning and construction of roads located on steep slopes must be carefully examined because of their impact on sedimentation. Complicated geographic conditions and thus road construction must be realistic considering the lower level of service (LOS) and environmental constraints.

Planning for road construction should consider all these factors and account for environmental and human change as the main factor forming processes against environmental policy (Ian McHarg 1969). The success of a design depends on the character design of the model and environmental responses that create a balance between the design and the overall environment (Hough 1989).

Road infrastructure in Indonesia is vital to national transportation: the existing road network serves approximately 92% of passengers and 90% of transportation modes. Continuous infrastructure development positively impacts the region's economic competitiveness in the national economy and expands the national economy an international level (Ministry of Public Works of Indonesia 2010). This purpose is appropriate for Indonesia's economic development strategy, which is pro-green, pro-jobs, and pro-poor. The best alternatives for infrastructure policies that are chosen by the public yield benefits that can alleviate the problem (Barnard and Simon 1947).

7.3   Objectives

Our objective is to evaluate the best type of construction for a regional road in Indonesia. The road passes through a critical geometric conservation area that is a barrier to development. There are two approaches to the attributes under consideration. One direction can be interpreted as "the best is better" and implies a maximization process; the other can be interpreted as "less is better" and implies a minimization process. Maximizing economic growth and minimizing the environmental damage and CO_2 emissions are typical examples of objectives within a public context.

7.4   Methodology

The type of construction is selected by the public, and the evaluation of the efficiency of the economic resources is determined using a public approach.

7.4.1   The Analytic Hierarchy Process (AHP) Approach

7.4.1.1   Decision Structure and Pairwise Comparison Method

This approach builds the formed matrix of relative weights among the criteria performed through the value of the preference. The AHP method is used to determine the type of construction. This method was first by developed by Saaty (1990) and is commonly used by decision-makers to determine policy by synthesizing several options in a single method. The main idea of this analysis is to transform a subjective assessment into a whole that has a value or weight. Acquisition of data weighting is derived from the analysis of the survey interview, which asks respondents the question of the weight of an interest rate criterion compared to other criteria. The criteria used are the results of the identification of the item that has a major influence on choice, not on achieving the goal. Relative weights among the criteria are used to obtain comparisons; weighting is normalized and importance is determined among the compared criterion variables. Relative preference values are obtained by analyzing interviews and questionnaires administered to respondents, who assess the importance level on a nine-point scale. Table 7.1 shows the scale of the interest rate criterion.

Respondents are assumed consistent in providing an assessment of each pairwise of criteria, and all n criteria have the same value when each is compared against itself. Each criterion has n elements, namely, $w_1, w_2, w_3, \cdots, w_n$, where the value of the comparison n criteria can be described by the equation: $1/2n(n-1)$. Overall comparison of each pairwise in this analysis forms the reciprocal square matrix illustrated below:

	A_1	A_2	A_3	$\cdots$	A_n
A_1	w_1/w_1	w_1/w_2	w_1/w_3	$\cdots$	w_1/w_n
A_2	w_2/w_1	w_2/w_2	w_2/w_3	$\cdots$	w_2/w_n
A_3	w_3/w_1	w_3/w_2	w_3/w_3	$\cdots$	w_3/w_n
$\vdots$	$\vdots$	$\vdots$	$\vdots$	$\ddots$	$\vdots$
A_n	w_n/w_1	w_n/w_2	w_n/w_3	$\cdots$	w_n/w_n

The results of calculation of each row in the matrix comparisons will obtain the value of the eigenvector which is the weighted value of the normalized average of each factor in each row.

The weight matrix of pairwise comparisons has a characteristic maximum value of n as positive, and both simple and characteristic vectors are associated with a positive (Theorem of Perron in Garminia 2010). Therefore, the pairwise comparison matrix has a consistency index of zero.

Table 7.1 The scale of assessment between criteria

Interest Rate	Definitions	Explanation
1	Equal importance	Two activities contribute equally to the objective
3	Moderate importance	Moderately favor one over the other
5	Essential importance	Strongly favor one over the other
7	Very strong importance	Strongly favored and dominant over the other
9	Extreme importance	Most favored
2, 4, 6, 8	Intermediate values	Indicate that compromise is required
Reciprocals	If the inverse element i has one of the above rates when compared to element j, then it has the reciprocal value when compared to the element i.	
Rational	Rations arising out of the scale	If consistency were to be forced by obtaining n numerical values to span the matrix

Source: Saaty (1990)

Table 7.2 Value of ratio index (RI)

N	1	2	3	4	5	6	7	8	9	10	11
RI	0	0	0.58	0.90	1.12	1.24	1.32	1.41	1.45	1.49	1.51

For the consistency index (*CI*) of the n matrix,

$$CI = \frac{\lambda_{max} - n}{n - 1} \tag{7.1}$$

where

CI = consistency index
λ_{max} = the largest eigenvalue of n matrix
and the consistency ratio is defined as

$$CR = \frac{CI}{RI} \tag{7.2}$$

where

CR = consistency ratio
CI = consistency index
RI = ratio index

The ratio index is the average value of the consistency index obtained randomly, as shown in Table 7.2.

The decision will be consistent if the value of the consistency ratio is no more than 10%.

7.4.1.2 Selection of Road Construction

The government and the previous study (Ibrahim 2010) have identified nine criteria for choosing a type of road construction. The problem is to decide which of the three candidate constructions to apply. Thus, we begin by structuring the problem as a hierarchy.

The top level shows where the selection is the best type of construction. At the second level are the nine criteria that contribute to the selection of the best type of road construction. The criteria are as follows:

1. Benefits: traffic safety, comfort and convenience
2. Environmental: minimization of pollutants, appreciation of natural environment, environmentally friendly material and technology
3. Economical: raising the economic growth of the region, increasing household income
4. Cost of construction: efficient and rapid rate return
5. Technology: safe, quiet, minimization of pollutants, and applicable
6. Maintenance costs: low cost, easy to repair, and durable
7. Aesthetic value: harmonized with area
8. Easy handling of implementation: simple and humble
9. Time of construction: self-explanation

These criteria are the important considerations used in the selection of construction based on the problem. Pairwise, the matrix of the criteria results in a vector of priorities, which is the principal eigenvector. This calculation gives the relative priority of the criteria measured on a scale of a ratio.

In the third level, pairwise comparisons of the types of construction with respect to the superiority of one over the other are suitable for each criterion at the second level. There are nine 3 × 3 matrices of judgments. We invited and collected preferences from the respondents, who are experts in the planning and development of road construction, and included government officials, planners, engineering supervisors, and academics. The respondents are not representative of the population as a whole because each group is represented by ten people. However, the respondents are considered to represent the entire community. Selection hierarchy is shown in Fig. 7.1.

Analyses were performed using the expert choice program in which respondents' perceptions made pairwise comparison matrices.

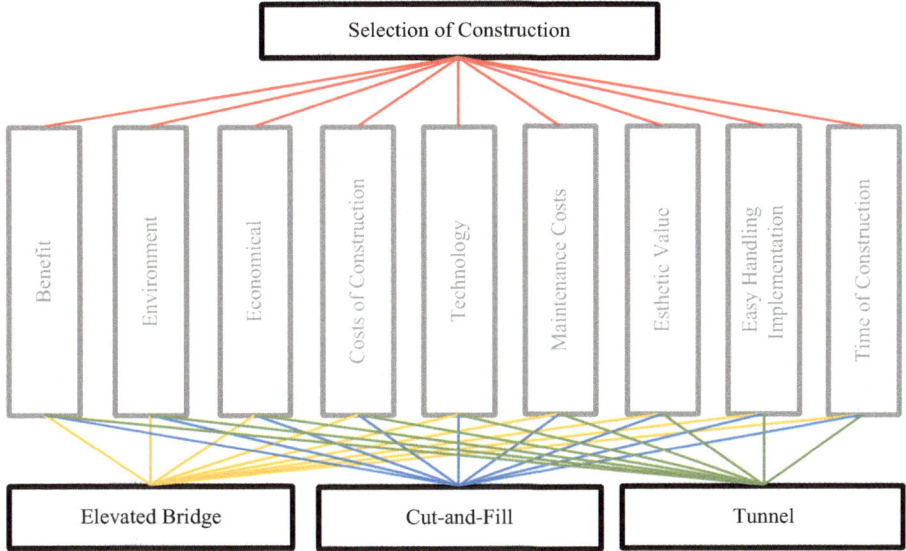

Fig. 7.1 Selection of the types of construction hierarchy

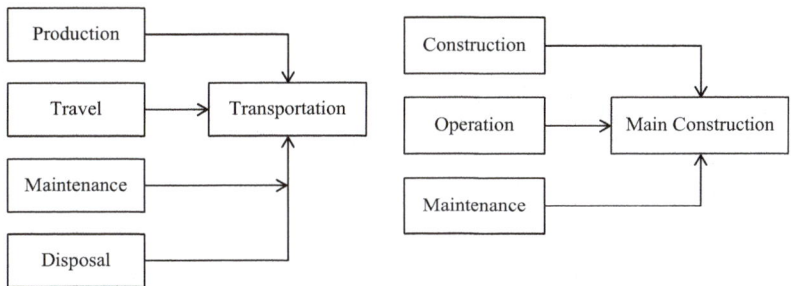

Fig. 7.2 Calculation of CO_2 emissions by investigation of qualification of environmental load emission

7.4.2 CO₂ Emission Calculation

Calculation of the approximate number of environmental impacts such as CO_2 emissions caused by the best type of construction uses the value of the emission factor results of several published, scientific studies, as shown in Fig. 7.2. Because of the limited data and literature available, we made many assumptions to simplify the calculation. We assumed that the value of the emission factors had indicators and geographical conditions similar to the previous research. The main construction used the results of the greenhouse gas calculations performed by Kato et al. (2005),

Table 7.3 Embodied CO_2 emissions for construction and road activities

Type of construction	Ton CO_2/KM			
	Main construction		Transportation	
	Construction	Maintenance	Construction	Maintenance
Elevated bridge	3680	120	0.000045	0.000039
Tunnel	5310	210		
Cut-and-fill	164.8–892.5	259		
Asphalt surface	47.09	10.41		

Source: Kato et al. (2005), Stripple (2001), Rajagopalan (2007), Rose (2010), and Forsyth (2011)

Stripple (2001), Rajagopalan (2007), and Forsyth (2011). Emissions caused by the transportation mode refer to the results of scientific research by Rose (2010). The calculation results depend on the actual construction design. Table 7.3 shows the embodied CO_2 emissions for construction and road activities.

7.4.3   Efficiency of Economic Evaluation

Cost–benefit analysis is a formal process for evaluating a project based on economists and government agencies seeking an efficient allocation of resources (Jones et al. 2014; World Bank 2004; Ninan 2008). Cost–benefit analysis, an important problem-solving tool in policy work, is one of the most widely accepted and applied methods because it provides many benefits. These benefits include a model of rationality, creating, evaluating, and comparing alternatives, including different scales for those alternatives, and monetizing costs and benefits (Munger 2000; Nickel et al. 2009). Cost–benefit analysis enumerates all direct costs and benefits to society of a particular project, assigns monetary values, discounts them to a net present value, and adds them into a single number to evaluate the project (Nickel et al. 2009).

The policy implementation calculated economic variables through an analysis of the B/C of the best construction, thus supporting decision-making. This analysis is used for activities that could potentially interfere with the environment and the public interest. The concept is measured by the value of the benefits and costs of a comparably sized activity. Activities will lead to the allocation of factors of production more efficiently if the value of the benefit is greater than cost. The highway development and management IV method calculated vehicle operating costs (VOC) based on the preliminary design simulations assuming the current price and geometric parameters. The value of time was calculated by using the integrated road management system (IRMS) and the gross output (human capital approach) approach to obtain the cost of accidents.

An expansion of the analysis of benefit–cost is to use the NPV to calculate investment feasibility, the IRR, and B/C ratio. Test sensitivity was calculated based on the optimistic scenario of eligibility conditions (increase in benefit cost of 25% and decrease in investment cost of 25%) and the condition of pessimism (decrease in the benefit cost of 25% and increase in investment cost of 25%).

7.5   Case Study

7.5.1   Project Descriptions

The Maros-Watampone Road is located in South Sulawesi, Indonesia. The road was built by the Dutch colonial government and is important for regional economic activity between the provinces of South Sulawesi and Southeast Sulawesi. This road is 145 km long with an average width of six meters in one line; it passes through several mountain areas with steep contour conditions. In general, the cross slope is more than 17%, the horizontal curvature radius is an average of 13 meters, and the critical length is greater than 175 meters. These features can slow vehicle to speed 4.6 km/h with limited visibility. Daily traffic has increased by 7.5%, which causes an accident rate that is 2.9% higher every year. The condition of the road has become damaged by a geometric path that is unsuitable to Indonesia's road construction standards. Geometric conditions of 40 kilometers must be repaired to maximize services on the road. The government performs maintenance only because the road is constrained by geographical conditions and is protected by natural habitat on the surrounding streets. Several segments have experienced a decrease in services such as regional economic flows, comfort, and safety.

From 2007 to 2009, the government conducted a study and discussion to improve the performance of Maros-Watampone Road. The plan recommended three alternate geometric road construction options: the elevated bridge, the cut-and-fill, and the tunnel system. Implementation of these three alternatives could negatively impact the environment. Thus, special attention must be paid to the topography and geology, along with the choice of construction techniques and methods to maintain the ecosystem sustainability in the national parks and heritage areas alongside the road. Figure 7.3 indicates the existing geometric conditions in the area of Babul National Park.

Fig. 7.3 Existing geometric conditions in the area of Babul National Park

The reason for the road development is to increase road capacity either by building new construction along the existing line or by constructing other lines, depending on road line conditions.

7.6 Analysis Results

7.6.1 Decision by AHP

The results of the pairwise comparison showed that the preferences of the respondents are consistent. This is evidenced by an inconsistency value of less than 0.10 (0.08) and the weight of the criterion and alternative options given in Table 7.4.

Benefits and the environment are the top sequence in the selection of criteria for consideration of construction type. This top sequence indicates that the type of construction chosen should provide maximum benefits to society and minimize environmental impact. The benefit criteria for consideration contributed the most to the respondents' construction choices because they understand the importance of the service that they will receive from this development. The road was built because of its benefit. The respondents prioritize benefits but still consider the resulting environmental effects, and therefore, they make the environmental criteria into their second consideration. People realize that the road's benefits must be balanced with its impact on development sustainability. Development of the road will increase mobility so that the economic growth of the area, traffic safety, and comfort will also be increased.

The use of environmentally friendly construction materials greatly affects the sustainability of biodiversity conservation in the surrounding area. The use of alternative materials is required to minimize the environmental impact. The

Table 7.4 The weighting of criteria and alternatives

| Criteria | Global weighting | Alternative weighting | | | Inconsistency |
		Elevated bridge	Cut-fill	Tunnel	
Benefit	0.300	**0.534**	**0.150**	**0.316**	0.03
Environment	0.224	0.519	0.304	0.177	0.02
Technology	0.130	0.493	0.311	0.196	0.05
Economical	0.104	0.570	0.270	0.160	0.03
Construction costs	0.081	0.550	0.210	0.240	0.02
Maintenance costs	0.054	0.523	0.284	0.193	0.09
Aesthetic value	0.041	0.489	0.332	0.180	0.09
Easy handling of implementation	0.038	0.581	0.282	0.137	0.04
Time of implementation	0.029	0.534	0.316	0.150	0.03
Inconsistency	0.090	0.528	0.248	0.223	**0.08**

technology criterion was chosen for the next sequence. This sequence shows that technology should be able to solve geometric problems without ignoring its impact on the environment.

The economic criterion and the cost of construction and maintenance costs concern the use of fund allocation for construction during the period of the plan. The community does not consider the appropriate construction and maintenance costs. This decision shows that the community understands the benefits and that the balance of natural resources requires environment-friendly technology with a significant implementation cost. These criteria can be calculated in several ways that will be discussed in the section on the efficiency of economic evaluation.

Harmony between construction and the environment must be considered by using aesthetic criteria to avoid the impression of a patchwork landscape. The criteria for easy handling and time of implementation tend to have an equal weight in terms of priority because they are directly proportional to one another. If construction is not difficult to implement, the work time will be faster as well as the opposite.

Synthesis analysis of the weight of the criteria and the weight of the alternatives showed that elevated bridge construction has the highest priority value at 0.528. This value shows that elevated bridge construction is suitable to solve geometric problems on that road. The cut-and-fill (0.428) and tunnel (0.223) approaches occupy the second and third priorities, respectively. The results of the sensitivity analysis are demonstrated in Fig. 7.4.

All the considerations criteria contributed the highest value for the elevated bridge construction. Criteria benefit (0.150) and the construction costs (0.210) give less priority to the cut-and-fill weights than the tunnel (0.316 and 0.240, respectively). However, other criteria contributed enough weight to cut-and-fill construction to make it the second priority for possible application.

The choice of elevated bridge construction as the most suitable to be applied for the Maros-Watampone Road is correct because its implementation will not change the landscape and will have little effect on nature. Wildlife habitat will be maintained in the conservation area. It is assumed that the construction pillar/abutment used with a high-tension electric tower can legally traverse several conservation areas. Using

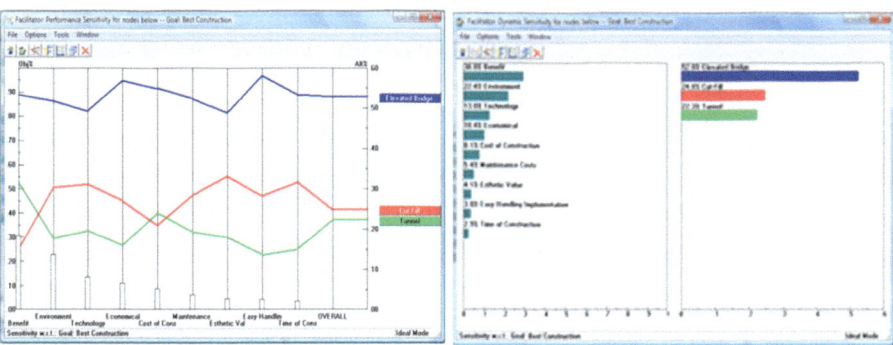

Fig. 7.4 Graph of sensitivity (Source: Authors' calculations)

environmental friendly technology, it will be possible to comply with appropriate geometric standards with limited land use. However, based on economic value, the cost of construction and maintenance is higher, and compared to other types of construction, elevated bridge construction requires special implementation expertise and considerable time. These criteria are not dominant influence on the value of contribution.

When compared to other types of construction, the tunnel and cut-and-fill approaches may destroy the balance of the ecosystem that surrounds the road. To obtain a road grade of 10%, both constructions must realign and extend the trace, thus requiring more land, which could damage the rock massif that is widely available around the site. Aesthetic value (0.489) renders the elevated bridge superior because it promotes harmony between development and high-value conservation areas that could eventually increase community incomes.

The most important advantage of road improvement includes greater potential for the transportation of goods, reduced costs pertaining to problems caused by low-quality roads, and a notable effect on the region's vitality.

7.6.2   Application of Elevated Bridge Construction

The assumptions regarding elevated bridge construction design are revealed by considering several parameters using the land development and 3dsMax programs, as seen in Fig. 7.5.

Table 7.5 shows the geometric changes in an existing conditions when construction of an elevated bridge is implemented. Several geometrical conditions cannot be adapted to the national road standard because we are trying to be realistic about conservation zones and critical areas that use lower levels of services.

Fig. 7.5 Simulation of elevated bridge construction

Table 7.5   Geometric change parameters

Road condition	Before implementation	After implementation	Unit
Length	10	11.5	Km
Width	4.5	7	M
Width shoulder	1	2	M
Topography condition	Hill	Flat	–
Average slope rise(RR)	22.5	2.5	m/km
Average slope falling (FR)	22.5	3.5	m/km
Slope rise + falling (TTR)	45	5	m/km
Degree of turn (DTR)	200	15	°/km
Surface condition (IRI)	5	7	m/km
Average speed	40	65	Km/jam

Table 7.6   Estimate of the total emissions produced by each type of alternative construction

	Ton CO_2/KM			
	Main construction			
Type of construction	Construction	Maintenance	Transportation	Total
Elevated bridge	1.05	0.03	0.23	1.31
Tunnel	1.50	0.07	0.23	1.79
Cut-and-fill	4.89–11.09	0.26	0.23	5.38–11.58
Asphalt surface	0.05	0.01	0.29	0.35

7.6.3   Construction Impacts on CO_2 Emissions

Considering the amount of CO_2 emissions generated by construction activities, transport must be considered because this road is in a conservation area, which is an oxygen and water reserve for the South Sulawesi province. The use of environmental construction materials can preserve the environmental sustainability of both the area and the region.

The study conducted by Horvath and Hendrickson (1997) shows that during the construction phase (e.g., during the concrete process), the bridge imposes a lower environmental burden. This is similar to the results of our simple calculation comparing the three types of construction, which shows that elevated bridge construction produces the lowest CO_2 emissions during its process and maintenance.

Table 7.6 illustrates the CO_2 emissions and relative contributions of construction, maintenance, and transportation related to both the existing construction and to the two construction alternatives. Cut-and-fill construction is post-dispatch construction, and therefore, we cannot display data about its resulting CO_2 emissions.

Overall CO_2 emissions resulting from elevated bridge construction (1.31 tCO_2/km) is lower than from tunnel construction (1.79 tCO_2/km). Contribution of CO_2 emissions from the process and maintenance of the main construction has a major impact on the value of the total emissions produced. The process and maintenance of tunnel construction (1.57 tCO_2/km) cause greater emissions than does the elevated bridge construction (1.08 tCO_2/km). Transport emissions contribute equivalent value to both types of construction because their concrete surfaces in the construction are the same. This construction is in accordance with Indonesian regulations that ban the use of two types of construction on road construction surfaces.

7.6.4   Construction Impacts on Benefits and Costs

7.6.4.1   Component of Benefit Cost

VOCs decreased after the construction was implemented. Table 7.7 shows that trucks incur many benefits from the project improvement. This condition supports of the smooth shipping of goods between the South and Southeast Sulawesi provinces, both of which use trucks. Regional economic activity will also increase. Public transport fare reductions (in the amount of 938, 537 or 3984) can also be implemented because of the large decline in value after the project is operational. Energy efficiency varies widely depending on the driving cycle and type of vehicle.

Private users of sedans/city cars (588) are not greatly impacted, and thus, it is likely that people will switch to using public transportation, which has a decreased tariff. If more people use public transportation, the energy consumption and emissions generated by transport activities will decrease. Thus, impact on the environment can be further reduced.

Geometric changes will have a major impact on travel time. Average vehicle travel times will be reduced by 20–30% compare with original condition. The accident rate will decrease. Overall changes in travel time before and after the project are set forth in Table 7.8.

Table 7.7 Operational cost of vehicle

Vehicle	Before project	After project	Different VOC
Sedan/city car	3720	3133	588
Sport utility vehicle	4678	3740	938
Mini bus	8140	7603	537
Bus	11,568	7584	3984
Light truck	7725	6670	1055
Medium truck	12,901	11,208	1693
Heavy truck	14,813	8671	6142

Table 7.8 Time value of travel before and after the project

Vehicle	Before project	After project	Time rate
Sedan/city car	73,821	45,428	28,393
Sport utility vehicle	53,176	32,724	20,452
Mini bus	100,352	65,447	40,905
Bus	212,703	130,894	81,809
Light truck	14,960	9206	5754
Medium truck	14,960	9206	5754
Heavy truck	14,960	9206	5754

Table 7.9 Sensitivity test on 25% change in profits and costs

Test	NPV (billion rupiah)	IRR (billion rupiah)	BCR (12%)	BCR (15%)
Scenario 1: No accident cost savings	899,849	20.07%	2.78	2.21
Condition				
Test 1: Cost investment up 25%, benefit down 25% (pessimistic)	385,052	17.91%	1.78	1.41
Test 2: Cost investment down 25%, benefit up 25% (optimistic)	1,459,639	21.32%	4.34	3.45
Scenario 2: With accident cost saving	1,078,678	20.36%	3.09	2.45
Condition				
Test 1: Cost investment up 25%, benefit down 25% (pessimistic)	563,881	18.60%	2.03	1.61
Test 2: Cost investment down 25%, benefit up 25% (optimistic)	1,638,468	21.43%	4.73	3.75

7.6.4.2   Feasibility and Sensitivity Analysis of Investment

Table 7.9 illustrates the value of the benefits arising out of the application of elevated bridge construction under different conditions. The values of the work implementation are evaluated according to a scale of feasible priorities and investments.

7.7   Concluding Remarks

An AHP method has been applied to select the best type of road construction on Maros-Watampone Road, Indonesia. To support decisions related to this, geometric construction on Maros-Watampone Road should consider economic and noneconomic aspects such as benefits, environment, technology, economy, construction costs, maintenance costs, aesthetic value, easy handling, and time of implementation. All the criteria must contribute significantly to the construction process and operation to keep development sustainable.

The results of the analysis showed that elevated bridge construction is the best alternative for geometric improvements on Maros-Watampone Road. This decision is supported by the results of a simple analysis of the environmental impact and evaluation of the economic aspects of the selected road construction. Overall, the selection of elevated bridge construction provided great benefits, but had little impact on the environment (as seen by its low level of carbon emissions), achieving geometric standards through technology. The value of BCR > 1.0 indicates that the cost of the benefit is greater than the cost of investing in an optimistic and pessimistic condition. In addition to these benefits, elevated bridge construction has an aesthetic value that can support increased conservation in an area of natural and cultural heritage.

If governments invest in road development, the quality and quantity of roads will increase. Therefore, the regional potential for transportation will be improved, which can increase economic growth and create greater income for the government. Furthermore, problems such as accidents and gradual damage to vehicles caused by low-quality roads will be reduced. Therefore, the roads will be safer, and drivers will incur less damage. Finally, a region with a vast number of high-quality roads is more likely to prosper; it will provide people with more opportunities for access to various resources and will lead to greater development.

The calculation of the project's ecological impacts will function, but it must be prepared as a follow-up to the calculation of CO_2 emissions. Future study should be concentrated on the environmental impact of energy consumption, especially in construction and transportation activities that involve all aspects of construction, maintenance, and transportation.

References

Barnard, C., & Simon, H. (1947). *Administrative behavior. A study of decision-making processes in administrative organization.* New York: Free Press.

Forsyth, P. (2011). Environmental and financial sustainability of air transport: Are they incompatible? *Journal of Air Transport Management, 17*(1), 27–32.

Glover, D. R., & Simon, J. L. (1975). The effect of population density on infrastructure: The case of road building. *Economic Development and Cultural Change, 23*(3), 453–468.

Horvath, A., & Hendrickson, C. (1997). *Estimation of environmental implications of construction materials and designs using life cycle assessment techniques.* Pittsburgh: Carnegie Mellon University.

Hough, M. (1989). *City form and natural process : Towards a New Urban Vemacular.* New York: Rouletedge.

Ian McHarg, L. (1969). *Design with nature.* New York: University of Pennsylvania.

Ibrahim, F. (2010). Pemilihan Trase Jalan dengan Pendekatan Analisis Multi Kriteria. In *Proceeding Konferensi Pascasarjana Teknik Sipil* (pp. 79–88). Bandung: Institut Tecknologi.

Jones, H., Moura, F., & Domingos, T. (2014). Transport infrastructure project evaluation using cost-benefit analysis. *Procedia-Social and Behavioral Sciences, 111*, 400–409.

Kato, H., Naoki, S., Motohiro, O., & Yoshitsugu, H. (2005). A life cycle assessment for evaluating environmental impacts of inter-regional high-speed mass transit projects. *Journal of the Eastern Asia Society for Transportation Studies, 6*, 3211–3224.

Mackay City Council. (2008). Geometric Road Design (Urban and Rural) (Planning Scheme Policy No. 15.01). http://www.mackay.qld.gov.au/__data/assets/pdf_file/0004/14773/15.01_-_Geometric_Road_Design_V2.pdf

Ministry of Public Works of Indonesia. (2010). *Strategic plan 2010–2014*. Jakarta: Author.

Miyata, Yuzuru, Hirobata, Yasuhiro, Nakanishi, Hitomi, and Shibusawa, Hiroyuki. (2005). *Rural Sustainable Development by Constructing New Roads in Advanced Country-A Case Study of San-en Region in Japan.*

Munger, M. C. (2000). *Analyzing policy: Choices, conflicts, and practices*. WW Norton, New York.

Nickel, J., Ross, A. M., & Rhodes, D. H. (2009, June). Comparison of project evaluation using cost-benefit analysis and multi-attribute tradespace exploration in the transportation domain. In *2nd international symposium on engineering systems.*

Ninan, K. N. (2008). *Cost-benefit analysis: An introduction*. Santa Barbara: Donald Bren School of Environmental Science and Management, University of California.

Rajagopalan, N. (2007). *Environmental life-cycle assessment of highway construction projects* (Doctoral dissertation, Texas A&M University).

Rose, B. J. (2010). *GHG-Energy Calc background paper.*

Saaty, T. L. (1990). How to make a decision: The analytic hierarchy process. *European Journal of Operational Research, 48*, 9–26.

Stripple, H. (2001). *Life cycle assessment of road*. A pilot study for inventory analysis (2nd Rev ed.). Report from the IVL Swedish Environmental Research Institute, 96.

Wicksell, K. (1977). *Lectures on political economy, Vol. I: General theory* (Vol. 1). Fairfield: Augustus M. Kelley.

Zheng, Z. R. (1997). *Application of reliability theory to highway geometric design*. Vancouver: University of British Columbia.

Chapter 8
Computable General Equilibrium Models for Economic and Environmental Policies

8.1 Introduction

Computable general equilibrium (CGE) modeling is an analysis that attempts to use the general equilibrium theory to empirically analyze resource allocation and the economy as a whole. The general equilibrium theory is a formalization of the simple but fundamental observation that markets in real-world economies are mutually interdependent (Bergman 2005). This theoretical analysis has provided important insights into the factors and mechanisms that determine relative prices and the allocation of resources within and among market economies.

8.2 Computable General Equilibrium: An Overview

With the development of fast computers and software suitable for policy analysis, Johansen (1960), who developed the Norwegian multi-sector growth model, presented the first CGE model. Since the beginning of the 1990s, many CGE models have been developed to analyze environmental policy and natural resource management issues, for example, development issues have been analyzed by Dervis and Robinson (1982), and taxation and international trade issues have been analyzed by Shoven and Whalley (1992) in a manner to that of Buehrer and Mauro (1995).

Today, the CGE model has been extended to analyze development planning, public finances, the environment and resource management, reconciliation of structural changes, and market transitions (Yeah et al. 1994). For example, the ORANI model is a CGE model of the Australian economy, built by Dixon et al. (1982), which analyzes the impact that policy has on resource allocation and economic structure, social welfare, and income distribution (Oktaviani 2000, 2011). CGE modeling has become popular because of the increasing need to analyze policies

© Springer Nature Singapore Pte Ltd. 2018
Y. Miyata et al., *Environmental and Natural Disaster Resilience of Indonesia*,
New Frontiers in Regional Science: Asian Perspectives 23,
https://doi.org/10.1007/978-981-10-8210-8_8

related to resource allocation issues, and it is often applied in many developing countries. A CGE model for Indonesia was first implemented in 2005 to calculate the impact of fuel price increases on income distribution and social welfare.

A CGE model is a nonlinear equation that stimulates the economy to accommodate price adjustments and quantities as the equilibrium market for production factors and commodities (Lewis 1991). Arrow (2005) has found that a CGE is the best method to analyze the economy-wide impact of policies, which is influenced by interlinkages between sectors and markets. Similarly, Hosoe et al. (2010) has proposed that CGE models can numerically depict a "world" in which a general equilibrium is attained by the price mechanism.

A CGE model is one of the rigorous quantitative methods that can be used to evaluate the impact of policy shocks throughout the economy. Today, this model is considered to provide the most realistic evaluation of the entire economic structure and all existing economic transactions among economic agents (production sectors, households, and the government, among others). This is because of the ability of CGE analysis to capture the economic impact derived from shocks or the widespread implementation of a specific policy reform. This approach is useful when the expected effects of policy implementation are complex and materialize through different transmission channels. Therefore, this model is the best option to evaluate a climate change shock, which involves analyzing static/dynamic, direct/indirect, and short- and long-term effects.

8.3 Computable General Equilibrium As Economy Modeling

The structure of the CGE model, in that it describes interactions among economic agents, was built on microeconomic theory in the form of a behavioral equation system. CGE models analyze the interaction between macroeconomic variables and the microeconomic sector and the impact of economic policy on the economy as whole. According to this model, the market is perfectly competitive, achieving efficiency in production and resource allocation. This relationship among utilities with respect to one another is known as the Pareto optimum condition. Three efficiencies in the Pareto optimum concept are fundamental to building a CGE model: efficiency of resource allocation (production equilibrium), efficiency of commodity distribution (consumption equilibrium), and efficiency of product combination (equilibrium of the production and consumption sectors).

To run the CGE model, three primary resources are required:

1. Time: constructing and running a CGE model take longer than performing an analysis through the use of alternative quantitative methods.
2. Special software to run the model.

3. A significant amount of data, such as productive sectors (i.e., input-output table), the existing flows of transactions among economic agents (i.e., social accounting matrix), and parameter values, among others.

8.4 Application of Computable General Equilibrium

The important step in CGE application for clearly defining the problem to be analyzed is how to choose the type, features, and detail level of the model. The type of problem to be analyzed will indicate the necessary degree of disaggregation, and the economic sectors that function must specify the most. The theoretical refinement of the model will also be affected by practical constraints such as information availability. Applied general equilibrium involves a trade-off between the researchers' intent to faithfully represent the economy's structure and the ad hoc constraints established by the available statistical information.

In any process model, to analyze various types of problems and to create the model's particularities, one should always use the following specifications (André et al. 2010):

- The number and type of goods (consumer goods, production goods, primary factors, etc.)
- The number and type of consumers (possibly classified by income, age, qualifications, tastes, etc.)
- The number and type of firms of productive sectors (simple or joint production, type of revenues of the production function, technological development, etc.)
- The characteristics of the public sector (attitude of the government as a demander or producer, fiscal system, budget, etc.)
- The characteristic of the foreign sector (related enterprises and sectors, degree of international integration, established tariffs and custom duties, etc.)
- The concept of equilibrium (with or without unemployment, with or without public and/or foreign deficit, etc.)

8.4.1 The Economic Agents

The following is a brief description of the economic agents of the applied CGE model (André et al. 2010; Hosoe et al. 2010; Varian 2014; Pauw 2003; Shoven and Walley 1992; Leontief 1986; Miyata 1995, 1997; Miyata and Shibusawa 2008; Shibusawa and Miyata 2011).

8.4.1.1 Industries

Industry is the production of a good or service within an economy, and therefore, it is often referred to as production or supply. Several factors can affect production: the price of the commodity, input prices, production costs, production factors, production technology, and government policies. Production is expressed as a mathematical relationship to the factors affecting it, known as the production function. Production technology is usually represented by a so-called nested production function. Producers are assumed to maximize their profits, and this maximization results in supply functions for each good.

Figure 8.1 shows a simple example of such a function. In this example, the domestic (or internal) production sector uses production inputs, which typically include intermediate outputs from other sectors (commodities) along with primary factors (labor and capital). Primary factors are combined using production technology to provide the value added by each sector. Total production (output) is the result of combining domestic production (production inputs) with imports using a specific function, which usually confirms Armington's (1969) hypothesis to simplify the analysis. This hypothesis considers that the analyzed country or economy is small enough to have an influence on foreign trade. At the first and second levels of the nest, either the Cobb–Douglas or the constant elasticity of substitution (CES) functions may be found. The activity output level (top level) is often defined as a Leontief function.

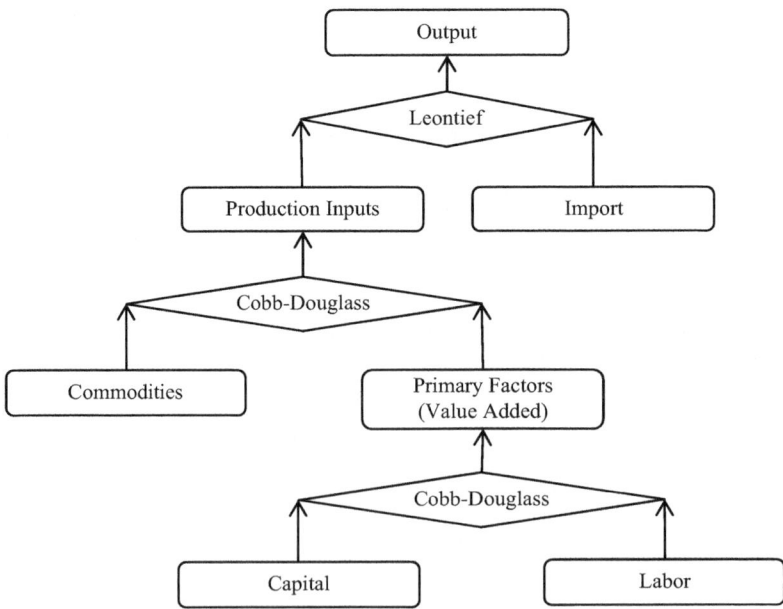

Fig. 8.1 Nested production structure (*Source: authors' elaboration*)

8.4.1.2   Consumer

The final demand comes from household demand for consumer goods and the nonconsumer demand sectors of investments and exports. Factors affecting consumer demand include commodity prices, input prices, preferences or utility, income, population, the estimated future prices, income distribution, and producer's efforts to increase sales. The demand function is the demand expressed as a mathematical relationship with the factors that influence it. It provides the optimal amounts of each good as a function of consumer prices and income.

In general, there are n possible types of goods identified by their productive sectors and one or more representative consumers (perhaps grouped by categories according to income source, income level, activity type, etc.) who demand consumer goods. Each consumer possesses initial endowments and a set of preferences. The representative consumer's purchases are primarily financed by revenues from the sale of the initial factor endowments. Available consumer income not used for consumption is savings. The representative consumer's disposable income is calculated by totaling all capital and labor earnings, plus transfers received, minus the direct taxes for which the consumer is liable:

$$\text{Disposable income} = \text{labor income} + \text{capital income} + \text{transfer} \\ - \text{direct taxes} \tag{8.1}$$

The consumer's objective is to maximize the utility function, U, which depends on consumer goods, CG_j, and savings, SG, subject to the budget constraint:

$$\text{Max } U(CG_1, \cdots, CG_n, SG) \tag{8.2}$$

Market demands are the result of adding all individual consumer demands together. Market demands are price dependent; they are also continuous, nonnegative, and homogenous of zero degree, and they satisfy Walras's law.

8.4.1.3   Public Sector

The public sector is usually represented by the government. This study focuses on policy-making; therefore, the model should include several hypotheses regarding how the government makes decisions. The government taxes economic transactions, thus collecting tax revenues and influencing the consumer's disposable income. It also makes transfers to the private sector and demands goods and services from different productive sectors j. The difference between the government's revenues and its outlays represents the balance (surplus or deficit) of the public (government) budget according to the following calculation:

$$\text{Government budget } (GB) = \text{revenues} - \text{public expenditures} \tag{8.3}$$

where both income and expenditures are measured in monetary terms. Expenditure is the aggregation of (the nominal value of) public consumption and transfers made to the private sector. The applications present in this study, the government activity (public expenditure and taxation) is perceived by economic agents as exogenous and by the government as decision variables. The government revenues will be transferred to the household: that is the specificity of our model.

8.4.1.4   External Sector

In the model, the focus will be on the domestic sphere; it will adopt the common simplifying assumption that the general equilibrium model is to take the activity of the foreign sector as fixed. This is consistent with Indonesia's status as a small country: the hypothesis is that the rest of the world is not affected by any domestic change introduced in our country. The external sector (Ex) is denoted by:

$$Ex = \text{exports} - \text{imports} \tag{8.4}$$

8.4.1.5   Investment and Savings

Introducing dynamic factors such as investment and savings is an inconsistency in the static model in which this study will be developed. However, investment cannot be ignored because it comprises a significantly large share of final demand. Our study incorporates an investment model in several ways, despite the fact that it is not completely consistent with economic theory.

Savings and investment normally use a so-called savings-driven model. This model is one in which the closure rule defines investment behavior. Usually, investment is taken to be exogenous; savings are determined by the public sector (or the government), the foreign sector, and consumers to maximize their utility and deficits; and public- and foreign-sector investments are left to be determined endogenously according to the following accounting identity:

$$INV = GB + SG.invp + Ex \tag{8.5}$$

where INV is the aggregated nominal value of investment and $invp$ is the price of investment goods.

8.4.1.6   Input Markets

Labor and capital demands are calculated assuming firms minimize the cost of producing value added in input markets. It is commonly assumed in the short term that total capital supply is inelastic, although more-complex specifications could also be used. Typically, labor supply is a difficult element to address. One problem is that CGE models are built on the assumption that all markets clear in equilibrium. Conversely, one of the aims of applied work is to reproduce reality as closely as possible. This implies the recognition of unemployment. However, such recognition is inconsistent with the equilibrium assumption because unemployment means an excess supply of labor. This study will solve the problem in our model.

8.4.2 Choosing Functional Forms

Various well-known functional forms, such as the Cobb–Douglas function, the Leontief function, and the constant elasticity of substitution (CES) function, are used frequently in economic modeling in which functions are often regarded as the family of "convenient" forms. The major constraints on the specification of demand and production functions in applied models are that they be consistent with the theoretical approach and be analytically tractable (Shoven and Whalley 1992). The first constraint involves choosing functions that satisfy several restrictions, such as Walras's law for demand functions. The second constraint requires that the economy's demand and supply responses be reasonably easy to evaluate for any price vector, considering a candidate equilibrium solution for the economy.

The specific form chosen typically depends upon how elasticities are to be used in the models (Table 9.1). This point is best illustrated by considering the model's demand side. The demand derived from Cobb–Douglas utility functions is easy to work with but has the restrictions of unitary-income and uncompensated own-price elasticities and zero uncompensated cross-price elasticities. These restrictions are typically implausible, given the empirical estimates of elasticities applicable to any

Table 9.1 Properties of function forms

Properties	Cobb–Douglas Functions	CES
Demand functions	$X_i = \frac{\alpha_i I}{P_i}$	$X_i = \dfrac{\alpha_i I}{P_i^{\sigma} \cdot \sum_j \alpha_j P_j^{(1-\sigma)}}$
Own-price (uncompensated) elasticity	-1	$-\sigma - (1-\sigma)\alpha_i P_i \gamma^{-1}$
Own-price (compensated) elasticity	$-(1-\alpha_i)$	$-\sigma\left(1 - \sigma_i P_i^{(1-\sigma)} \cdot \gamma^{-1}\right)$
Income elasticity	1	1
Cross-price (uncompensated) elasticities	0	$-(1-\sigma)\alpha_j P_j^{(1-\sigma)} \gamma^{-1}$
Indirect utility function	$U = I \cdot \prod \left(\frac{\alpha_i}{P_i}\right)^{\alpha_i}$	$U = I \cdot \left(\sum_j \alpha_j P_j^{(1-\sigma)}\right)$
Expenditure function (true cost-of-living index)	$E = \prod \left(\frac{P_i}{\alpha_i}\right)^{\alpha_i}$	$U = \left(\sum_j \alpha_j P_j^{(1-\sigma)}\right)^{(1-\sigma)}$

Source: Shoven and Whalley (1992)

particular model, but can only be relaxed by using additional general functional forms. With CES functions, unitary own-price elasticities no longer apply. However, if all expenditure shares are small, the compensated own-price elasticities equal the elasticity of substitution in preferences, and it may be unacceptable to model all commodities as having essentially the same compensated own-price elasticities.

Once all these elements have been specified, it is time to apply the equilibrium hypothesis. We assume that markets tend to equilibrium in the sense that supply equals demand in all markets as long as consumers and producers make optimal decisions. We applied the model for finding the equilibrium fit and solving a system equation using a computational program. The complexity of this system is model dependent but must include, at least, the supply functions (one for each output and input), the demand functions, the market-clearing conditions, and all the relevant accounting identities.

The zero-degree homogeneity of the demand functions and the linear homogeneity of profits in relation to the prices mean that only relative prices are significant; absolute prices have no impact on the resulting equilibrium. Therefore, equilibrium is characterized by relative prices and by certain production levels in each industry in which market demand equals supply for all goods. The assumption that producers maximize their profits means that in the case of constant-scale revenues, no activity offers positive economic profits at market prices.

There is not one single general equilibrium model; rather, there are as many models as there are different combinations of decisions to be made (number of sectors, functional forms, etc.). The choice of specific functional forms usually depends on how elasticities are used in the model. The method most often applied is to select the functional form that best accounts for the key parameter values (such as price and income elasticities) without damaging the model's feasibility.

8.5   Model Closure

CGE models always contain more variables than equations, which have a relation to one another that enable to be both endogenous and exogenous. Several of the variables set outside the model are called exogenous. Variables determined by the model are termed endogenous. The choice of which variables are to be exogenous is called the model closure. Strategies for the choice of model closure include:

1. Identifying variables that describe each equation
2. Automatically deeming variables that are not described in the equation system as exogenous
3. Accounting for matrix size variables

8.6   Building Benchmark Equilibrium Data Sets

The benchmark equilibrium data set for the model is crucial in the calibration process. The data set is constructed under the assumption of an observable equilibrium and meets the equilibrium conditions for the model being studied. If equilibrium is to be reflected in an assembled set of national accounts, demand must equal market supply for all commodities, and supply and demand must be separately disaggregated by agent. Ultimately, each agent has incomes and expenditures consistent with his or her budget constraints.

Equilibrium conditions must be satisfied by most of the constructed benchmark equilibrium data sets (Shoven and Whalley 1992) as follows:

1. Demands equal supplies for all commodities.
2. Nonpositive profits are made in all industries.
3. All domestic agents (including the government) have demands that satisfy their budget constraints.
4. The economy is in external sector balance.

The benchmark data sets are constructed for use as a business-as-usual condition in applied general equilibrium models. Various adjustments are necessary to block data that are available separately but are not arranged on a micro-consistent basis. The nature of these adjustments, which are made on a case-by-case basis, varies.

8.7   The Advantages and Disadvantages of Applied CGE Models

CGE modeling (Hosoe et al. 2010; Horison 1997; Ayres and Kneese 1969a; Debreu 1959) has certain advantages:

- Its potential to capture a much wider set of economic impacts that includes all transactions of economic agents as a whole and, therefore, the effect of a policy that can be quantitatively analyzed with respect to macro- or microeconomic performance
- Its potential to include substitutions between production factors so that price changes in the production factor will cause the consumer to change his or her composition in the consumption of production factors
- Its ability to evaluate not only the implementation of a policy reform but also its distributive effects within the economy at different levels of disaggregation
- Its relatively small data requirements considering the size of the model (for particular benchmark years)
- Its high level of rigor and elegance analysis, which extend to compass externalities and environmental resources with public goods characteristics

However, CGE modeling also has several disadvantages:

- Its significant data and time requirements. Collecting updated, high-quality, multiregional data, building a social accounting matrix, and programming and calibrating a CGE model are very time-consuming processes.
- The CGE model is complicated, and using many assumptions causes the black box problem to appear, which makes it difficult to explain why the estimation result may not correspond to the economic theory or prediction.
- The CGE model requires the primary assumption of perfectly competitive market equilibrium with a constant return to scale condition.
- The CGE model depends on calibration of the parameter's benchmark with the value calculated from other model calculations. Therefore, for a developing country, it is difficult to obtain precise data. Interpretation of results focuses on magnitudes, directions, and distributive patterns, not the numeric outcomes themselves. Therefore, results from CGE models should be complemented with additional analytical work using alternative quantitative methods for policy implementation.

References

André, F. J., Cardenete, M. A., & Romero, C. (2010). *Designing public policies: An approach based on multi-criteria analysis and computable general equilibrium modeling* (Vol. 642). Berlin: Springer.

Armington, P. S. (1969). The geographic pattern of trade and the effects of price changes. *Staff Papers, 16*(2), 179–201.

Arrow, K. J. (2005). Personal reflections on applied general equilibrium models. In T. J. Kehoe, T. N. Srinivasan, & J. Whalley (Eds.), *Frontiers in applied general equilibrium modeling in honour of Herbert Scarf.* Cambridge: Cambridge University Press.

Ayres, R. U., & Kneese, A. V. (1969a). Production, consumption, and externalities. *The American Economic Review, 59*(3), 282–297.

Ayres, R. U., & Kneese, A. V. (1969b). Production, consumption, and externalities. *The American Economic Review, 59*(3), 282–297.

Bergman, L. (2005). CGE modeling of environmental policy and resource management. *Handbook of Environmental Economics, 3*, 1273–1306.

Buehrer, T., & Di Mauro, F. (1995). *Computable general equilibrium models as tools for policy analysis in developing countries: Some basic principles and an empirical application.* Rome: Banca d'Italia.

Debreu, G. (1959). *Theory of value: An axiomatic analysis of economic equilibrium* (Vol. 17). New Haven: Yale University Press.

Dervis, K., & Robinson, S. (1982). *General equilibrium models for development policy.* Cambridge: Cambridge University Press.

Dixon, P.B., B.R. Parmenter, Sutton, J., & and Vincent, D.P.(1982), ORANI: A multisectoral model of the Australian economy, contributions to economic analysis 142, North-Holland Publishing Company.

Horison, W. J. (1997) *Computable general equilibrium models.* (October 12, 2008) Retrieved from http://www.mobidik.dk/mobi.cge.html (2014.6.1).

Hosoe, N., Gasawa, K., & Hashimoto, H. (2010). *Textbook of computable general equilibrium modeling: Programming and simulations*. London: Springer.

Johansen, L. (1960). *A multisectoral study of economic growth*. Amsterdam: North-Holland.

Leontief, W. (1986). *Technological change, prices, wages, and rates of return on capital in the USA economy, Input-Output economics* (2 nd ed.). New York: Oxford University Press.

Lewis, J. D. (1991). *Computable General Equilibrium (CGE) Model of Indonesia (No. 378)*. Harvard Institute for International Development, Harvard University.

Miyata, Y. (1995). A General equilibrim analysis of the waste-economic system. *Infrastructure Planning Review, 12*, 259–270.

Miyata, Y. (1997). An intertemporal general equilibrium analysis of the waste-economic system. *Infrastructure Planning Review, 14*, 421–432.

Miyata, Y., & Shibusawa, H. (2008). Does a decrease in the population prevent a sustainable growth of an environmentally friendly city? –A comparison of cases of decreasing and increasing populations of Obihiro metropolitan area, Japan by an intertemporal CGE-Modeling approach. *Interdisciplinary Information Sciences, 14*(1), 1–24.

Oktaviani, R. (2000). *The Impact of APEC Trade Liberalization on Indonesia Economy and its Agricultural Sector*. PhD Thesis. Department of Agricultral Economics University of Sydney, Sydney. 473 p.

Oktaviani, R. (2011). Economic model of general equilibrium. Theory and application in Indonesia. Bogor: IPB Press. 335(656.8585411), 0.1.

Pauw, K. (2003). *Functional forms used in CGE models: Modelling production and commodity flows* (No. 15606). PROVIDE Project.

Shibusawa, H., & Miyata, Y. (2011). Evaluating the dynamic and spatial economic impacts of an earthquake: A CGE Application to Japan. *Regional Science Inquiry, 3*(2), 13–25.

Shoven, J. B., & Whalley, J. (1992). *Applying general equilibrium*. Cambridge: Cambridge University Press.

Varian, H. R. (2014). *Intermediate microeconomics: A modern approach* (9th ed.). New York: WW Norton and Company.

Yeah, K. L., Yanagida, J. F., & Yamauchi, H. (1994). Evaluation of external effects and government intervention in Malaysia's agricultural sector: A computable general equilibrium framework. *Agricultural Economics, 11*, 237–256.

Chapter 9
Constructing a CGE Model for Economic and Environmental Policies in Makassar City

9.1 Introduction

Our study introduces a standard structure of CGE model that conforms to a basic of the Walrasian equilibrium to perform a joint analysis of economic and environmental policies; moreover, the model incorporates information about both the key economic variables and the environmental impact of economic activity. Taxes and government activity are taken to be exogenous for households and industries, whereas they are considered as decision variables for the government.

We present the industrial behavior by the technology structure in a nested production function. Consumer behavior is represented by a single household that makes decisions about consumption and savings while trying to maximize his or her utility function subject to a budget constraint. CO_2 emissions are introduced following a short-term approach according to which the intensity of CO_2 emission is assumed to be fixed. The basic structure of the model is completed by a description of input markets, the external sector, commodity prices, and the closure rule, which links investment, saving, and government balances. The model also assumes that the activity level of the external sector is fixed in the sense that imports and exports are not sensitive to policy changes implemented by the government. This assumption is consistent with a small-country hypothesis and a short-term approach to policy design.

The relative prices and the activity levels of the production sectors are endogenous variables. The equilibrium of the economy is given by a price vector for all goods and inputs, a vector of activity levels, and a value for government income such that the household is maximizing his or her utility, the production sectors are maximizing their profits (net of taxes), the government income equals the payments of all economic agents, and supply equals demand in all markets.

The main database used in the calibration process is Makassar's social accounting matrix.

© Springer Nature Singapore Pte Ltd. 2018
Y. Miyata et al., *Environmental and Natural Disaster Resilience of Indonesia*,
New Frontiers in Regional Science: Asian Perspectives 23,
https://doi.org/10.1007/978-981-10-8210-8_9

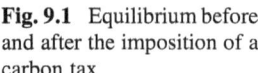

Fig. 9.1 Equilibrium before and after the imposition of a carbon tax

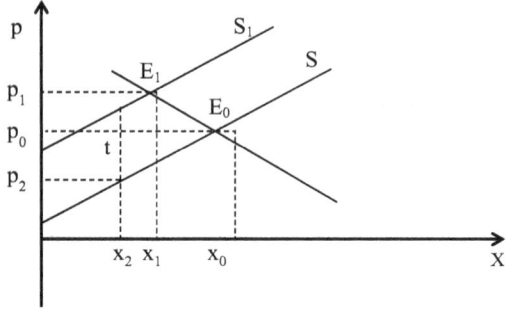

9.2   Model Framework

The results of the simulations produced using the CGE comparative static model were reported as deviations from a baseline scenario (BAU). Instead of presenting changes over time, the model reports differences with respect to the baseline scenario at a given point in 2006. Such results are generally considered to represent economic responses over a period of approximately 2 years (McDougall 1993). The model is consistent with price levels and real economic activity. The price is determined exogenously and acts as the numeraire in the model.

Figure 9.1 presents an example of a comparative static model. The figure depicts the equilibrium relationships between demand and supply before and after the imposition of a carbon tax. This study assumed that the city's industries produce products and CO_2 emissions as a by-product. In the figure, x is a commodity, p is the price of the commodity, t is the tax per unit of the commodity, and the commodity supply function will shift upward by t.

This figure indicates that the price of the commodity before the tax has been imposed (x_2) is p_2 and that the price of the commodity after the tax has been imposed (x_2) becomes $p_2 + t$. Equilibrium is achieved when the demand function (D) and the supply function (S) intersect at point $E(x_0, p_0)$. After the tax is imposed, equilibrium occurs at point $E_1(x_1, p_1)$, which is the intersection of the demand function (D) and the supply function (S_1) after the tax has been imposed.

The model simulations indicate that the tax will result in percentage changes in industrial output of $100 \times (X_1 - X_0)/X_0$ and demonstrate how the policy might affect industrial output and economic performance.

9.3   Setup of the Economy

In the model, production requires the use of two production factors: one unit of labor and one unit of capital. In the model economy, there are 28 industry representative firms that produce 28 commodities. There is a single representative household that consumes all the commodities in the economy in a way that maximizes its utility.

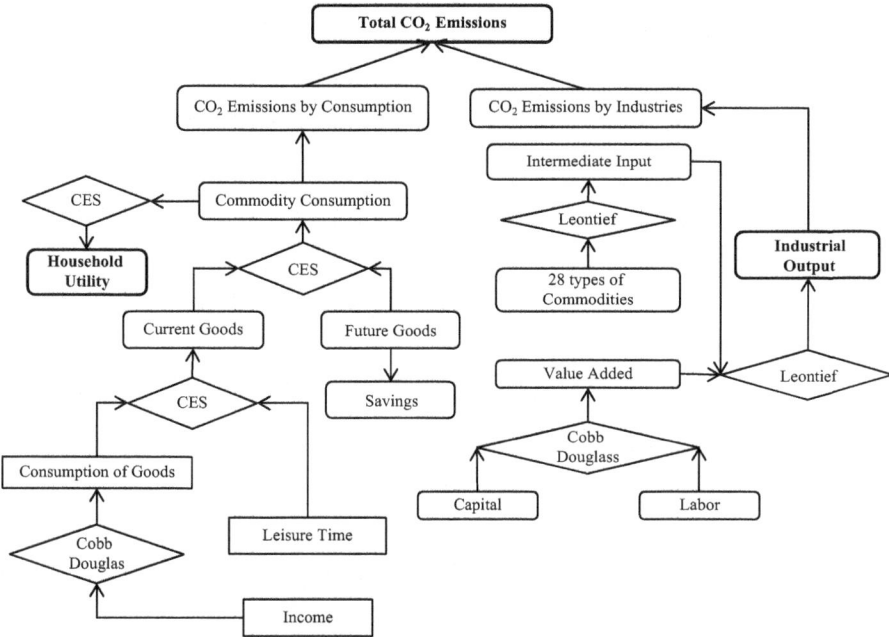

Fig. 9.2 Hierarchical structure of the model

The household supplies the firms with two production factors in return for income. The supply and demand for these commodities and production factors are in perfectly competitive equilibrium in 2006. Figure 9.2 indicates the hierarchical structure of the model.

9.4 Behavior of Economic Agents

9.4.1 Industries

The model comprises 28 production sectors matching the aggregate 2006 Social Accounting Matrix (SAM) of Makassar City, which is used to calibrate the model. The production technology is given by a nested production function.

The industries use intermediate inputs, labor, and capital to produce goods. Industries combine the intermediate labor and capital inputs using the Leontief production function and apply a Cobb–Douglas production function for the value-added inputs (see Fig. 9.3). The firm's cost minimization problem can be written as follows:

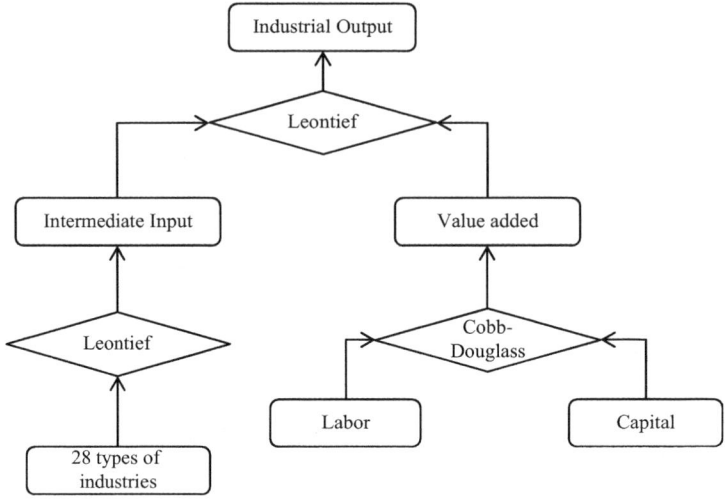

Fig. 9.3 Hierarchical structure of industries

$$\min_{\{x_{ij}, L_j, K_j\}} \sum_{i=1}^{28} p_i x_{ij} + \left(1 + tp_j\right)\left(wL_j + rK_j\right) \quad (j = 1, ..., 28) \qquad (9.1)$$

subject to

$$X_j = \min\left[\frac{1}{a_{0j}} f_j\left(L_j, K_j\right), \frac{x_{1j}}{a_{1j}}, ..., \frac{x_{ij}}{a_{1j}}, ..., \frac{x_{28j}}{a_{28j}}\right] \qquad (9.2)$$

$$f_j\left(L_j, K_j\right) \equiv A_j L_j^{\alpha_j} K_j^{\left(1 - \alpha_j\right)} \qquad (9.3)$$

where

p_i: price of commodity i

x_{ij}: intermediate input of industry i's product in industry j

tp_j: net indirect tax rate imposed on industry j's product (indirect tax rate-subsidy rate)

w: wage rate

r: capital return rate

L_j: labor input in industry j

K_j: capital input in industry j

X_j: output in industry j

a_{0j}: value-added rate in industry j

a_{ij}: input coefficient

A_j, α_j: technological parameters in industry j

The conditional demands for intermediate goods, labor, and capital in the production process are as follows:

$$x_{ij} = a_{ij}X_j \tag{9.4}$$

$$LD_j = \left[\frac{(1-\alpha_j)r}{\alpha_j w}\right]^{\alpha_j} \frac{a_{0j}X_j}{A_j} \tag{9.5}$$

$$KD_j = \left[\frac{\alpha_j w}{(1-\alpha_j)r}\right]^{(1-\alpha_j)} \frac{a_{0j}X_j}{A_j} \tag{9.6}$$

where

LD_j: conditional demand for labor in industry j
KD_j: conditional capital demand in industry j

The industries conform to the zero-profit condition under perfect competition.

$$\text{profit} = p_j X_j - \sum_{i=1}^{28} p_i x_{ij} - (1 + tp_j)(wLD_j + rKD_j) = 0 \tag{9.7}$$

9.4.2 Households

A fixed number of households in Makassar City are assumed to be homogenous. Thus, these households are assumed to share a common aggregate utility function. The households share a *CES* utility function with respect to the consumption of current and future goods. In this model, the current good is defined as a *CES* composite of current consumption goods and leisure time, and the future good is derived from savings. The household utility function is thus illustrated in Fig. 9.4.

Households select a bundle of current and future goods to maximize their utility function subject to a budget constraint. The current good is then divided into a composite consumption good and leisure time (labor supply).

Household income consists of full wage income (which is obtained when households supply their entire labor endowment), capital income after capital depreciation, current transfers from the government, labor income, property income, and other current transfers from the external sector. A share of household wage and capital income is transferred to the external sector.

A direct tax is imposed on household income upon receiving transfers. Households are then assumed to allocate their after-direct-tax income to current and future goods. Here, for purposes of simplicity, the direct tax is assumed to include all current transfers from households to the government.

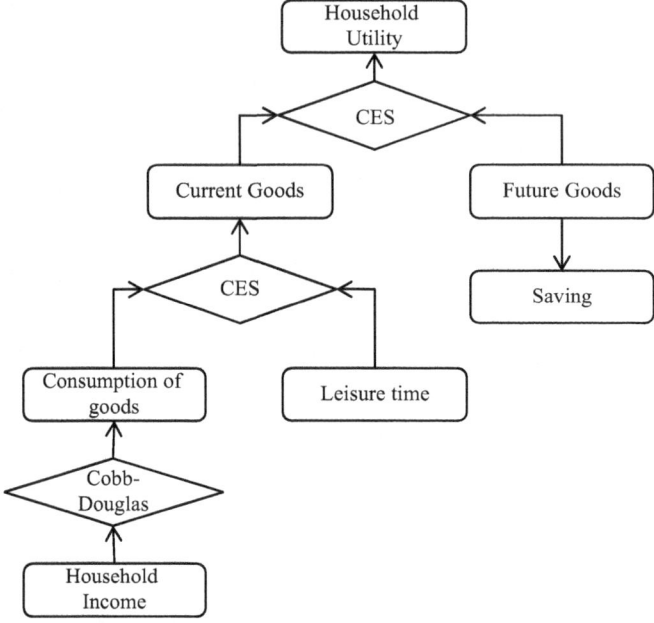

Fig. 9.4 Hierarchical structure of households

To explain household behavior, future goods consumption is derived here. The future goods indicate future household consumption derived from household savings; however, household savings also form the basis for capital investment. Therefore, the capital good can be interpreted as a saving good. Investment is made using produced goods, and their shares in total investment are denoted by b_i. When the price of the investment good is denoted by p_I, $p_I I = \sum_{i=1}^{28} p_i I_i$ is realized. The price of the investment good is then expressed as $p_I I = \sum_{i=1}^{28} b_i p_i$. This price can be regarded as the price of the saving good p_s.

Because the returns to capital net of the direct tax on a unit of capital investment is expressed by $(1 - ty)(1 - k_o)(1 - k_r)r\delta$, the expected rate of return on the price of saving good p_s, that is, the expected net return rate of household saving r_s, is written as follows:

$$r_s = (1 - ty)(1 - k_o)(1 - k_r)r\delta/p_s \qquad (9.8)$$

where

ty: direct tax rate imposed on households
k_o: rate of transfer of property income to the external sector
k_r: capital depreciation rate
δ: ratio of capital stock in units of a physical commodity to that in units of capital
service

Here, the assumption is that the expected returns to savings finance future consumption. Interpreting the price of the future good as the price of the current consumption good under myopic expectations and denoting real household savings S, we observe that the following equation holds

$$p \cdot H = (1 - ty)(1 - k_o)(1 - k_r)r\delta \cdot S \tag{9.9}$$

This equation yields $\frac{p_s p}{(1-ty)(1-k_o)(1-k_r)r\delta} H = p_s S$, and setting the price of the future good p_H associated with real savings S yields the following:

$$p_H = \frac{p_s p}{(1 - ty)(1 - k_o)(1 - k_r)r\delta} \tag{9.10}$$

Then, $p_s S = p_H H$ is realized.

Employing the abovementioned future good and its price, the household utility maximization problem is now specified as follows. The maximization of household utility with respect to current good consumption will be described in a subsequent section.

$$\max_{\{G,H\}} u(G,H) \equiv \left\{ \alpha^{\frac{1}{v_1}} G^{\frac{v_1-1}{v_1}} + (1-\alpha)^{\frac{1}{v_1}} H^{\frac{v_1-1}{v_1}} \right\}^{\frac{v_1}{v_1-1}} \tag{9.11}$$

subject to

$$p_G \cdot G + p_H \cdot H = (1 - ty)FI - TrHO \tag{9.12}$$

$$FI \equiv (1 - l_o)w \cdot E + LI + (1 - k_o)(1 - k_r)r \cdot KS + KI + TrGH + TrOH \tag{9.13}$$

where

α: share parameter
v_1: elasticity of substitution between the current good and future good
G: current household consumption
H: future household consumption
p_G: price of the current good
p_H: price of the future good
FI: household full income
$TrHO$: current transfers from households to the external sector
l_o: rate at which labor income is transferred to the external sector
E: initial household labor endowment, which is specified as twice the actual working time based on actual working and leisure time in Makassar City
LI: labor income transferred from the external sector to households (exogenous variable)
KS: initial household endowment of capital stock
KI: property income transferred from the external sector to households (exogenous variable)

TrGH: current transfers from the government to households
TrOH: current transfers from the external sector to households

By solving this utility maximization problem, we obtain the demand functions for the current and future goods, which yield a household saving function.

$$G = \frac{\alpha[(1 - ty)FI - TrHO]}{p_G^{v_1} \cdot \Delta} \tag{9.14}$$

$$H = \frac{(1 - \alpha)[(1 - ty)FI - TrHO]}{p_H^{v_1} \cdot \Delta} \tag{9.15}$$

$$S = \frac{p_H H}{p_s} \tag{9.16}$$

$$\Delta \equiv \alpha p_G^{1-v_1} + (1 - \alpha)p_H^{1-v_1} \tag{9.17}$$

We then describe the derivation of demands for composite consumption and leisure time from the current good G. The current good G is a composite of consumption and leisure time, and G is obtained from the following optimization problem.

$$\max_{\{C,F\}} G \equiv \left\{ \beta^{\frac{1}{v_2}} C^{\frac{v_2-1}{v_2}} + (1 - \beta)^{\frac{1}{v_2}} F^{\frac{v_2-1}{v_2}} \right\}^{\frac{v_2}{v_2-1}} \tag{9.18}$$

subject to

$$p \cdot C + (1 - ty)(1 - l_o)w \cdot F = (1 - ty)FI - TrHO - SH \tag{9.19}$$

where

β: share parameter
v_2: elasticity of substitution between composite consumption and leisure time
C: composite consumption
F: leisure time
p: price of the composite consumption good
SH: household nominal savings ($=P_s \cdot S$)

Solving this utility maximization problem yields the demand functions for composite consumption, leisure time, and labor supply.

$$C = \frac{\beta[(1 - ty)FI - TrHO - SH]}{p^{v_2} \cdot \Omega} \tag{9.20}$$

$$F = \frac{(1 - \beta)[(1 - ty)FI - TrHO - SH]}{[(1 - ty)(1 - l_o)w]^{v_2} \cdot \Omega} \tag{9.21}$$

$$LS = E - F \tag{9.22}$$

$$\Omega = \beta p^{1 - v_2} + (1 - \beta)[(1 - ty)(1 - l_o)w]^{1 - v_2} \tag{9.23}$$

where LS reflects the household labor supply

Substituting composite consumption (9.20) and leisure time (9.21) into (9.18), we derive the price index of the current good as follows:

$$p_G = \left\{ \beta p^{1 - v_2} + (1 - \beta)[(1 - ty)(1 - l_o)w]^{1 - v_2} \right\}^{\frac{1}{v_2 - 1}} \tag{9.24}$$

Moreover, the composite consumption good is disaggregated into produced goods by maximizing a Cobb–Douglas sub-sub utility function given household income and leisure time.

$$\max_{\{C_i\}} C \equiv \prod_{i=1}^{28} C_i^{\gamma_i} \quad \left(\sum_{i=1}^{28} \gamma_i = 1 \right) \tag{9.25}$$

subject to

$$\sum_{i=1}^{28} p_i \cdot C_i = (1 - ty)Y - TrHO - SH \tag{9.26}$$

where

C_i: household consumption good produced by industry i
C_i: the price of good i
Y: household income

$$(= (1 - l_o)w \cdot LS + LI + (1 - k_o)(1 - k_r)r \cdot KS + KI + TrGH + TrOH)$$

Consumption good i is derived from this optimization problem.

$$C_i = \frac{\gamma_i}{p_i}[(1 - ty)Y - TrHO - SH] \quad (i = 1, ..., 28) \tag{9.27}$$

The price of composite consumption is calculated as follows:

$$p = \prod_{i=1}^{28} \left[\frac{p_i}{\gamma_i} \right]^{\gamma_i} \tag{9.28}$$

9.4.3 The Government

The government sector in this study consists of the activities of the national and local governments in Makassar City. Thus, the concept of government that we employ corresponds to the definition used in the SAM framework. The government sets taxes for public revenue, makes transfers to the private sector, and demands goods and services from each sector, which leads to the final balance (surplus or deficit) of the government budget.

The government obtains its income from direct and net indirect taxes collected in Makassar City and current transfers from the external sector. Tax revenue includes revenue raised by all direct and indirect taxes, including CO_2 emission taxes. The government then spends this income on government consumption, current transfers to households, and current transfers to the external sector.

The government saves the difference between income and expenditures. Nominal consumption expenditures on commodities/services are assumed to be proportional to the government revenue with a constant sectorial share. These expenditures are denoted by the following balance of payments.

$$\sum_{i=1}^{28} p_i \cdot CG_i + TrGH + TrGO + TrGO + SG$$

$$= ty \cdot Y + \sum_{i=1}^{28} tp_i(w \cdot LD_i + r \cdot KD_i) + TrOG \tag{9.29}$$

where

CG_i: government consumption expenditures on commodity I
$TrGH$: current transfers to households
$TrGO$: current transfers to the external sector
SG: government savings
$TrOG$: current transfers from the external sector

9.4.4 The External Sector

The external sector gains its income from Makassar City's imports, current transfers from the government, labor income transfers, and property income transfers. The sector then spends this income in financing Makassar City's exports and imports, current transfers to households and the government, labor (employees in Makassar City), and property income transfers. These expenditures are also expressed by the following balance of payments.

$$\sum_{i=1}^{28} p_i \cdot EX_i + TrOH + TrOG + KI + LI + SO$$

$$= \sum_{i=1}^{28} tp_i \cdot EM_i + TrHO + TrGO + KIO + LIO \tag{9.30}$$

where

EX_i: export of commodity I
EM_i: import of commodity I
SO: savings of the external sector (= national current surplus)
LIO: labor income transfers to the external sector ($=l_o \cdot w \cdot LS$)
KIO: property income transfers to the external sector ($=k_o \cdot r \cdot KS$)

9.4.5 Balance of Investment and Savings

Savings accumulated by the representative household, the government, the local department, and total capital depreciation determine the total investment.

$$\sum_{i=1}^{28} p_i \cdot I_i = SH + SG + SO + \sum_{i=1}^{28} DR_i \tag{9.31}$$

where

I_i: demand for commodity i by other investments
DR_i: amount of fixed capital consumption in industry i

9.4.6 Commodity Prices

Given the zero-profit condition imposed on industry, we can determine commodity prices from the following equation:

$$p_j X_j = \sum_{i=1}^{28} p_i \cdot x_{ij} + (1 + tp_j) [w \cdot LD_j + r \cdot KD_j] \tag{9.32}$$

Given a wage and a capital return rate, we can calculate commodity prices as follows:

$$P = (I - A')^{-1} [(1 + tp_j)(w \cdot ld_j + r \cdot kd_j)] \tag{9.33}$$

where

P: vector of commodity prices
A': transposed matrix of industries' input coefficients
$[\cdot]$: a column vector whose elements are presented in parentheses:

$$ld_j \equiv LD_j/X_j \text{ and } kd_j \equiv KD_j/X_j$$

9.4.7 Derivation of Equilibrium

The equilibrium conditions in the model can be summarized as follows:

Commodity Market

$$
\begin{bmatrix} X_1 \\ \vdots \\ X_{28} \end{bmatrix} =
\begin{bmatrix} a_{1,1} & \cdots & a_{1,28} \\ \vdots & \ddots & \vdots \\ a_{28,1} & \cdots & a_{28,28} \end{bmatrix}
\begin{bmatrix} X_1 \\ \vdots \\ X_{28} \end{bmatrix} +
\begin{bmatrix} C_1 \\ \vdots \\ C_{28} \end{bmatrix} +
\begin{bmatrix} CG_1 \\ \vdots \\ CG_{28} \end{bmatrix} +
\begin{bmatrix} I_1 \\ \vdots \\ I_{28} \end{bmatrix}
$$
$$
+ \begin{bmatrix} EX_1 \\ \vdots \\ EX_{28} \end{bmatrix} -
\begin{bmatrix} EM_1 \\ \vdots \\ EM_{28} \end{bmatrix}
\tag{9.34}
$$

$$
\begin{bmatrix} X_1 \\ \vdots \\ X_{28} \end{bmatrix} =
\begin{bmatrix} a_{1,1} & \cdots & a_{1,28} \\ \vdots & \ddots & \vdots \\ a_{28,1} & \cdots & a_{28,28} \end{bmatrix}
\begin{bmatrix} X_1 \\ \vdots \\ X_{28} \end{bmatrix} +
\begin{bmatrix} C_1 \\ \vdots \\ C_{28} \end{bmatrix} +
\begin{bmatrix} CG_1 \\ \vdots \\ CG_{28} \end{bmatrix} +
\begin{bmatrix} I_1 \\ \vdots \\ I_{28} \end{bmatrix}
$$
$$
+ \begin{bmatrix} EX_1 \\ \vdots \\ EX_{28} \end{bmatrix} -
\begin{bmatrix} EM_1 \\ \vdots \\ EM_{28} \end{bmatrix}
$$

Labor Market

$$LS = \sum_{j=1}^{28} LD_j \tag{9.35}$$

Capital Market

$$KS = \sum_{j=1}^{28} KD_j \tag{9.36}$$

Reference

McDougall, J. N. (1993). *Politics and economics of Eric Kierans: A man for all Canadas*. Montreal: McGill-Queen's Press-MQUP.

Chapter 10
Database for a Computable General Equilibrium

10.1 Introduction

The primary data used in this study are based on an input–output (I–O) table for Makassar City. Data from the social accounting matrix table along with other data sources such as elasticity values, exchange rate, and others are used to complete the I–O table data. The integration of sector aggregation in input–output and social accounting matrix tables uses mapping between the sectors contained in the primary data sources. This chapter explains how to construct the data for a CGE model. The explanation will be started with an understanding of the data structures of the I–O and social accounting matrix tables. The model's coefficients and exogenous variables are estimated using the social accounting matrix tables. The CGE model requires elasticity parameter data and several of parameters.

The CO_2 emission data also required by our CGE model represent the intensity of each sector's CO_2 emissions. Those data are derived from I–O tables and each sector's energy consumption. The study assumes that one industry produces one commodity and, therefore, each commodity generates CO_2 emissions through the energy consumption caused by its production.

10.2 Input–Output (I–O) Table for Makassar City

The I–O table developed by Leontief (1936) is a table of matrix transactions that describes the flows of production of all industries in each sector. This table depicts the relationship between supply and demand among the various sectors in the regional economy. The equilibrium in the I–O table is included in the general equilibrium model.

© Springer Nature Singapore Pte Ltd. 2018
Y. Miyata et al., *Environmental and Natural Disaster Resilience of Indonesia*,
New Frontiers in Regional Science: Asian Perspectives 23,
https://doi.org/10.1007/978-981-10-8210-8_10

The 2006 I–O table for Makassar City comprised 28 industries listed in Table 10.1 by producer price. Those sectors include the following:

Food crops
Plantation crops
Livestock
Forestry
Fishery
Mining of oil and gas and non-oil and gas
Manufacture of food, beverages, and tobacco
Manufacture of textiles, clothing, and leather
Manufacture of wood, bamboo, and furniture
Manufacture of paper and paper products, printing, and publishing
Manufacture of chemicals, petroleum, coal, rubber, and plastic products
Manufacture of cement and non-metallic minerals
Manufacture of basic metals
Manufacture of fabricated metal
Other manufactures
Electricity, gas, and water supply
Construction/building
Trade
Hotels
Restaurants
Highway and other transportations
Communications
Banks and other financial institutions
Leasing, real estate, and business services
Education
Health
Social and other services

All the data in the I–O tables are presented in Indonesian rupiah.

The table describes the flow of goods and services in all the individual sectors of Makassar City's economy during 2006. The classification of 28 sectors is aggregated from the Statistics Indonesia I–O Table (2000), which contains 175. In principle, aggregation is the process of grouping a number of sectors into a single sector.

Every column in the I–O table shows an economic agent, namely, 28 industries, one household, government, investments, and exports. Each row shows the origin of the economic agents' commodity purchases shown in each column, such as flow of materials, taxes, capital, labor, and other costs. Each commodity is derived from local production or import from outside the city, outside the region, or a foreign country. The industry used commodity as an input of current production and capital formation. Only domestically produced goods are included in the export column.

There are two demands: intermediate products and final demand. For intermediate input, we assumed that production used two production factors: capital and labor. The final demand consists of household consumption, government consumption,

Table 10.1 I–O table for Makassar City, 2006

	001	002	003	004	005	006	007	008	009	010	011	012	013
Sector	FC	PC	L	Fo	Fi	MOG and NOG	MFBT	MTCL	MWBF	MP&PP, P&P	MCPCR & PP	MCNMM	MBM
001 Food crops	0	0	1332	0	36	0	66,894	0	0	4	0	0	0
002 Plantation crops	15	1058	287	0	0	0	21,145	7	30	0	924	0	0
003 Livestock	720	73	303	0	35	0	1916	198	0	0	0	0	0
004 Forestry	68	184	36	3	129	8	8	0	5125	76	0	11	0
005 Fishery	0	0	0	0	8600	0	19,304	0	0	0	0	0	0
006 Mining of oil and gas and non-oil and gas	0	0	0	0	0	2	173	3	0	8	0	2222	15
007 Manufacture of food, beverages, and tobacco	0	48	652	0	6824	0	14,238	3	23	4	3	3	0
008 Manufacture of textiles, clothing, and leather	160	128	17	0	559	1	280	1750	325	1	15	60	0
009 Manufacture of wood, bamboo, and furniture	43	94	34	0	246	13	175	1	1448	1935	9	28	25
010 Manufacture of paper and paper product, printing, and publishing	6	56	21	0	102	0	81	27	30	15	2215	1527	176

(continued)

Table 10.1 (continued)

Sector		001 FC	002 PC	003 L	004 Fo	005 Fi	006 MOG and NOG	007 MFBT	008 MTCL	009 MWBF	010 MP&PP, P&P	011 MCPCR & PP	012 MCNMM	013 MBM
011	Manufacture of chemicals, petroleum, coal, rubber, and plastic products	10,853	5080	2063	5	9635	27	2768	236	1583	468	754	3760	944
012	Manufacture of cement non-metallic mineral	0	5	17	0	5	0	16	1	3	13	1	744	477
013	Manufacture of basic metals	335	278	20	1	344	8	120	1	62	4	2	9	781
014	Manufacture of fabricated metal	7	33	6	2	3375	37	263	5	113	3	3	54	2
015	Other manufacturing	20	6	3	0	31	0	5	4	9	1	0	4	0
016	Electricity, gas and water supply	0	15	14	0	43	1	218	17	206	10	1	200	9
017	Construction/ building	12	102	1	1	18	71	3	1	11	0	1	135	2
018	Trade	630	199	345	0	3821	3	16,089	129	984	182	58	387	64
019	Hotel	1	8	1	0	17	5	22	2	70	6	1	171	1
020	Restaurants	119	52	13	1	343	91	43	59	165	13	3	459	6
021	Highway transportation	268	146	44	1	338	172	1486	31	466	61	6	738	19

Code		115	72	74	1	659	8	2714	71	262	28	7	275	18
022	Other transportations	115	72	74	1	659	8	2714	71	262	28	7	275	18
023	Communication	5	16	3	0	43	2	210	7	62	12	3	209	4
024	Banks and other financial institutions	128	110	34	0	425	15	152	13	108	25	2	72	4
025	Leasing, real estate, and business services	2583	256	333	5	5245	107	336	16	129	34	8	511	16
026	Education	0	0	0	0	0	0	9	0	4	2	0	29	0
027	Health	0	0	11	0	9	2	15	1	5	5	0	15	1
028	Social services and other services	38	88	15	0	24	11	32	1	10	2	0	18	0
190	Total intermediate demands	16,126	8107	5679	20	40,906	584	148,715	2584	11,233	2912	4016	11,641	2564
201	Wage/salary	24,970	8740	4060	30	38,444	2210	8518	314	2968	598	106	5708	197
202	Surplus of business	134,332	26,864	16,757	113	124,722	2917	22,324	1116	6522	1457	138	9399	303
203	Depreciation	1709	867	426	9	7707	493	3281	112	1399	132	27	3463	48
204	Indirect taxes	1330	317	234	2	773	123	2789	27	311	83	21	2994	50
205	Subsidy	0	0	0	0	0	0	0	0	0	0	0	0	0
209	Total of primary demand	162,341	36,788	21,477	154	171,646	5743	36,912	1569	11,200	2270	292	21,564	598
210	Total input	178,467	44,895	27,156	174	212,552	6327	185,627	4153	22,433	5182	4308	33,205	3162

(continued)

Table 10.1 (continued)

Sector		014 MFM	015 OM	016 EGWS	017 C/B	018 Tr	019 Ht	020 R	021 HT	022 OT	023 C	024 BOFI	025 LREBS	026 E	027 He
001	Food crops	0	0	0	0	2	0	990	0	0	0	0	23	0	21
002	Plantation crops	0	0	0	0	0	0	95	0	0	0	0	0	1	2
003	Livestock	0	0	0	0	0	0	187	0	0	0	0	99	0	10
004	Forestry	6	0	0	2228	0	0	13	0	0	0	0	0	0	0
005	Fishery	0	0	0	0	0	0	1451	0	0	0	0	0	0	1
006	Mining of oil and gas and non-oil and gas	0	0	4195	8961	0	0	0	0	0	0	0	0	0	0
007	Manufacture of food, beverages, and tobacco	0	0	0	0	13	6	7688	3	13	1	16	12	0	57
008	Manufacture of textiles, clothing, and leather	12	3	2	25	267	0	14	41	1	20	20	28	2	4
009	Manufacture of wood, bamboo, and furniture	1004	0	1	4481	101	0	0	1	0	2	27	6	13	1
010	Manufacture of paper and paper product,	5	0	38	166	6	0	1	109	10	4	5854	40	1589	103

		1	2	3	4	5	6	7	8	9	10	11	12	13	14
	printing, and publishing														
011	Manufacture of chemicals, petroleum, coal, rubber, and plastic products	251	1	1790	6944	120	2	163	130	361	90	1890	170	1718	31
012	Manufacture of cement non-metallic mineral	9	0	2	22,666	231	0	4	2	0	0	20	2	30	0
013	Manufacture of basic metals	319	68	5	5617	4	0	14	1	0	13	2	20	0	0
014	Manufacture of fabricated metal	454	0	384	1492	43	0	5	18	20	59	141	283	3	1
015	Other manufacturing	125	6	1	120	28	0	3	16	1	3	94	22	7	2
016	Electricity, gas and water supply	9	0	133	26	114	0	49	1129	291	43	973	24	0	4
017	Construction/building	27	0	214	104	207	0	34	45	14	567	1997	4228	10	5
018	Trade	303	7	5	5990	114	1	2048	10	6	17	324	41	9	17
019	Hotel	9	0	5	143	230	0	10	39	7	44	2011	68	0	1
020	Restaurants	29	0	2	439	455	0	14	262	36	31	1305	78	1	1
021	Highway transportation	23	1	31	786	790	0	169	619	1	49	928	106	1	1

(continued)

Table 10.1 (continued)

Sector		014 MFM	015 OM	016 EGWS	017 C/B	018 Tr	019 Ht	020 R	021 HT	022 OT	023 C	024 BOFI	025 LREBS	026 E	027 He
022	Other transportations	51	2	11	1472	580	0	356	343	146	355	920	154	2	2
023	Communication	44	1	30	207	1026	1	53	76	19	808	1575	258	0	5
024	Banks and other financial institutions	19	0	25	258	39	0	16	83	5	31	12,184	114	1	5
025	Leasing, real estate, and business services	30	2	115	659	2895	0	71	981	16	158	8023	362	11	10
026	Education	0	0	0	18	13	0	1	0	1	12	305	12	9	8
027	Health	8	0	12	53	8	0	0	3	1	16	17	16	0	4
028	Social services and other services	2	0	9	16	27	0	6	2492	1	12	1852	56	0	2
190	Total intermediate demands	2739	91	7010	62,871	7313	10	13,455	6403	950	2335	40,478	6222	3407	298
201	Wage/salary	1192	17	1774	22,417	16,095	3	1964	5445	251	2744	11,510	4935	493	84
202	Surplus of business	589	22	3217	13,757	46,320	7	2506	14,729	348	4473	7263	35,685	179	76
203	Depreciation	104	2	3143	2862	4159	1	298	3996	290	2885	17,851	3795	27	70
204	Indirect taxes	110	4	101	2172	4847	1	402	396	22	143	418	2451	15	6
205	Subsidy	0	0	0	0	0	0	0	0	0	0	0	0	0	0
209	Total of primary demand	1995	45	8235	41,208	71,421	12	5170	24,566	911	10,245	37,042	46,866	714	236
210	Total input	4734	136	15,245	104,079	78,734	22	18,625	30,969	1861	12,580	77,520	53,088	4121	534

Sector	028 SSOS	180	301	302	303	304	305	309	310	409	509	600	700
001 Food crops	431	69,733	88,248	0	0	6744	13,743	108,736	178,469	1	0	178,467	178,469
002 Plantation crops	27	23,591	21,113	0	0	533	30,525	52,170	75,763	30,867	0	44,895	75,763
003 Livestock	135	3676	8675	0	2691	−230	17,949	29,085	32,762	5605	0	27,156	32,762
004 Forestry	5	7900	104	0	0	−26	192	270	8171	7996	0	174	8171
005 Fishery	41	29,397	86,248	0	0	3004	94,323	183,575	212,973	420	0	212,552	212,973
006 Mining of oil and gas and non-oil and gas	0	15,579	19,541	0	0	−13,799	1007	6749	22,331	16,001	0	6327	22,331
007 Manufacture of food, beverages, and tobacco	1027	30,634	100,270	0	0	4157	66,333	170,760	201,395	15,767	0	185,627	201,395
008 Manufacture of textiles, clothing, and leather	467	4202	36,418	0	74	131	1473	38,096	42,299	38,145	0	4153	42,299
009 Manufacture of wood, bamboo, and furniture	42	9730	47,458	0	0	716	26,439	74,614	84,344	61,910	0	22,433	84,344
010 Manufacture of paper and paper product, printing, and publishing	583	12,764	235,651	0	0	0	105	235,755	248,520	243,338	0	5182	248,520

(continued)

Table 10.1 (continued)

Sector	028 SSOS	180	301	302	303	304	305	309	310	409	509	600	700
011 Manufacture of chemicals, petroleum, coal, rubber, and plastic products	1334	53,171	191,378	0	0	0	2219	193,597	246,768	242,460	0	4308	246,768
012 Manufacture of cement non-metallic mineral	9	24,257	70,806	0	0	46	17,568	88,420	112,678	79,472	0	33,205	112,678
013 Manufacture of basic metals	160	8188	25,940	0	4094	−2496	413	27,950	36,140	32,977	0	3162	36,140
014 Manufacture of fabricated metal	2706	9512	90,389	0	289,015	705	923	381,032	390,546	385,810	0	4734	390,546
015 Other manufacturing	936	1447	63,522	0	0	7855	84,752	156,129	157,578	157,440	0	136	157,578
016 Electricity, gas, and water supply	896	4425	10,818	0	0	0	2	10,818	15,245	0	0	15,245	15,245
017 Construction/building	2758	10,568	0	0	134,258	0	0	134,258	144,824	40,747	0	104,079	144,824
018 Trade	1026	32,809	17,720	0	774	0	27,433	45,927	78,737	2	0	78,734	78,737
019 Hotel	1848	4720	127	0	0	0	3	130	4850	4828	0	22	4850
020 Restaurants	4800	8820	9984	0	0	0	20	10,005	18,826	199	0	18,625	18,826
021 Highway transportation	4029	11,310	14,096	0	89	0	6127	20,312	31,621	653	0	30,969	31,621
022 Other transportations	4232	12,930	1198	0	5	0	325	1528	14,459	12,597	0	1861	14,459
023 Communication	12,442	17,121	9655	0	0	0	13	9669	26,789	14,209	0	12,580	26,789

Code														
024	Banks and other financial institutions	392	14,260	97,606	0	0	0	2265	99,871	114,130	36,611	0	77,520	114,130
025	Leasing, real estate, and business services	755	23,667	31,302	0	0	0	11	31,312	54,980	1892	0	53,088	54,980
026	Education	69	492	3630	0	0	0	0	3630	4122	1	0	4121	4122
027	Health	21	223	320	0	0	0	0	320	542	9	0	534	542
028	Social services and other services	219	4933	23,283	181,321	0	0	4	204,609	209,540	24,535	0	185,006	209,540
190	Total intermediate demands	**41,390**	**450,059**	**1305,500**	**181,321**	**431,000**	**7340**	**394,167**	**2,319,327**	**2,769,402**	**1,454,492**	**0**	**1,314,895**	**2,769,402**
201	Wage/salary	136,000	**301,787**											
202	Surplus of business	595	**476,730**											
203	Depreciation	6992	**66,148**											
204	Indirect taxes	29	**20,171**											
205	Subsidy	0	**0**											
209	Total of primary demand	143,616	**864,836**											
210	Total input	185,006	**1,314,895**											

Source: Makassar City Statistical Bureau, 2008. Table code description: *301* household consumption, *302* government consumption, *303* capital, *304* changing stock, *305* export, *309* total of final demand, *409* import, *310* total demand, *599* margin trading and transportation, *600* total output, *700* total supply

capital, changing stock, exports, and imports. Value added consists of wage/salary, surplus, depreciation, indirect taxes, and subsidies. Intermediate input consists of a 28 × 28 matrix transaction of 28 industries. The structure of an intermediate input matrix is such that some cells are zero. This means that some sectors do not correspond to other sectors. One of the sectors may use only a portion of intermediate input from the other sectors.

10.3   Construction of the Social Accounting Matrix (SAM) Table for Makassar City

A social accounting matrix (SAM) is a matrix that compiles all the monetary flows among the agents and sectors in a particular economy. It includes information about most transactions, such as the wages that firms pay to households, consumption of goods by households, and taxes and transfers administrated by the government. A SAM is a representation of all of an economy's existing monetary transactions. Each cell represents a flow of funds from a source (column) to a recipient (row) (Breisinger et al. 2009).

CGE models analyze economic activities, which are transactions that involve goods and factors, and the concurrent flows of funds between economic agents. The flows of goods and services from the agents listed in the rows to the counterpart agents listed in the columns are described in the SAM data. The SAM data extend data from I–O tables that are comprehensive and consistent with a macroeconomic database written in a matrix-form table where agents are used as both row labels and column labels.

For empirical CGE analysis, we must construct our own SAM tables. Various coefficients and exogenous variables for developing a CGE model based on real data must be estimated by using the SAM. Therefore, this study estimated the SAM table for Makassar City based on the 2006 I–O table for Makassar City, the 2005 SAM table for Indonesia, and related data such as Indonesia's 2005 National Account table in the same year.

The SAM of our CGE model consists of "Production Activity," "Institution," "Production Factors," "Capital Accumulation," and "External Sector." In this SAM, "Production Activity" is subdivided into 28 industries, "Institution" is subdivided into government and households, and "Production Factors" is subdivided into capital and labor.

Almost all the data included in the SAM tables are provided in a 2006 I–O table for Makassar City. Data in the I–O tables can be transferred into the correct cells in the SAM table. In the SAM table construction, all the cells contained in the first row and the first column "Households–Capital" and "Households–Labor" can be copied from I–O tables. The important issue is how to fill the cells of SAM construction where the data cannot be derived from the I–O tables. To address this issue, column sums are equal to the corresponding row sums in the SAM tables. The empty cells can be filled immediately by applying the row-sum and column-sum equality rule (Hosoe et al. 2010). The following explanation will describe how to fill the cells based on data from I–O tables.

In the SAM table, "Production Activity" includes intermediate input demand for 28 industries in addition to the capital and labor input for production. In the column lines, all transactions are expenditure, including included intermediate input, wages, and value added from tax. The row lines illustrate all transactions assumed as revenue from domestic production along with revenue. The total intermediate inputs of 28 industries production appear in the cell "Production Activity–Production Activity" (Rp. 450,059). Government consumption and household consumption appear in the cells "Production Activity–Government" (Rp. 181,321) and "Production Activity–Households" (Rp. 1,305,500), respectively. The cell labeled "Production Activity–Capital Accumulation" shows the total of capital and changing stock (Rp. 438,340), and the cell labeled "Production Activity–External Sector" shows the domestic production (Rp. 1,060,325).

"Institution" consists of government and households, which consume "Production Activity." "Government" cell shows that government expenditures (column lines) include subsidies, consumption of goods and services, and some transfers. The government revenue (row lines) comes from tax and transfers from household. The "Households" cell shows household revenue from the production factors of revenue and transfers. Household expenditure is indicated for household consumption of goods and taxes and for saving a portion of capital. The transaction shown in the "Government–Production Activity" (Rp. 20,171) cell demonstrates indirect taxes can be regarded as the production taxes collected by the 28 industries. The cell labeled "Households–Capital" (Rp. 476,730) shows business surplus, and the "Households–Labor" (Rp. 301,787) cell shows household wage/salary from industry activity.

"Production Factors" consists of the capital and labor used for "Production Activity." In the row lines, those cells show revenues derived from wages and illustrate the revenue of remittances and capital. The corresponding column lines indicated the revenue distributed to households as labor income, business surpluses as industry profits, and depreciation. The cell labeled "Capital–Production Activity" (Rp. 476,730) illustrates the expenditure of industries to capital, and "Labor–Production Activity" (Rp. 301,787) shows expenditures from industries to households.

The cell labeled "Capital Finance–Production Activity" (Rp. 66,148) shows depreciation in industry capital. The cells labeled "Capital Finance" and "External Sector" are exogenous and include capital. The corresponding row lines show the revenues from government and household savings. The column lines illustrate expenditures such as payment of production factors.

If there are unknown cells after the other cells are filled by applying the row-sum and column-sum equality rule, we seek data sources from the 2005 SAM table and Indonesia's 2005 National Account table. We determine Makassar City's government savings and transfer to households, which are entered into the "Households–Government" (Rp. 180,499) and the "Capital Finance–Government" (Rp. 139,899) cells, respectively. Next, direct tax revenues and household savings are entered into the "Government–Households" (Rp. 46,925) and the "Capital Finance–Households" (Rp. 130,039) cells, respectively.

The row sums and the column sums in the SAM table show the total revenue and the total expenditure, and each row sum must match its corresponding column sum. That indicates that each cell transaction in the SAM tables is always in equilibrium. Finally, the compilation of the 2006 SAM table for Makassar City is complete, as shown in Table 10.2.

10.4   Elasticity Parameters

In determining the results of policy simulations generated by any applied model, parameter values for functional forms are crucial. The procedure most commonly used to select parameter values has come to be labeled "calibration" (Mansur and Whalley 1981).

The elasticity parameters used are elasticity of substitution for current goods and household utility. Other necessary parameters include shared parameters in household utility, household expenditure (current and future consumption), and leisure time. In theory, the value of the parameter can be estimated from time series data by using econometric analysis.

Elasticity of substitution shows how current goods and household utility respond in each sector by change in price input. For a CES utility function, goods consumption substitutes for leisure time, and current goods substitute for future goods in the constant elasticity substitutions. This research applied elasticity substitution for all commodities (0.5) from a literature search, followed by calibration as needed, as is commonly performed in Indonesian case studies.

10.5   Estimation of Carbon Dioxide Intensity

An additional database was compiled from data collected by Nansai et al. (2002). The National Greenhouse Gas Inventory guidelines published by Indonesia's Ministry of the Environment (2012) were used as a reference and to adjust the results regarding embodied energy and emission intensity in each sector.

These data used an I–O approach to calculate production induced by final demand for energy consumption and CO_2 emissions in a life cycle assessment (LCA) inventory in the context of an environmental analysis (Nansai et al. 2002; Kondo et al. 1998). The I–O table provides input and output on inventory with minimal processing and without modification. The values and quantities table accompanying the I–O tables described the input for each sector in the form of quantities of key

Table 10.2 The 2006 SAM table for Makassar City

Economic sectors (in million rupiah)		Production activities	Institution		Production factors		Capital	External	Total
		28 industries	Government	Households	Capital	Labor	Accumulation	sector	
Production activities	28 industries	450,059	181,321	1305,500	0	0	438,340	1,060,325	1,314,895
Institution	Government	20,171	0	46,925	0	0	0	434,623	501,719
	Households	0	180,499	0	476,730	301,787	0	523,448	1,482,464
Production factors	Capital	476,730	0	0	0	0	0	0	476,730
	Labor	301,787	0	0	0	0	0	0	301,787
Capital finance		66,148	139,899	130,039	0	0	0	102,254	438,340
1,314,895		0	0	0	0	0	0	0	0
Total		1,314,895	501,719	1,482,464	476,730	301,787	438,340	0	

material, including energy products. In principle, material input per unit production by each sector can be obtained from a physical amount of total production for each commodity.

By using the I–O tables, we obtain embodied environmental burden intensity (embodied intensity) from the direct environmental burdens linked to goods' unit production activity.

In this database, the CO_2 emissions were calculated by multiplying the energy consumption value obtained for each fuel type by its corresponding carbon dioxide emission factor. Furthermore, in addition to fossil fuel emissions, the CO_2 emissions emanating from limestone were considered. The direct emission and CO_2 emission intensity of each sector were aggregated for each sector in the I–O table.

Using data from Miyata et al. (2009), we then used I–O analysis to calculate emission intensities for consumption expenditures in the household sector, as shown in Fig. 10.1.

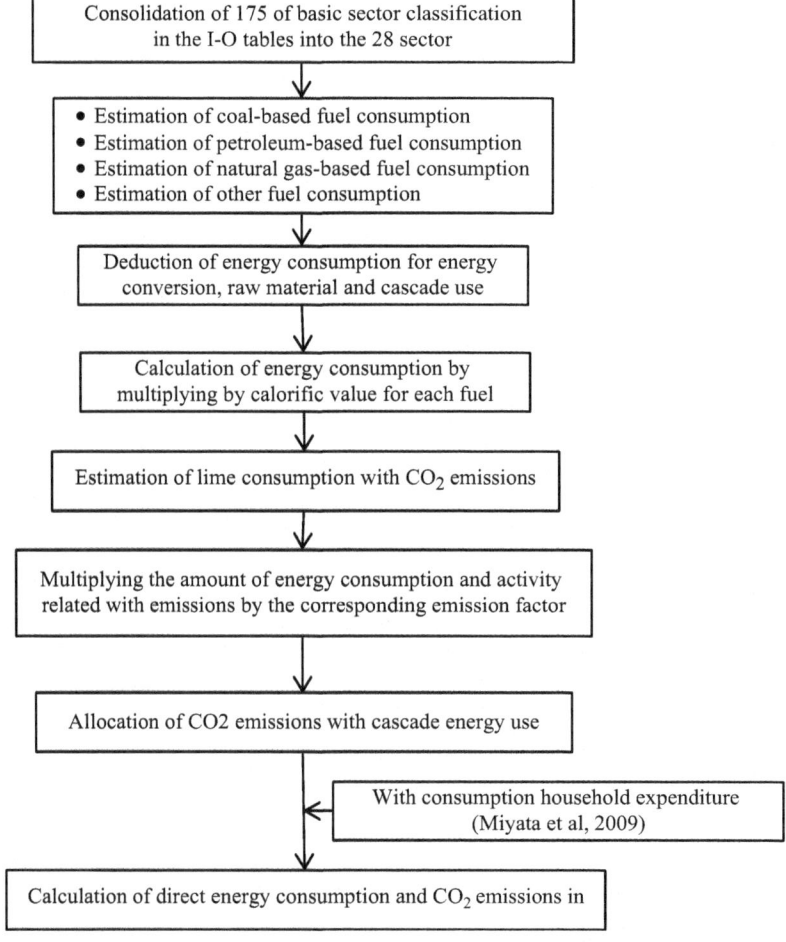

Fig. 10.1 Calculation process for embodied energy and emission intensity in each sector (*Source*: Modification of Nansai et al. 2002)

Table 10.3 presents emission intensities and CO_2 emissions based on the I–O table for Makassar City.

This research used the 2012 Handbook of Energy and Economic Statistics of Indonesia (Ministry of Energy and Mineral Resources of Indonesia 2012). However, not all necessary data were available, and thus, this research used information data

Table 10.3 Emission intensities and carbon dioxide emissions for each sector in 2006

No	Sectors	Intensity of CO_2 emissions t-CO_2/MRp	CO_2 emissions t-CO_2
001	Food crops	0.319	56,988.308
002	Plantation crops	0.495	22,219.434
003	Livestock	0.251	6807.967
004	Forestry	0.525	91.387
005	Fishery	1.386	294,518.322
006	Mining of oil and gas and non-oil and gas	0.495	3130.547
007	Manufacture of food, beverages, and tobacco	3.341	620,137.117
008	Manufacture of textiles, clothing, and leather	1.071	4448.002
009	Manufacture of wood, bamboo, and furniture	0.126	2826.503
010	Manufacture of paper and paper product, printing, and publishing	1.782	9232.334
011	Manufacture of chemicals, petroleum, coal, rubber, and plastic products	20.364	87,726.732
012	Manufacture of cement non-metallic mineral	24.691	819,867.193
013	Manufacture of basic metals	7.173	22,680.110
014	Manufacture of fabricated metal	0.139	659.182
015	Other manufacturing	0.035	4.748
016	Electricity, gas, and water supply	10.305	157,096.064
017	Construction/building	0.249	25,868.746
018	Trade	0.036	2866.157
019	Hotel	0.044	0.972
020	Restaurants	0.168	3122.555
021	Highway transportation	2.870	88,892.113
022	Other transportation	5.184	9648.165
023	Communication	0.077	969.255
024	Banks and other financial institutions	0.008	639.886
025	Leasing, real estate, and business services	0.037	1955.915
026	Education	0.712	2936.175
027	Health	0.246	131.187
028	Social services and other services	1.288	238,198.137
	Total of intermediate sectors	83.416	2,483,663.210
	Consumption expenditures of households	0.065	85,264.657
	Total	83.481	2,568,927.867

adjusted from the Japan data (Nansai et al. 2002). We assumed that Indonesia's technology is similar to that of Japan because most of Indonesia's sectors use technology made in Japan, especially automobiles, which consume a large amount of fuel. Japan's 399 sectors adjust to Indonesia's 175 sectors.

References

Breisinger, C., Thomas, M., & Thurlow, J. (2009). *Social accounting matrices and multiplier analysis: An introduction with exercises* (Vol. 5). Washington, DC: International Food Policy Research Institute.

Hosoe, N., Gasawa, K., & Hashimoto, H. (2010). *Textbook of computable general equilibrium modeling: Programming and simulations*. London: Springer.

Kondo, Y., Moriguchi, Y., & Shimizu, H. (1998). CO_2 emissions in Japan: Influences of imports and exports. *Applied Energy, 59*(2), 163–174.

Leontief, W. W. (1936). Quantitative input and output relations in the economic systems of the United States. *The Review of Economics and Statistics, 18*, 105–125.

Mansur, A., & Whalley, J. (1981). *Numerical specification of applied general equilibrium models: Estimation, calibration, and data*. London: Department of Economics, University of Western Ontario.

Ministry of Environmental of Indonesia. (2012). *Guidelines for national greenhouse gas inventory, Book II, Vol. 1: Methodology of energy procurement and use*. Jakarta: Author.

Miyata, Y., Hirobata, Y., Nakanishi, H., & Shibusawa, H. (2009). Economy-transport-environment interactive analysis: A spatial modeling approach. *Studies in Regional Science, 39*(1), 109–130.

Nansai, K., Moriguchi, Y., & Tohno, S. (2002). *Embodied energy and emission intensity data for Japan using input-output tables (3EID) – Inventory data for LCA*. Tsukuba: National Institute for Environmental Studies.

Chapter 11
The Impact of a Carbon Tax
on the Economy of Makassar City

11.1 Introduction

A carbon tax is a policy instrument that can be applied to help constrain greenhouse gas emissions. Indonesia's policy goals in this respect were articulated in the Ministry of Finance Indonesia's Green Paper on Climate Change Commitment of the President of the Republic of Indonesia, presented at a G-20 conference (2010). The country's target is to reduce CO_2 emissions in 2020 to the equivalent of 6% to 24% below 2005 levels. The tax will be introduced at a rate that is calculated to reduce emissions to meet long-term goals.

The degree of abatement achieved is measured based on the estimated emission level in 2006, which is considered the business-as-usual (BAU) scenario. In principle, the degree of abatement applies to all CO_2 emissions generated as a result of economic activity in a city. The use of fossil fuel accounts for 68.7% of total emissions in Indonesia (2010).

Under the BAU scenario, the CO_2 emissions generated by the energy sector in Makassar City are estimated at 2.57 million tons for 2006. To achieve the target in the Green Paper, it will be necessary to reduce emissions by 154,000 to 616,000 tons relative to the BAU scenario. Under the scenarios considered in this study, a carbon tax is introduced at a rate that is calculated to reduce CO_2 emissions by 7% to 8% relative to 2006 levels. The tax applies to all commodities consumed in the city. However, to avoid double taxation, the tax does not apply to either the export or distribution sectors.

© Springer Nature Singapore Pte Ltd. 2018
Y. Miyata et al., *Environmental and Natural Disaster Resilience of Indonesia*,
New Frontiers in Regional Science: Asian Perspectives 23,
https://doi.org/10.1007/978-981-10-8210-8_11

11.2   Objectives

This study aimed to evaluate the impact of the carbon tax on urban economic performance which can be estimated in the change in household welfare.

11.3   Methodology

The study provides a detailed evaluation of the impacts of the carbon tax on production, consumption, and urban economic performance. This research uses a computable general equilibrium (CGE) model, which is a quantitative method to estimate the impact of economic and policy shocks, particularly those affecting the entire economy. The model realistically reproduces the structure of the overall economy and therefore the nature of all existing economic transactions among diverse economic agents (productive sectors, household, the government, and external sectors). The results from the CGE model are expected to reveal that the carbon tax will have significant impact throughout the economy.

The main data used in this study are based on the 2006 input-output table with 28 sectors and a social accounting matrix table (SAM) for Makassar City. Data from other sources (such as elasticity values, exchange rate, etc.) are used to complete input-output table data.

The carbon tax will initially be set at a rate of Rp. 10,000/t-CO_2, which is equivalent to US \$1/t-CO_2. The model employs the carbon tax rate applied in India and operates under the assumption that Makassar City exhibits an economic structure that is sufficiently similar to that of India. The results presented below estimate the effects of the carbon tax on the city's economic activity.

11.4   Simulation Scenarios

This article considers two representative CO_2 restriction policies, a carbon tax without transfers and a carbon tax in which all revenues are transferred to households. The impacts of these policies are compared with the BAU scenario. This study considers three scenarios:

1. Baseline scenario (BAU): this scenario was simulated to reproduce the baseline SAM of Makassar City, Indonesia.
2. Scenario 1: a carbon tax of 0.01 MRp/t-CO_2 is imposed on all industries emitting CO_2.
3. Scenario 2: a carbon tax of 0.01 MRp/t-CO_2 is imposed on all industries, and the revenues are transferred to households.

11.5   Business-As-Usual (BAU) Condition

The BAU (the baseline or benchmark) condition is the starting point equilibrium. This scenario implies no policy when the economic growth has no limits. The BAU was determined by calibrating all the function's forms for all the economic agents in the model.

Table 11.1 shows that CO_2 emissions that are generated by industries and households are estimated at 2.57 million ton for 2006.

The largest CO_2 emissions were derived from the following: the manufacture of cement non-metallic minerals (819,867.19 t-CO_2); the manufacture of food, beverages, and tobacco (620,137.12 t-CO_2); and the fishery (294,541.32 t-CO_2). These sectors are assumed the greatest energy users in their industry technology process. On the production side, the sectors with the largest output are the fishery (212,552); the manufacture of food, beverages, and tobacco (185,627); and social services and other services (185,006). The greatest income for the city is that collected from the fishery (171,646), the food crops (162,341), and social services and other services (143,616).

The largest demand for labor is predicted to come from food crops (136,000), the fishery (38,444), and the manufacture of food, beverages, and tobacco (24,970). The largest capital demand comes from food crops (136,041), the fishery (132,429), and the trade (50,479).

11.6   Simulation Results

The effects of the simulated scenarios were analyzed in terms of their impact on economic variables.

This section presents the simulation results with respect to certain important economic variables which are explained below.

11.6.1   CO₂ Emissions

The manufacture of cement and non-metallic minerals and the manufacture of food, beverages, and tobacco generated the greatest CO_2 emissions in the baseline scenario: 819,867.19 tCO_2 and 620,137.12 t-CO_2, respectively. The carbon tax reduced overall CO_2 emissions by 8.04% (scenario 1) and 8.25% (scenario 2). Household responses to the carbon tax policies resulted in increased CO_2 emissions of 7.78% in scenario 1 and 7.94% in scenario 2.

CO_2 emissions declined in 13 sectors in scenario 1 and 14 sectors in scenario 2. The decline ranged from 0.17% to 19.81%. The largest changes occurred in the manufacture of cement and non-metallic minerals (19.81% in scenario 1 and 19.77%

Table 11.1 Economic conditions under the BAU scenario

Industries	Denoted	CO_2 emissions	Industrial outputs	Municipal GDP	Labor demand of industry	Capital demand of industry
	Total	2,483,663.210	1,314,895	864,836	301,787	542,878
Food crops	**Sector 1**	56,988.308	178,467	162,341	24,970	136,041
Plantation crops	**Sector 2**	22,219.434	44,895	36,788	8740	27,731
Livestock	**Sector 3**	6807.967	27,156	21,477	4060	17,183
Forestry	**Sector 4**	91.387	174	154	30	122
Fishery	**Sector 5**	294,518.322	212,552	171,646	38,444	132,429
Mining of oil and gas and non-oil and gas	**Sector 6**	3130.547	6327	5743	2210	3410
Manufacture of food, beverages, and tobacco	**Sector 7**	620,137.117	185,627	36,912	8518	25,605
Manufacture of textiles, clothing, and leather	**Sector 8**	4448.002	4153	1569	314	1228
Manufacture of wood, bamboo, and furniture	**Sector 9**	2826.503	22,433	11,200	2968	7921
Manufacture of paper and paper products, printing and publishing	**Sector 10**	9232.334	5182	2270	598	1589
Manufacture of chemicals, petroleum, coal, rubber, and plastic products	**Sector 11**	87,726.732	4308	292	106	165
Manufacture of cement non-metallic minerals	**Sector 12**	819,867.193	33,205	21,564	5708	12,862
Manufacture of basic metals	**Sector 13**	22,680.110	3162	598	197	351
Manufacture of fabricated metal	**Sector 14**	659.182	4734	1995	1192	693
Other manufactures	**Sector 15**	4.748	136	45	17	24
Electricity, gas, and water supply	**Sector 16**	157,096.064	15,245	8235	1774	6360

(continued)

Table 11.1 (continued)

Industries	Denoted	CO_2 emissions	Industrial outputs	Municipal GDP	Labor demand of industry	Capital demand of industry
Construction/ building	**Sector 17**	25,868.746	104,079	41,208	22,417	16,619
Trade	**Sector 18**	2866.157	78,734	71,421	16,095	50,479
Hotels	**Sector 19**	0.972	22	12	3	8
Restaurants	**Sector 20**	3122.555	18,625	5170	1964	2804
Highway transportation	**Sector 21**	88,892.113	30,969	24,566	5445	18,725
Other transportation	**Sector 22**	9648.165	1861	911	251	638
Communications	**Sector 23**	969.255	12,580	10,245	2744	7358
Banks and other financial institutions	**Sector 24**	639.886	77,520	37,042	11,510	25,114
Leasing, real estate, and business services	**Sector 25**	1955.915	53,088	46,866	4935	39,480
Education	**Sector 26**	2936.175	4121	714	493	206
Health	**Sector 27**	131.187	534	236	84	146
Social services and other services	**Sector 28**	238,198.137	185,006	143,616	136,000	7587

in scenario 2) and in the manufacture of chemicals, petroleum, coal, rubber, and tobacco (17.71% in scenario 1 and 17.39% in scenario 2).

However, CO_2 emissions increased in 15 sectors in scenario 1 and in 14 sectors in scenario 2. The increase from 0.002% to 656.86% and the largest changes were observed in other manufactures (335.42% in scenario 1 and 656.86% in scenario 2) and forestry (101.98% in scenario 1 and 125.65% in scenario 2). Figures 11.1 and 11.2 depict the changes in each sector.

11.6.2   Industrial Outputs

The baseline scenario indicates that the largest sectors in terms of output were fishery; the manufacture of food, beverages, and tobacco; and social services and other services. Conversely, the hotels, other manufactures, and forestry sectors

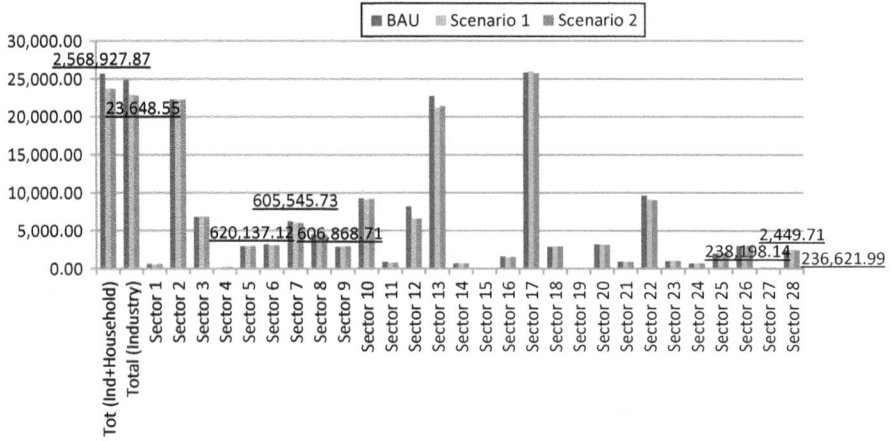

Fig. 11.1 CO_2 emission

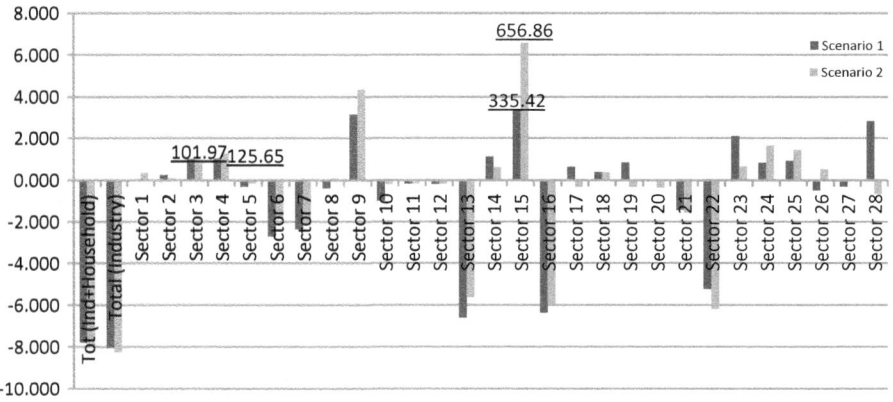

Fig. 11.2 Changes in CO_2 emissions

produced slightly higher output. The imposition of the carbon tax resulted in changes to output. The changes in industrial outputs are depicted in Figs. 11.3 and 11.4. Total industrial outputs of industry declined in each scenario by 0.38% in scenario 1 and 0.74% in scenario 2.

Nearly identical numbers of sectors experienced changes in output (both positive and negative) in scenario 1 and scenario 2. The following sectors exhibited increased output: food crops, plantation crops, livestock, forestry, the manufacture of fabricated metal, other manufactures, constructions/buildings, trade, hotels, restaurants, communications, banks and other financial institutions, leasing, real estate and business services, and social services and other services. The other manufactures (335.42%) and forestry (101.98%) sectors exhibited the greatest increases in output in scenario 1. Small increases were observed in other sectors. These increases

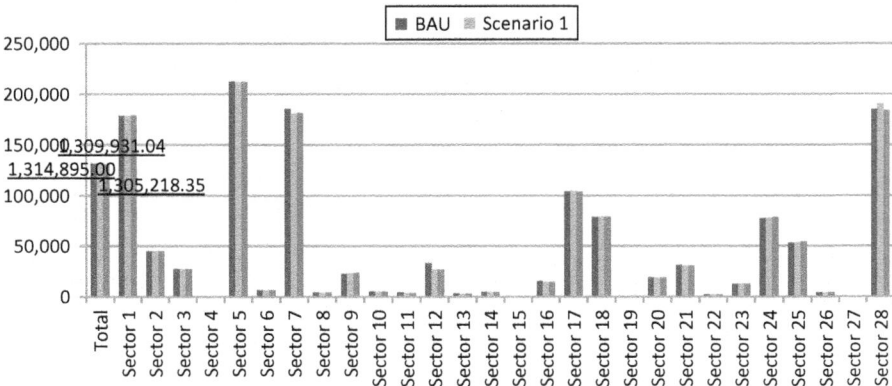

Fig. 11.3 Industrial output

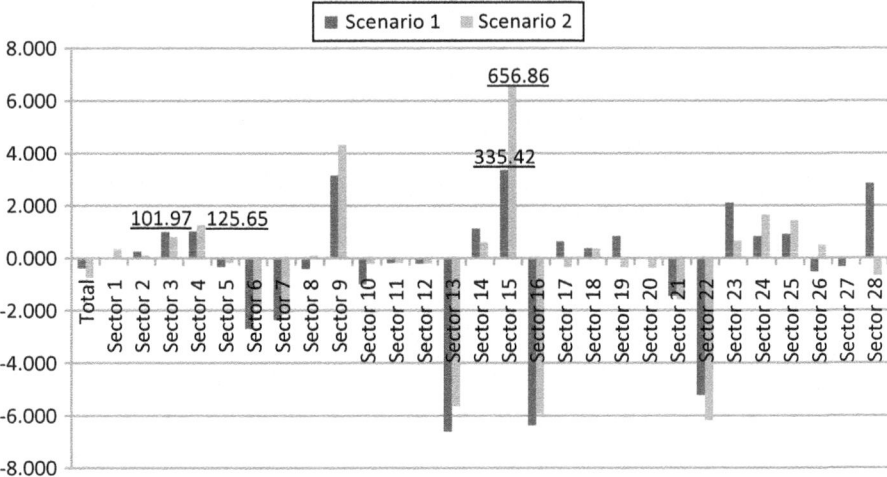

Fig. 11.4 Changes in industrial output

indicate that these sectors benefited from the imposition of the tax. In contrast, the manufacture of cement and non-metallic minerals (19.81%) and the manufacture of chemicals and paper products, printing and publishing (17.71%), were harmed by the carbon tax, and these sectors exhibited the greatest declines in outputs. The declines observed in other sectors were relatively small.

The simulation results for scenario 2 exhibited relatively small differences from the values observed for scenario 1. Similar to scenario 1, increases in outputs occurred in food crops; plantation crops; livestock; forestry; the manufacture of fabricated metal; other manufactures; trade; communications; banks and other financial institutions; leasing, real estate, and business services; education; and healthcare. The other manufactures and forestry sectors presented the largest increases in output

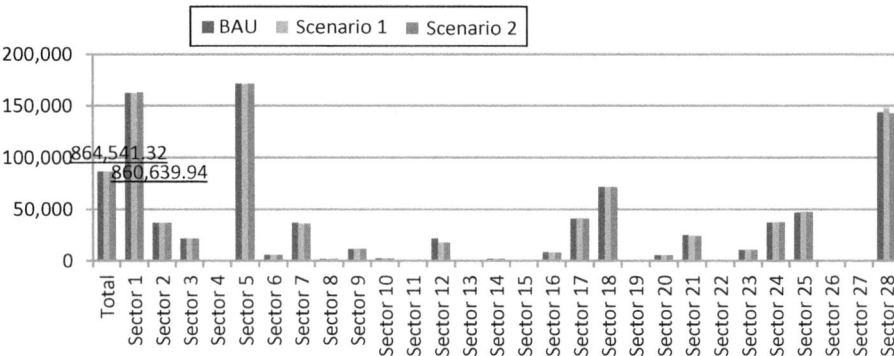

Fig. 11.5 Municipal GDP

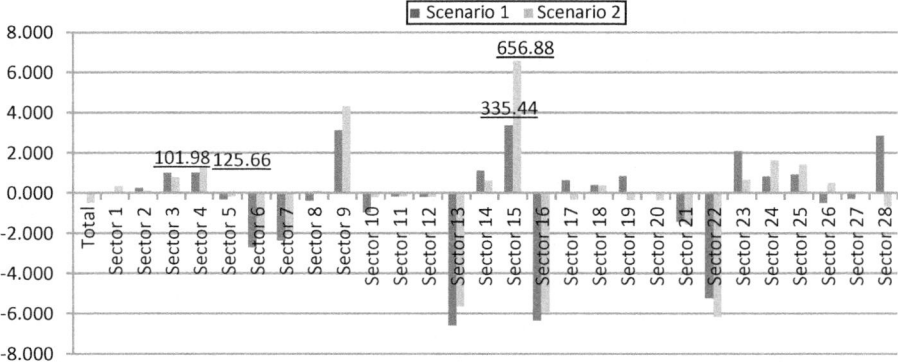

Fig. 11.6 Changes in municipal GDP

in response to the city's policy: 656.86% and 125.65%, respectively. Conversely, the largest declines were observed in the manufacture of cement and non-metallic minerals (19.77%) and in the manufacture of chemicals and paper products, printing and publishing (17.39%).

11.6.3 Municipal GDP

The largest contributions to the municipal GDP under the BAU scenario were made by following sectors: fishery; manufacture of food, beverages, and tobacco; and social services and other services. The impacts of the carbon tax policy are presented in Figs. 11.5 and 11.6. Overall, the GDP has declined by more than 19% for each scenario. In scenario 1, 13 sectors contributed to the decline in GDP, compared with 14 sectors in scenario 1. Sectorial declines ranged from approximately 0.17% to 19.80%. The manufacture of cement and non-metallic minerals and the manufacture of chemicals, petroleum, coal, rubber, and plastic products exhibited the largest declines in each scenario.

However, these declines were accompanied by increases in other sectors. Contributions to an increased GDP were observed in 15 sectors in scenario 1 and 14 sectors in scenario 2, ranging in magnitude from approximately 0.004% to 656.88%. The largest changes occurred in the other manufactures (335.44% in scenario 1 and 656.88% in scenario 2) and forestry (101.98% for scenario 1 and 125.66% for scenario 2) sectors.

11.6.4 Labor Demand

Figures 11.7 and 11.8 indicate that labor demand generally responded negatively to the carbon tax policies in the sectors considered. Labor demand declined in 22 sectors in scenario 1 and 21 sectors in scenario 2; overall, labor demand declined by approximately 0.01% to 1.2%. The greatest changes occurred in the manufacture of cement and non-metallic minerals (20.90% in scenario 1 and 20.54% in scenario 2) and the manufacture of chemicals, petroleum, coal, rubber, and tobacco (18.70% in scenario 1 and 18.09% in scenario 2).

Certain sectors responded positively to the carbon tax policies in terms of labor demand. In particular, six sectors in scenario 1 and seven sectors in scenario 2 exhibited increased labor demand, ranging from 0.1% to 650.73%. The other manufactures (98.80% in scenario 1 and 123.15% in scenario 2) and forestry sectors (330.41% in scenario 1 and 650.73% in scenario 2) exhibited the greatest increases in labor demand.

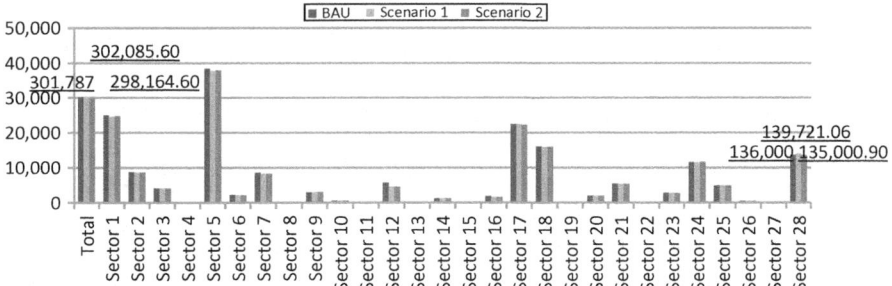

Fig. 11.7 Labor demand

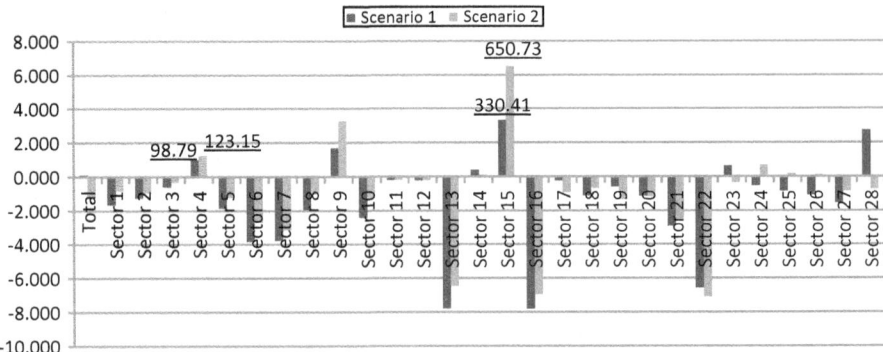

Fig. 11.8 Changes in labor demand

11.6.5 Capital Demand

Regarding the changes in the demand for capital by industry depicted in Figs. 11.9 and 11.10, the pattern of changes differs substantially from that observed for labor demand. Increased demand for capital is observed in 19 sectors in scenario 1 and in 20 sectors in scenario 2. Thus, the demand for capital responded positively to the carbon tax programs. The largest positive responses were observed in the other manufactures (339.007% in scenario 1 and 661.23% in scenario 2) and forestry (102.77% in scenario 1 and 126.27% in scenario 2) sectors.

Declines in the demand for capital were observed in nine sectors in scenario 1 and in eight sectors in scenario 2; these declines range from 0.44% to 19.43%. The manufacture of cement and non-metallic minerals (19.32% in scenario 1 and 19.43% in scenario 2) and the manufacture of chemicals, petroleum, coal, rubber, and tobacco (17.07% in scenario 1 and 16.94% in scenario 2) exhibited the largest declines.

11.6.6 Commodity Prices

Figure 11.11 shows price changes for all sectors. The carbon tax increased output prices by an average of 2.32% in scenario 1 and 2.61% in scenario 2, and these changes were particularly pronounced in sectors characterized by the heavy use of energy-intensive commodities. The differences between scenarios 1 and 2 with respect to price changes are not large.

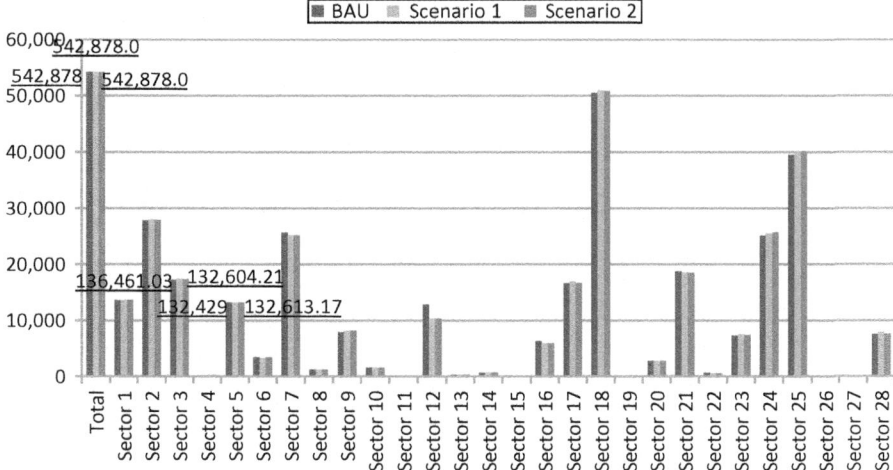

Fig. 11.9 Capital demand

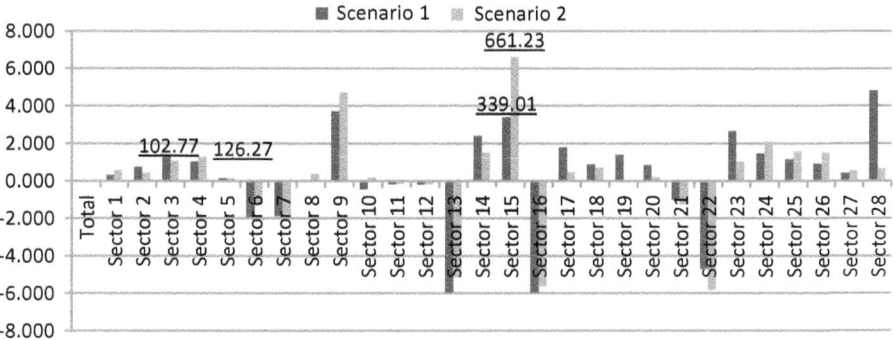

Fig. 11.10 Changes in capital demand

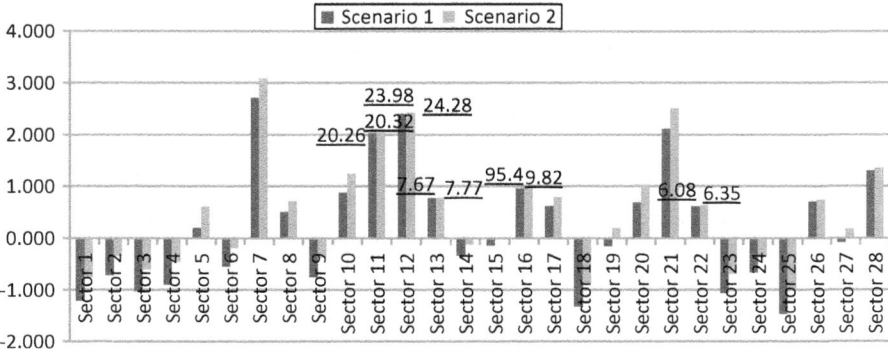

Fig. 11.11 Commodity prices

11.6.7 Other Variables

As depicted in Figs. 11.12 and 11.13, household income did not change significantly, exhibiting an increase of 0.12% in scenario 1. However, as the price of the composite consumption good increased by 0.34%, household consumption declined by 0.17%. Moreover, leisure time increased by 0.01%, and household savings declined by 0.42%. As a result, equivalent variation reveals a welfare gain/loss of 0.5 billion rupiah.

Regarding the government sector, in scenario 1, the imposition of a carbon tax reduced revenue from net indirect taxation by 4.3%. However, total government

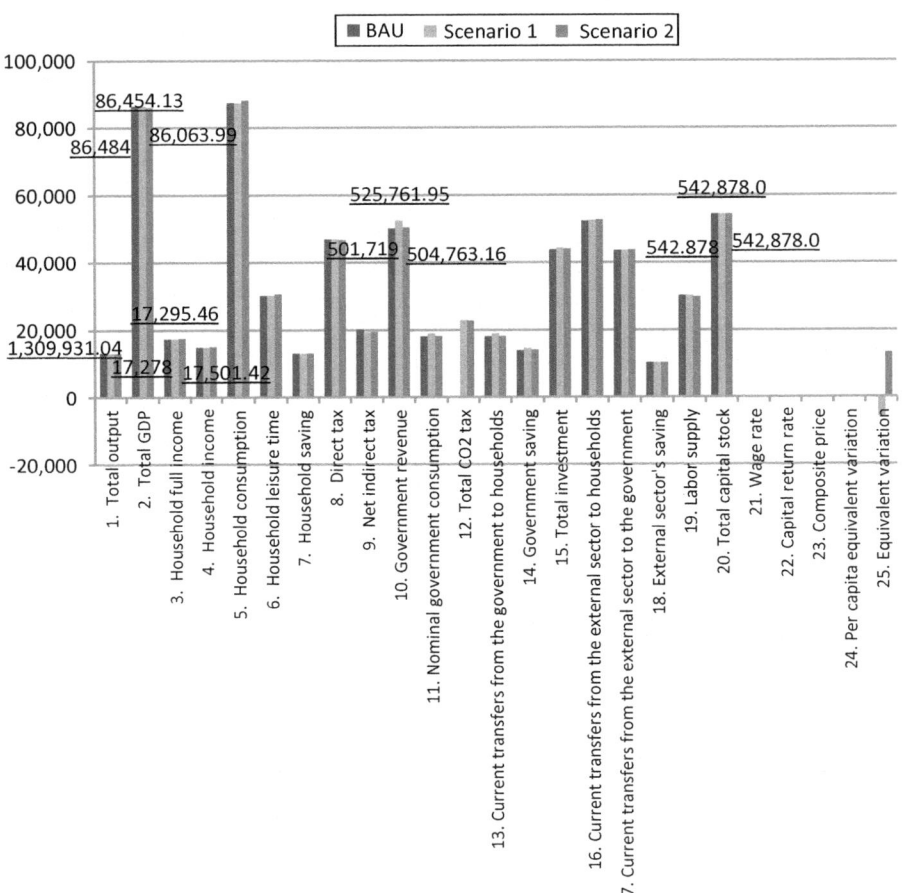

Fig. 11.12 Other variables

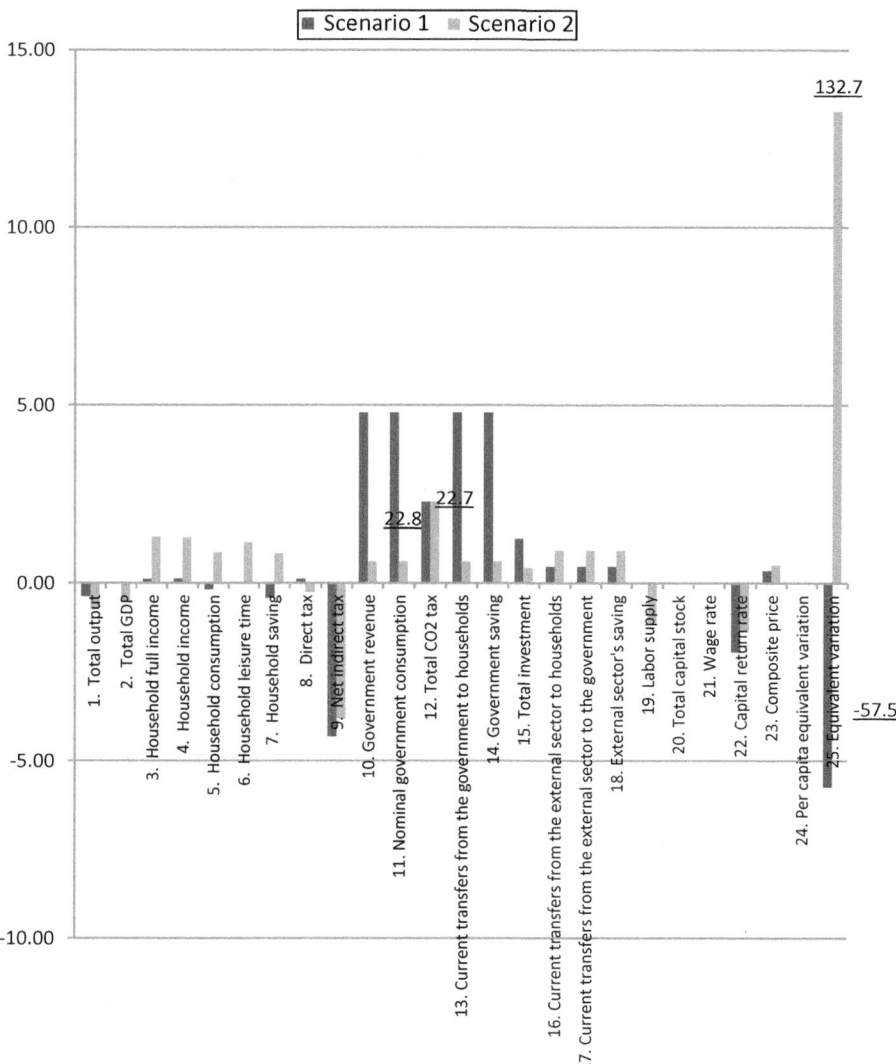

Fig. 11.13 Changes in other variables
Note: (1) industrial output, (2) GDP, (3) full income, (4) household income, (5) composite consumption, (6) leisure time, (7) household saving, (8) direct tax, (9) net indirect tax, (10) government revenue, (11) government consumption, (12) total CO_2 tax, (13) current transfers from the government to households, (14) government saving, (15) total investment, (16) current transfers from the external sectors to households, (17) current transfers from the external sector to the government, (18) external sector's saving, (19) labor supply, (20) total capital stock, (21) wage rate, (22) capital return rate, (23) composite price, (24) per capita equivalent variation, and (25) equivalent variation

revenue increased by 4.79%, which led to increased government consumption and current transfers to households and the external sector and led to reduced government savings.

In scenario 2, household income increased by 1.3%, including the effect of the direct tax on households. The household income net of the direct tax was increased by 1.28% relative to the baseline scenario. Following the increase in household income, household composite consumption increased by 0.86%, leisure time increased by 1.14%, and household savings increased by 0.82%. As result, equivalent variation indicates a welfare gain of 1.33 billion rupiah.

Regarding the government sector, revenue from the net indirect tax declined by 3.82%. Government revenues from households decreased by 0.26%, whereas total government revenue increased by 0.61%. Because of this increase, government expenditures, current transfers to households and to the external sector, and government savings increased.

11.7   Conclusion and Policy Implications

11.7.1   Conclusion

In 2003, fossil fuels accounted for approximately 95% of primary energy used in Indonesia, which indicates that a carbon tax would thus impose costs on the economy. Simulating these scenarios against the baseline/benchmark shows the following:

– The impact of a carbon tax in scenario 1.

The carbon tax in scenario results in reduced CO_2 emissions (7.8%), but it increases the prices of fossil fuels, which, in turn, raises production costs and ultimately drive up prices (2.39%) for goods and services throughout the economy. The changes in prices encourage the household to use less or to make changes that result in preferring and selecting commodities that involve lower emissions of commodities; using savings to consume such goods leads to a reduction in savings of 0.4%.

The increased prices of fossil fuels also result in lowering the economy's total industrial outputs (0.378%), thus reducing the real wages and the amount that people work, which ultimately decrease the overall supply of labor (characterized by an increase in labor demand of 0.1%).

In summary, the carbon tax under scenario 1 reduces CO_2 emissions but also reduces economic growth, as shown in municipal GDP decreasing by 0.03% and because welfare as characterized by the equivalent variation value is negative during the same period.

– The impact of a carbon tax on all revenue in scenario 2.

The amount of CO_2 emissions continues to decline. Facing the rise in commodity prices (2.69%), all revenues from a carbon tax transferred to households lead to increased household income (1.3%) and savings (0.8%), which thus encourage households to raise consumption (0.9%).

Lower real wage effects include decreasing labor supply (1.1%) and labor demand (1.2%).

In summary, all revenues from a carbon tax reduce CO_2 emissions (8%) and keep economic growth in decline, as shown by decreasing municipal GDP 0.5%, but the welfare of society increases, as shown by the positive value of equivalent variation.

Based on the study results, it can be concluded that an urban economic change occurs and affects household welfare, which is characterized by the value of equivalent variation. As a result, the implementing of carbon tax policies generally had a negative impact on the economy of Makassar City in scenario 1 and a positive impact in scenario 2, despite the fact that the total municipal GDP declined in all the simulation scenarios. Because of the effects of government transfers on households, household consumption declined in scenario 1 but increased slightly in scenario 2. As a result, savings in the external sector increased.

Government revenue increased in all scenarios. The costs of production increased following declines in output prices. The declines in sectorial outputs resulted in a negative impact on household utility in scenario 1.

11.7.2 Policy Implications

The results of this study show that the implementing of a carbon tax to reduce CO_2 emissions will reduce economic growth. The tax levy motivates industries and households throughout the economy to undertake the least costly reductions in emissions. Strong efforts are required to encourage the application of the tax in manner that increases economic growth.

The government might allow certain types of exemption without jeopardizing the goal of minimizing the cost of reducing emissions. For example, it already exempts some sources of emission from the tax, such as commercial vehicles. The increase in production costs can be reduced by providing industrial incentives. Such incentives might be combined with the use of low-carbon intermediate inputs such that industry is able to raise the capital that ultimately raises real wages and encourages increases in labor supply. The energy supply side must reduce emissions and engage in carbon capture and storage.

The government should also impose regulations that encourage utilizing renewable energy resource and innovative low-carbon technologies to ensure that carbon emissions targets are met.

Chapter 12
Conclusion, Discussion, and Recommendations for Future Research

12.1 Conclusion

This dissertation studied environmental economic analysis based on an AHP using a structural economic model to establish efficient economic and environmental policy. Economic and environmental policy is efficient if the achievement is obtained with the minimum possible environmental impact without compromising its economic purposes. This study achieved its three primary objectives. The first contribution of this study is its normative importance of evaluating the economy and the environment to achieve sustainable development. Theoretically, this study evaluated an environmental economic system through the efficiency of economic and environmental integration. The second achievement is its application of a standard approach to policy-making, and the efficiency is demonstrated by sharing it with other approaches. This study empirically evaluated decision-making based on the economic and environmental indicators of community preferences for a regional road construction project in Makassar, Indonesia. The third achievement is its empirical simulation of how to reduce CO_2 emissions through carbon tax policy without sacrificing Makassar City's economic welfare. The final chapter summarized the primary results of this study.

Chapter 1 evaluated environmental economics through economic and environmental interaction for sustainable development. This interaction is the basis for environmental and economic accounting.

The study then took an AHP approach to policy-makers who set tentative targets to optimize decisions characterized by the existence of multiple conflicting objectives and interests. These observations were described in Chap. 2. This chapter presented the approach using criteria that significantly contribute to the operation and in road construction process to maintain environmental sustainability. This study broadened the method's scope to consider both its economic and environmental dimensions. This approach is particularly relevant to and suitable for current

© Springer Nature Singapore Pte Ltd. 2018
Y. Miyata et al., *Environmental and Natural Disaster Resilience of Indonesia*,
New Frontiers in Regional Science: Asian Perspectives 23,
https://doi.org/10.1007/978-981-10-8210-8_12

environmental concerns. Therefore, it stressed the joint determinant of environmental and economic policies. The approach can be helpful to make environmental and economic policy decisions in practice and to support policy-makers in the decision-making process. Chapter 2 demonstrated how to estimate the amount of CO_2 emissions caused by economic activities. The results showed that public preferences consider environmental sustainability without sacrificing economic growth, proven efficient through economic resource. The economic and environmental efficiency presented in the concept of the model showed that output production used resources with a lower environmental impact.

Chapter 3 reviewed general equilibrium theory beginning with its origins and discussed how the theory evolved into applied models. Chapter 3 also reviewed the economic agents of an applied equilibrium model and how to choose a functional form and build the benchmark equilibrium counterfactual for the simulation scenario model.

Chapter 4 developed the standard structure of the static CGE model that followed the Walrasian tradition of Makassar City. All the models used in these studies confirm the basic principles of the Walrasian equilibrium. Taxes and the government are considered exogenous by both households and industries. The model also includes an external sector, the activity level of which is assumed fixed in that total imports and exports are not sensitive to government policy changes. This assumption is consistent with the small-country hypothesis and a short-term approach to policy design. The equilibrium of the economy is given by a price vector for all goods and inputs, a vector of activity levels, and a value for public income. Accordingly, the industry sector maximizes its profits, the household maximizes his or her utility, government income equals the payments of all economic agents, and supply equals demand in all markets. The model depicted that allocative efficiency is the economic unit's ability to minimize the cost of production for input prices that replace the inputs.

Apart from constructing a CGE model, this methodology requires several additional elements, such as a suitable database to calibrate the model and to make it applicable to and consistent with reality. These elements were described in Chap. 5, which presented several applications using data from Makassar. Chapter 5 also discusses an SAM table suitable for the model and considered CO_2 emission intensity based on an I-O table for Makassar City in 2006.

Chapter 6 showed the simulation results of scenarios after calibration. Chapter 6 also depicted counterfactual, business-as-usual scenarios and how emission changes are incorporated into the model. These simulations described the impact of CO_2 emission reduction by imposing a carbon tax on industries, with all revenue from taxes transferred to households. The impact of the implementation of the carbon tax varies among industries and the performance of Makassar City. The results showed that a carbon tax had a negative impact on industry outputs, the commodity price increased, and the level of household consumption and welfare decreased. The change in welfare was quantified by equivalent variation. Equivalent variation is the adjustment in income that changes the household's utility equal to the level that would occur if the event had taken place. The welfare of households increased after receiving transfer carbon tax revenues from the government.

12.2   Discussion and Recommendations for Future Research

Several problems and limitations of this study and its analysis should be emphasized.

1. This research collected public preferences from professionals who were experts in road planning and development. These experts were government officials, planners, engineering supervisors, and academics. Additional types of professionals would further develop the environmental criteria.
2. This research used simplified assumptions to keep the CGE model manageable, understandable, and plausible to future developments. Simplifications were made regarding how different market interaction has been modeled. These generalizations included the small-country hypothesis and overlooking international relationship both at the economic and the environmental levels.
3. This research was confined to a static, short-term approach. Upgrading the model would be too complicated at this stage. A dynamic framework that could be developed in future extensions would address a variety of interesting additional issues such as the long-term sustainability of environmental issues.
4. This research assumed that CO_2 emission intensity is constant. More industry activity implies that more CO_2 emissions are a unidirectional effect of the economy on the environment. This assumption implicitly neglects the possibility that industries engage in abatement activities in clean technology. It might be relevant to conduct a long-term analysis that considers the opposite effect, i.e., the impact of environmental quality on the economy.

Printed by Printforce, the Netherlands